ROUTLEDGE LIBRARY EDITIONS:
EGYPT

EGYPT'S ECONOMIC POTENTIAL

EGYPT'S ECONOMIC POTENTIAL

Edited by
ROBERTO ALIBONI, ALI HILLAL DESSOUKI,
SAAD EDDIN IBRAHIM, GIACOMO LUCIANO AND
PIERCARLO PADOAN

Volume 7

Routledge
Taylor & Francis Group
LONDON AND NEW YORK

First published in 1984

This edition first published in 2013
by Routledge
2 Park Square, Milton Park, Abingdon, Oxon, OX14 4RN

Simultaneously published in the USA and Canada
by Routledge
711 Third Avenue, New York, NY 10017

Routledge is an imprint of the Taylor & Francis Group, an informa business

British Library Cataloguing in Publication Data
A catalogue record for this book is available from the British Library

ISBN: 978-0-415-63747-3 (Set)
eISBN: 978-0-203-07914-0 (Set)
ISBN: 978-0-415-81120-0 (Volume 7)
eISBN: 978-0-203-06941-7 (Volume 7)

Publisher's Note
The publisher has gone to great lengths to ensure the quality of this reprint but points out that some imperfections in the original copies may be apparent.

Disclaimer
The publisher has made every effort to trace copyright holders and would welcome correspondence from those they have been unable to trace.

EGYPT'S
ECONOMIC POTENTIAL

EDITED BY:

Roberto Aliboni
Ali Hillal Dessouki
Saad Eddin Ibrahim
Giacomo Luciano
Piercarlo Padoan

CROOM HELM
London • Sydney • Dover, New Hampshire

Croom Helm Ltd, Provident House, Burrel Row,
Beckenham, Kent BR3 1AT
Croom Helm Australia Pty Ltd, First Floor, 139 King Street,
Sydney, NSW 2001, Australia
Croom Helm, 51 Washington Street,
Dover, New Hampshire, 03820 USA

British Library Cataloguing in Publication Data

Egypt's economic potential.
1. Egypt–Economic conditions– 1952-
I. Aliboni, Roberto
330.962'055 HC830

ISBN 0-7099-1319-2

Printed and bound in Great Britain
by Billing & Sons Limited, Worcester.

CONTENTS

TABLES

FIGURES

ABBREVIATIONS

ARE	Arab Republic of Egypt
AWAC	Airborne Warning and Control System
CAPMAS	Central Agency for Public Mobilisation and Statistics
EGPG	Egyptian General Petroleum Company
ESU	Economic Studies Unit
GDP	Gross Domestic Product
IBRD	International Bank for Reconstruction and Development
IDA	International Development Association
IEOC	International Egyptian Oil Company (a subsidiary of Italy's AGIP)
IISS	International Institute of Strategic Studies
ILO	International Labour Organisation
IMF	International Monetary Fund
LDCs	Less Developed Countries
MEES	Middle East Economic Survey
OAPEC	Organisation of Arab Petroleum Exporting Countries
ODEP	Open Door Economic Policy
OECD	Organisation of Economic Co-operation and Development
OPEC	Organisation of Petroleum Exporting Countries
PIW	Petroleum Intelligence Weekly
UNECWA	United Nations Economic Commission for Western Asia
USAID	United States Agency for International Development

NOTE ON AUTHORS

Roberto Aliboni is the Director of IAI. An expert on international relations in the Mediterranean, North Africa and the Middle East, he edited a volume on "Arab Industrial Integration" (Croom Helm, 1979).

Ali E. Hillal Dessouki is Professor of Political Science at Cairo University. He was a visiting professor at UCLA and Princeton University. His publications include "Islam and Power" (Croom Helm, 1982) "Islamic Resurgence in the Arab World" and "Foreign Policies of the Arab States".

Saad Eddin Ibrahim is Professor of Sociology at the American University in Cairo. He was a visiting professor at the AUB and UCLA. Wrote extensively in Arabic and English on Egyptian and Arab society, and is the author of "The New Arab Social Order" (Westview - Croom Helm, 1982).

Giacomo Luciani is the Director of Studies of IAI. An economist by training, has written extensively on oil, the multinational enterprises and the Arab and Mediterranean economies. Is the author of "International Oil Companies and Arab Countries" (Croom Helm, 1984) and editor of "The Mediterranean Region" (Croom Helm, 1984).

Piercarlo Padoan is Associate Professor of Economics at the University of Rome. He is the author of contributions to "Qualitative Analysis and Econometric Estimation of Continuous Time Dynamic Models" (North Holland, 1980), "Non-Linear Models of Fluctuating Growth" (Springer Verlag, 1984) and of other articles on major international journals.

ACKNOWLEDGEMENTS:

This book is the result of a research project undertaken by the Istituto Affari Internazionali with funds kindly provided by the Istituto Bancario S. Paolo of Turin. The IAI wishes to express its gratitude for this support to Prof. Luigi Coccioli, who was at the time the President of S. Paolo, and has since moved to become President of the Banco di Napoli. We also wish to thank Dr Ruggero Fossati, head of the International Division, and Dr Alfonso Iozzo, head of the Research Department of the Istituto Bancario S. Paolo.

The five authors team met in Cairo in November 1982 and extensively discussed preliminary drafts of the various chapters. During their stay in Cairo, the Italian members of the team also conducted numerous interviews and discussions on specific aspects with the following persons: Abdel Moneim Abu Saad, Ahmed Youssef Ahmed, Peter W. Amato, Galal Amin, Hamied Ansari, Nabya Asfahani, Ahmed Baha Eldine, John Bentley, Boutros Boutros-Ghali, Mostafa K. El Ayouty, Mahmoud Abdel Fadil, John Gerhart, Mughtar Halouda, Heba Handoussa, Nabil A. Hilmy, Fawzi Ibrashi, Hafez Ismail, Walid Kazziha, Mustapha Khalil, Moustafa Mahir Amin, Osman Mohammed Osman, Ismail Sabri Abdallah, Ibrahim Sakr, El Sayed Yassin. While the help and cooperation of all the persons listed above is gratefully acknowledged, they cannot in any way be held responsible for opinions and judgements expressed in this book.

The work of the team was immensely facilitated by the friendly support of Mrs Bertha Badr of the Ford Foundation; and Mrs Nancy Cylke, who at the time was in charge of the library of USAID in Cairo.

Translation of parts of this manuscript that were originally written in Italian was performed by Tony Fletcher and Roger Meservey.

As already mentioned, extensive discussions held in Cairo allowed for in-depth coordination of the individual efforts of the five authors; in this sense this book reflects the joint work of the team. Nevertheless the final drafting of each part was due to its individual author, and each is responsible for the details. In particular, Roberto Aliboni wrote the Introduction and section 3 of Chapter Three; Saadeddin Ibrahim wrote section 1 of Chapter Three; Ali Hillal Dessouki wrote section 2 of Chapter Three; Giacomo Luciani wrote Chapter Two; and Piercarlo Padoan wrote Chapter One.

INTRODUCTION

Over the past ten years the Egyptian economy has undergone a major transformation, which has partially done away with the centralised and protective measures of Nasser's time and led to greater decisional decentralisation and international competition. This transformation, along with changing circumstances in the surrounding Arab areas, and the end of military hostilities with Israel, has given rise to the tremendous change in the Egyptian economy.

Without underestimating the obstacles that still stand in the way of sustained economic growth and development, this work foresees a more optimistic overall outlook for Egypt than do other such studies carried out by international organisations such as the World Bank. Our optimism is based on a wider and more interdisciplinary approach than that which normally characterises such studies.

Although Egypt is still a very poor country, it is in fact richer than its Arab neighbours in terms of human and industrial capital. It is also helped by a series of structural factors which keep the deficit of its balance of payments under control (oil; Suez Canal; tourism; emigrants' remittances; foreign aid); and there are many opportunities in Egypt for profitable investment. However in spite of this in order to maintain the political consensus the government must resort to public expenditure policies and in particular to a policy of subsidising foodstuffs. These expenditure programmes are very costly and use up valuable public resources. In fact, the main problem facing the Egyptian economy is the need to close a savings gap which prevents the authorities from channelling savings towards financing the great potential for growth.

The difficulties of overcoming this problem are to be found in the political situation. The present regime is fundamentally stable and even a further change at the top would be unlikely to alter the institutional framework of the economy or the basic economic philosophy of the country. In spite of the fact that many economic policy changes need to be made, the main features of the open door policy are here to stay. Although policy innovations will have to plot a very fine course between the opposing needs - on the one hand the need to increase both savings and investments and on the other hand the need to maintain the consensus of those affected by the changes - it is our opinion that the Egyptian economy has the potential for stable and rapid growth.

How easy it will be to achieve growth, will depend to a great extent on developments in the wider regional and global settings of which Egypt is part. Such developments will help to determine the path that the Egyptian economy will follow. No simple economic formula seems capable of solving all Egypt's problems, rather, a series of flexible policies and careful mediation will be needed.

Even though Mubarak is not the overwhelming leader that Sadat and Nasser were, his position is not weak. The present situation calls for other qualities and so far Mubarak has maintained the consensus of important sectors of Egyptian society.

The Transformation of Egypt

As noted above, Egypt has changed much in the last ten or fifteen years. Sadat, who during the first years of his mandate carried on many of Nasser's policies, gradually moved the country towards other goals.

In 1967 Egypt was an ally of the Soviet Union and led the other Arab countries in the fight against Israel. Then in 1979, having broken away from the rest of the Arab world, and by now a close ally of the US, Egypt signed a peace treaty with Israel.

On the eve of the 1967 war, Egypt was a country

tending towards socialism. There was much state intervention in the economy, and attempts were being made to redistribute income in favour of the poor and to create channels for greater social mobility.

Now in the 1980s the private sector is alive and flourishing and the economy is open. Any income redistribution now taking place favours the wealthier classes or those benefitting (directly or indirectly) from emigration, and lowers the real income of the traditional middle classes.

These socioeconomic changes have been paralleled by changes on the political front. Egypt passed from Nasser's charismatic leadership which, due to its mass consensus, had effectively eliminated all opposition, to Sadat, who, having wished to build a more open and articulate society, had allowed a certain level of pluralism to creep in. However, this attempt at controlled democracy which Sadat had hoped might accompany the new 'Open Door Economic Policy' (ODEP) was a failure; the increasingly repressive posture of the regime finally led to Sadat's assassination.

The many changes introduced under Sadat have outraged or at least irritated a great many Egyptians. The circumstances which accompanied Sadat's funeral, which took place before the indifferent eyes of his countrymen and in a country under martial law, are testimony to this bad feeling. However there was no institutional breakdown nor was there a significant discontinuity in the political life of the country. Mubarak came to power in accordance with the Constitution and he too aims at continuity, albeit with proposals for improvements and corrections.

Many among the left wing opposition advocate a return to Nasser's socialist and pan-Arab policies. However, although Mubarak has much more in common with Nasser than meets the eye, he is unlikely to consider a return to Nasser's socialist policies, or waging another war with Israel, or centralising the economy or taking up a neutral (non-aligned) position in international affairs. More likely Mubarak would attempt to evolve a synthesis, or a middle ground between the policies of his two predecessors. Mubarak wants to correct rather than radically change Sadat's policies, and he will succeed in this if international conditions and the domestic sociopolitical situation allow him to proceed with the necessary restructuring of the economy and the political institutions. In any case the political and economic transformation of Egypt has gone too far to be easily turned back now.

The Problems Facing the Egyptian Economy

The growth of the Egyptian economy depends mainly on fixed investments, but political and economic constraints limit their expansion.

In particular there are two constraints which often stand in the way of increased investment: the savings gap (i.e. a shortage of savings with respect to investments); and the foreign exchange gap (i.e. the current deficit). In Egypt it is the savings gap which is at the root of the problem. Since signing the peace with Israel, Egypt has been able to count on four important sources of foreign exchange: oil, the Suez Canal, emigrants' remittances and tourism. These receipts, together with the considerable inflow of foreign aid, guarantee funds to pay for import needs. However, the foreign exchange gap can only be kept under control in the short-medium term. To overcome the problem in the long term it will be necessary to increase exports, especially manufactured goods. In order that this may be done, it will be necessary to increase savings in the short term to allow greater investment, but it is in this respect that the problem of the savings gap become evident. These savings are not forthcoming. In Egypt the propensity to save is low, not only on the part of private individuals but also on the part of the public authorities. This is due to the fact that a large slice of the government's expenditure goes to subsidise subsistence goods, many of which are imported.

This shortage of private and, above all, public savings is at the root of Egypt's economic problems. Today, as in the past, economic growth is being held back by the excessive growth of public consumption, which uses up resources which could otherwise be turned to productive investment. In order to increase investments it will be necessary to contain not only private but also public consumption.

Any attempt to fix a high target for investments (and for the savings to finance them) could cause conflict between private and public consumption and given the nature of the public subsidies designed to help the poorer classes, problems concerning income redistribution could arise - as indeed they did in 1977 when consumption subsidies were eliminated - causing serious social disturbances.

Given the crucial effect of subsidies on public expenditure, and their inverse relation with savings, the main dilemma confronting Egyptian society may be seen as a trade-off between short term social benefits (directly proportional to the expenditure on subsidies), and long term development possibilities (directly proportional to investment expenditure).

The existence of a savings gap has other implications for the Egyptian economy. One of these is the problem of financing the public deficit. Given that Egypt has an underdeveloped capital market and that the economy suffers from persistent bouts of financial repression (interest rates are held at artificially low levels) the public deficit can only be financed (given the amount of income originating abroad) by creating liquidity. Recourse has often been made to this method in recent years, resulting in a considerable expansion of the money supply.

In an economy such as Egypt's, characterised by a growing opening up of the economy to Western markets, and by an inadequate domestic industrial sector, such a practice runs the risk of building up inflationary pressures and pressure on the balance of payments. Both of these outcomes adversely affect the exchange rate and cause serious problems for the monetary authorities in the short term. The Egyptian financial market is further complicated by its 'dual' nature: it permits a free circulation of both the dollar and Egyptian pound.

This brings us to another central aspect of the Egyptian economy, the terms of trade. Here too the authorities are faced with a trade-off: in this case between making Egyptian exports more competitive by way of a currency devaluation, and the increase in import costs which devaluation would cause. Although many feel that the current exchange rate for the Egyptian pound is high, many factors suggest against devaluing in order to increase competitiveness.

One of these reasons is that the low growth of Egyptian exports is due more to the limits on supply (and therefore to the low rate of capital accumulation) than to factors on the demand side which might be affected by devaluation. A second reason is that the worsening of the terms of trade would have the immediate effect of increasing the costs of imports necessary to increase Egypt's productive capacity.

A third, and possibly more important, reason is that a devaluation could set the Egyptian economy off on a vicious circle. The devaluation would increase the cost of imported consumption goods, including those necessary for subsistence, and this would increase the public debt by increasing the burden of subsidies. This would inevitably bring about an acceleration of the monetary expansion which (as noted above) would adversely affect the balance of payments to the point of necessitating another devaluation.

In view of these considerations, it seems unlikely that the Egyptian authorities will adopt a policy of devaluation in order to increase competitiveness. However, it cannot be excluded that inflationary problems might necessitate periodical revisions of the exchange rate.

It is clear from the above that public expenditure plays a crucial role in the Egyptian economy. With total public expenditure remaining constant, any possibilities of accelerating development will depend on a greater share of public expenditure going to finance investment projects, as private investment is not yet in a position to take on the role of main engine of the economy.

The Egyptian economy must follow a growth path which enables it to profit from the increasing opening of the economy, and attract foreign capital and private investment; but at the same time it must also avoid causing problems of income redistribution which could arise either due to inflation or due to the workings of public finance.

Industrial Growth and Export Development

Of all the Arab countries Egypt has the most diversified industrial sector and that with the longest history.

Nasser's industrialisation policies brought heavy industry to Egypt and led the way for the expansion of the public industrial sector. Although it had registered many major successes, this model was in trouble by the mid-Sixties, by which time output growth had fallen significantly. Sadat's open door economic policy (ODEP) was an attempt to inject new life into the industrial sector by decentralising decision making and opening the economy to international competition. The policy was a success and in recent years industrial output has grown rapidly (recording an annual increase of around 10 per cent in real terms) and has become the most important factor for the development of the Egyptian economy.

The springboard for industrial growth is to be found in the legislation behind the ODEP, that is Law 43 of 1974 and Law 32 of 1977. Although these laws were passed in order to stimulate foreign investment, they have become key instruments in boosting industrialisation and reforming public industry. Fiscal incentives and administrative facilities, which were originally intended to help only joint ventures between Egyptian and foreign firms, have since been extended to benefit also all-Egyptian concerns. And further, joint ventures between private and public firms are treated as private concerns. This process, which has been encouraged by the authorities, has encouraged domestic investors in the private sector, and has convinced many public sector managers of the worth of restructuring their organisation and increasing investments. Recent studies have shown a considerable increase in domestic investments whereas foreign investment has been modest.

The same studies show a growing tendency to export. There is considerable agreement on the need to increase exports, but there also exist important differences of opinion concerning how this should be done. It has been suggested that aggressive export-led industrialisation policies should be followed such as those implemented in South-East Asia. Further, it has been suggested that Egypt devalue its currency, and we have already alluded to the dangers associated with such a move. Even without following aggressive policies Egyptian industry is showing a growing propensity to export. In the long run, when investments will have increased the supply of manufactured goods, devaluation policies designed to favour exports might be more seriously considered.

It should be stressed however that although the future of the private sector seems bright and that it promises to attract a flow of foreign investments to Egypt, most of the burden of increasing productive investments in the short-medium term will be borne by the public sector, which is still dominant in the economic structure of the country.

Economic Assets and the Obstacles to Development

Alongside the rapid industrial development witnessed in recent years, and the optimism over the future of the Egyptian economy, attention must also be given to certain structural factors which epitomise Egypt and which will influence the economic development throughout the rest of this century. Like most other developing countries Egypt will have to overcome many serious obstacles. However, unlike most other LDCs Egypt is in a position to benefit from several favourable structural factors.

Although often seen in a bad light by the Egyptians themselves, Egypt's assets include the population, agriculture, hydrocarbons, tourism, the Suez Canal and the desert. Although often thought of as a useless space, the Egyptian desert, well situated as it is, near important fertile areas, will bring with it long term advantages to the country such as tourism, space for urban development and wide open land for isolated nuclear and industrial plants. It will also offer a location for the production of energy from alternative sources and it may contain valuable minerals.

The hydrocarbons will continue for many years to help Egypt's balance of payments just as they will continue to help the industrialisation process, which has already reached notable levels of experience and diversification.

For geopolitical reasons the Canal is not simply

destined to generate foreign income: it will also attract investments and create value added.

Finally, the intrinsic value of Egypt's cultural, historic and artistic heritage is so great as to guarantee the country a prosperous tourist trade.

Although agriculture and the population are Egypt's two main assets, their position as such is not generally acknowledged. Many see Egyptian agriculture as being a necessarily declining activity, and note that over the last hundred years or so the cultivated areas have increased less quickly than the population and that, in spite of the many land reclamation projects carried out, the possibility for further expansion is limited. Unit outputs are already very high with respect to other developing Arab countries and it would be difficult to increase them further.

On the other hand however, expert observers and the specialised literature are both optimistic as regards the possibility of further expanding agricultural output. Their optimism is based on the excellent irrigation offered by the Nile and the improvements that could be made by introducing new drainage techniques, a greater use of fertilisers and greater crop diversification.

However, the state of Egypt's agricultural sector depends on market prices, incentives, and the crops farmed, which in turn are tied to government subsidies and which distort competition, especially at the international level, and dampen both the initiative and control of Egyptian farmers. If domestic agricultural prices were closer to international prices and guaranteed as they are to farmers in the EEC, agricultural output in Egypt would increase considerably.

In Egypt there exists the widespread opinion that an excessive dependence on imports of essential foodstuffs could undermine the country's security. It has been this concept of food security which has stopped Egypt from concentrating on those products in which it has an international comparative advantage.

A programme of agricultural cooperation with Sudan has been agreed upon by the Egyptian authorities, and this cooperation with a close neighbour might contribute to overcoming the various objections which have hitherto blocked agricultural specialisation in Egypt.

In October 1982, Egypt had a total population of 45 millions and registered a growth rate of one million every ten months. The size, quality and rapid growth of the population are factors which have both aided and obstructed economic development in the country.

The fact that Egypt is the most populous of all the Arab countries and the one with the greatest absolute number of skilled persons is of great political and economic importance, in both the short term and the long term. This gives Egypt a major role in the socioeconomic development process of the Arab world and makes its collaboration necessary in any regional initiatives.

Thanks to high levels of emigration - which increased from 100,000 in 1973 to a current level of two million - the Egyptian economy has shared in the wealth of the Arab oil-producing countries in the form of emigrants' remittances. In 1980 these totalled three billion dollars, that is 70 per cent of all Egyptian exports in the same year. Emigration also promises to bring about an important structural benefit in the long term. It is likely that, when they return to Egypt, the emigrants will invest their savings in small firms or professional activities and in this respect emigration generates a process of unprecedented primitive accumulation. Signs that such a phenomenon is under way are already visible.

At the same time however there is a risk that Egypt's many assets may be rendered worthless by the rapid population growth. Whilst Egypt has many opportunities for development, it should not be forgotten that a large part of the population still lives in conditions of great poverty. A higher population growth, ceteris paribus, means that in order to reach a given growth target for individual income, it is necessary to invest a higher percentage of current income. The problem in Egypt regards the political and social feasibility of laying such a heavy burden on such a poor population. The rapid population growth influences not only the total sum of investments but also their allocation: along with population will grow the need to provide housing, public services and education. This risks generating a situation in which there are not sufficient resources left over to invest in industry and other productive sectors, which, as we have seen, offer the best opportunities for development.

Such a vicious circle already exists between the provision of social infrastructure and population intensity. The great numbers which have gathered in the urban areas have put enormous pressures on the inadequate public services. The high cost involved in increasing services at the same rate as the population means that fewer and fewer resources will be available to invest in productive sectors.

The high population growth will cause the labour force to increase and this will necessitate the creation of new jobs in the long term. However, although there are many difficulties involved in estimating the state of the labour market beyond 1985, it is probable that, barring a mass return of emigrants, Egypt will avoid serious unemployment problems and indeed might even register labour shortages in certain sectors. A labour rehabilitation scheme could attempt to benefit from the excess demand to re-employ Egypt's many underemployed, especially those in the public sector.

It is clear, however, that the outlook for the labour market is one of the most delicate matters facing the Egyptian economic authorities. In fact it will have a determining effect on the optimum capital intensity of new investments and on opinions concerning which sectors to promote in the domestic economy.

A recent study on Egypt's industrial sector, carried out by a research team from Boston University, suggests that highly labour intensive technologies be adopted in order to maximise the number of new jobs created, in view of the rapid population growth.

Although such proposals are designed to combat legitimate fears about mass unemployment, current industrial trends tend to paint a somewhat brighter picture for the future, based on increased efficiency in the public sector and expansion of the private sector and exporting firms.

Public Expenditure and the Social Background

Excessive public expenditure on current account is at the root of Egypt's savings gap and is therefore one of the main obstacles to economic development in the country. Any restraint of this current expenditure is made difficult by the many sociopolitical and international demands made on it. In fact domestic transfer payments and military expenditure account for most of the public sector deficit.

Income subsidies to families play a crucial role in Egyptian public finance and in the country's economy in general. The share of expenditure on subsidies in the public sector deficit accounts for roughly 14 per cent of total public expenditure, with subsidies on foodstuffs playing a particularly important role. These have increased steadily since the international price rise of 1973. This is due to the fact that, with the exception of rice, most of the important foodstuffs that the government subsidises are wholly or increasingly imported.

The subsidies have many effects on the Egyptian economy. They play an important role in determining:

(a) income distribution, maintaining salaries at subsistence levels for large numbers of the population;
(b) the relative price structure and the allocation of resources that this implies;
(c) the pattern of the inflationary process;
(d) the public sector deficit and the fact that it is financed almost totally by liquidity creation;
(e) the effects of the BOP.

Over the years the Egyptian economy has suffered many problems due to this system of subsidies.

The income distribution has caused a worsening of the relative position of the poorest groups over the past few years. Although the subsidies have been able to maintain income at subsistence levels, they have not in themselves been able to narrow the gap between the higher and lower income groups. Further, given the structure of the system (which includes subsidies on such goods as petrol and electricity) the higher income groups (and in some cases only the higher income groups) can benefit from the subsidies.

Many of the existing subsidies are no more than inappropriate prices for public services, which are insufficient to cover the costs of offering the service, and distort the entire structure of the costs of productive inputs. In this case the structure of the subsidies system contributes to bringing about a poor allocation of resources and therefore stands in the way of productivity growth and industrial competitiveness.

A similar but more general argument concerns the effect that the subsidies have on the terms of trade between agriculture and industry. Holding domestic farm prices well below those on the international market discourages agricultural production and encourages migration towards the urban centres. This makes for social as well as economic problems.

In general, therefore, the maintaining of a structure of subsidies can increase inflationary pressures in that it does not allow productivity levels to dictate resource allocation.

But Egypt's system of subsidies also fuels inflationary pressures by increasing the public deficit, given that any such measure would necessarily be accompanied by an increase of the salaries and incomes of public sector employees.

Due to these inherent inflationary pressures, Egypt's policy of subsidising goods and incomes in order to defend the real income of the poorer classes runs the risk of aggravating the problem, and worsening the relative position of the poor. The subsidies have not met with much success in their objective of creating a greater social equilibrium.

There is widespread agreement in Egypt regarding the need eventually to abolish the subsidies. However the various plans and projects that have so far been suggested have lacked political realism. In circumstances of growing inequality and poverty, the subsidies are seen as the minimum acceptable welfare policy and the sociopolitical situation could rapidly worsen if they were withdrawn. Recent studies have shown however, that in the medium-long term it will be possible to make gradual reforms to the system.

The problem of subsidies has assumed greater importance over the years because the gap between rich and poor has been growing steadily. This has been due to many factors, amongst which the most important have been migration towards the urban centres, the high concentration of wealth and the lack of social mobility.

Urban slums have been a result of the large numbers heading for the cities. The first generation of migrants found slightly better conditions in the city than they had left in the countryside. However, having been educated in the cities and having seen relative wealth at close quarters, their children have formed higher expectations. The gap between expectations and results is a general problem. The level of professional and academic preparation of the younger generations has increased over the years. In 1952 only one Egyptian in ten went to school, whereas by 1982 school was attended by one in five. This higher preparation however is often not matched by improved job opportunities and leads to frustration, not unlike that felt by the graduates from universities and colleges who are drafted into the public administration. The young graduates still accept these jobs but with respect to the opportunities offered by emigration or the ODEP, they are only second best solutions. The financial and non-financial rewards of migration, working for a foreign concern in Egypt, working in the domestic private sector, or working for a public firm are all higher than those to be earned in a public administration job. This suggests that, although the expectations of Egypt's youth are frustrated by current conditions, a return to a policy of bureaucratic expansion would not do much to improve the situation.

The most significant data however concern the growing concentration of income. With respect to 1970 the number of urban and rural families with an income below the poverty line has grown, and often conditions are similar to those in the 1950s. It has been the middle-lower income groups, and in some instances the middle groups, which have lost ground. The youngsters in the middle-low income urban areas are the social counterparts of those born in the 'slums'.

The problem is not simply one of subsidies and the problem of social control is not simply restricted to street disturbances. Income distribution is a function of both overall economic growth, and government policies. The positive effect of the higher economic growth, witnessed during the early years of the ODEP, has been nullified by the absence of some form of policy to correct the new income distribution, and by the abandonment of the socialist policies which characterised the phase of economic development and social promotion in the 60s.

It is clear the the ODEP cannot reasonably be followed without some parallel domestic income redistribution policy. Such a policy will be needed to dampen what could become a potentially explosive situation. The youngsters in the slums, the middle-low urban groups and the dissatisfied graduates and professionals also happen to be the militants of the Islamic groups. The Islamic resurgence is the result of many factors but in particular it is the result of social unrest.

Political Consensus and Military Expenditure

Although the vast majority of Egyptians do not agree with the violent tactics of some Islamic groups, they have not as yet explicitly condemned them nor have they shown much support for the establishment and its institutions. The indifference that followed the assassination of Sadat is evidence of this lack of support for the institutions. This is due to the absence of a democratic dialectic and is one of the main problems still to be overcome in modern day Egypt. What has already been said as regards armed opposition and terrorism, also holds true for the political economy. The more the authorities ask for sacrifices in order to reform the economy, the more they will depend on the political consensus of the population.

One of the major tasks facing Mubarak is to combine a suitable social coalition and a normal democratic style of government in the country. In other words, the solution to the problem of social control (which influences the launching of policies designed to overcome the savings gap) is to construct the basis of a real political consensus. However, with those who would like to see Sadat's policies followed to the letter on one side and those who call for a return to Nasser's socialist policies on the other, the future for Mubarak's intermediate coalition will not be without its problems.

There is little doubt that the armed forces will be called upon to play an important role in the future of Mubarak's coalition. Military expenditure will be important as a consequence. This however depends neither on the fact that Mubarak is a soldier nor on a desire for absolute power.

Just as the need to maintain public order constitutes the main obstacle to a cut in public expenditure, pressing demands made on Egypt's armed forces (in spite of the peace with Israel) by the international situation and fears for national security constitute the obstacles to a cut in military expenditure.

In order to regain its previous position in the international sphere and in particular in the Arab World, Egypt will have to increase its military strength. The policy taken on by Sadat, with the backing of the major Arab states, at the beginning of the 1970s was that of allying with the United States in order to be able to put pressure on Israel and arrive at a comprehensive settlement of the Middle East question.

To be feasible, this political process should have been accompanied by a credible military option. The military option would not have been used to win, but to maintain Egypt's leadership over the other Arab countries and, above all, to threaten a reopening of hostilities and the involvement of the superpowers if the USA did not push for a final settlement between Egypt and Israel. However the military option was gradually abandoned. After Camp David, Egypt was wholly dependent on the goodwill and ability of the USA to impose a solution on Israel, and had no power to influence American behaviour. At the same time Egypt found itself isolated and estranged from the Arab world.

Sadat's death left Egypt totally dependent on the United States and with no leverage with which to influence its policy towards Israel and the Arab World.

A credible military option is not attainable in the short term. On the other hand, the restoration of such an option would only be of value if it were backed up politically by the re-establishment of an Arab coalition. Any return to a relationship of effective collaboration with the other Arab countries is blocked by the Camp David agreements, and if the Egyptians were to disavow Camp David in order to rejoin an Arab coalition they would only be able to do so in an unacceptably weak position.

Thus Egypt is forced to follow a narrow policy which must overcome Camp David but which must also underline the continuity of the peace policy inaugurated by Egypt at Camp David in such a way as to maintain its prestige and authority at the regional level. Egypt's way is also blocked by its loss of influence on the United States and Reagan's Middle East policy. President Mubarak feels that the 'Reagan Plan' and the 'Jordan option' put the continuity of the Camp David policy at risk, and risk undermining Egypt's status at the regional level.

The cautious and pragmatic diplomacy with which Mubarak has faced this difficult situation is worthy of note. He has made the necessary gestures to reintegrate Egypt in inter-Arab relations - his presence at King Khaled's funeral, and his refusal to go to Jerusalem - but rather than formalise any relationship he is waiting until Egypt's position grows stronger. Without formally entering into an alliance he supported the Gulf countries and Iraq in the war against Iran and in so doing helped to re-establish the image of the military indispensability of Egypt in regional disturbances. He initiated a policy of diversification of Egypt's arms suppliers and now arms are also bought from Western Europe and work has been going on in collaboration with several European countries (France in particular) in the armaments industry, leading to the production of an excellent combat aircraft. But in order that the benefits of this diplomacy, which is aimed at increasing flexibility, may be reaped in the medium term, Egypt will have to re-establish its military credibility. This however will pose further problems for the Egyptian economy as regards the compatibility between economic development and the availability of resources, for in order to re-establish military credibility the Egyptian authorities will have to increase public expenditure and this will aggravate the savings gap which characterises the Egyptian economy.

Chapter One

THE EGYPTIAN ECONOMY AND FINANCIAL STRUCTURE: AN OVERVIEW

FROM PLANNING TO THE OPEN DOOR ECONOMIC POLICY

To understand Egypt's economic and financial problems and the policy options open to it today, it is necessary briefly to review the various phases into which the nation's recent political and economic history can be divided. Each of these phases, profoundly different from one another, has in fact left a deep imprint on the country's economic and social structure. The interweaving of these imprints makes the problems Egyptian economic policymakers face today all the more complex and difficult to resolve.

This can, of course, be said of any economic system, but it is especially relevant in Egypt's case, for in less than thirty years the economy has passed from a pre-industrial market system to widespread planning, which sharply accelerated industrialisation, and then back to a market economy, open to foreign capital, but also characterised by widespread state intervention and an apparatus to bolster the people's living standard which, at least in some respects, could be said to make Egypt a sort of 'welfare state'.

The initial phase, from 1952 to 1956, saw the economy almost entirely in private hands with the state's role limited to infrastructure investments and the provision of social services. The 1952 revolution brought

Nasser to power but at first the new government seemed to accentuate rather than diminish the relative weight of the private sectors. Private industry demanded and obtained lower taxes and more protection from the world economy, through a lowering of duties on imported raw materials and capital goods and higher tariffs on other imports which resulted in lower costs and higher prices, hence higher profits. In addition the flow of foreign capital into the country was encouraged, allowing foreign businessmen to hold majority interests in Egyptian companies.

One of the first elements of change was the agrarian reform, which set limits on the extent of rural landholdings and offered incentives for the formation of cooperatives.

From 1957 to 1960, policy options changed and there was a decided new impetus towards progressive nationalisation of the economy. In this phase the major foreign-owned enterprises were nationalised - French and British companies in particular - and so were Egyptian banks. At the same time the first five year plans for agriculture and industry were launched as well as general plans for economic and social development. In the wake of these measures capital formation in Egypt came rapidly under the control of the government authorities.

From 1961 to 1973 the Egyptian economy became an almost completely planned system and the private sector was relegated to a marginal role. In particular, very little room was allowed for private investment decisions. Infrastructures, mining and basic manufacturing, banking and insurance, all imports and three-quarters of exports came under the control of the public sector, while only domestic commerce, real estate, construction and light industry remained in the hands of the private sector. An important innovation of this phase, perhaps the one that more than any other would condition subsequent development, was the implementation of a policy of social welfare devised to govern income distribution and guarantee a minimum subsistence level to the population. The decisive element in this strategy was, and still is, the policy of price controls and the system of subsidies.

As Table 1.1 indicates, during the period of most rapid industrialisation, GDP growth accelerated to an annual rate of 10 per cent while the share of GDP absorbed by investment rose to 16.8 per cent. This trend was accompanied by a rise in the deficit for goods and services which went up to 4.1 per cent of GDP. After 1967, however, the year of the war with Israel and the closure of the Suez Canal, the economic expansion slowed down.

Between the two Arab-Israeli wars (1967-73) the Egyptian economy experienced an arrest of the tumultuous growth of previous years. A number of structural problems thus came to the surface, both domestic and external in nature, which would later prompt the changes introduced by Sadat under the 'Open Door Economic Policy' (ODEP).

International economic relations may be considered within the same division.

In the early 1950s the management of the external equilibrium (see Table 1.2) was aimed at stabilising the balance of payments, the main positive item on which was cotton exports, though Egypt also earned revenue from tourism and the Suez Canal. In spite of an initial encouragement of the inflow of foreign capital, successive nationalisation soon halted this source of currency and as a consequence the current account was financed mainly by the utilisation of reserves (see Table 1.3).

AN OVERVIEW OF THE EGYPTIAN ECONOMY AND FINANCE

By the late 1950s the progressive isolation of the Egyptian economy and its continuing dependency on imported goods led to a substantial deficit in the balance of payments which in turn led to the devaluation of the Egyptian pound in 1962. However, this measure was largely ineffective due to the rigidity of the economy. The value of exports (the volume of which was not increased) fell due to the worsening of the terms of trade and the cost of importing factors of production necessary to the industrialisation process

Table 1.1: Aggregate Domestic Expenditure, 1952/53 - 1973-76

Period (yearly averages)	GDP rate of growth at current prices	Expenditure as percentage of GDP			Deficit for goods and services as percentage of GDP
		Gross investment	Public consumption	Private consumption	
1952/53-1957/58	7.1	14.2	17.0	69.9	1.2
1958/59-1965/66	10.1	16.8	18.7	68.5	4.1
1966/67-1971/72	6.2	13.5	23.9	66.5	3.9
1973/76	15.3	21.2	25.4	66.3	12.9

Sources: Egyptian Ministry of Planning, CAPMAS, World Bank estimates.

Table 1.2: Balance on Goods and Services, 1952-72 (millions of US dollars)

	1952-58		1959-66		1967-72	
	Cumulated total	Yearly average	Cumulated total	Yearly average	Cumulated total	Yearly average
Trade balance	-942	-135	-2,475	-310	-2,007	-335
Exports (fob)	2,963	423	4,115	514	4,475	745
(Cotton, textiles)	(2,417)	(345)	(2,895)	(362)	(2,786)	(464)
Imports (cif)	-3,905	-558	-6,590	-824	-6,482	-1,080
(Cereals)	(-365)	(-52)	(-968)	(-121)	(-782)	(-130)
Services	435	62	865	108	-243	-40
Inflows	1,600	229	2,471	309	1,235	206
(Suez Canal)	(617)	(88)	(1,314)	(164)	(108)	(15)
(Tourism)	(706)	(101)	(775)	(97)	(463)	(77)
Outflows	-1,165	-166	-1,606	-201	-1,478	-246
(Interests and dividends)	(-245)	(-35)	(-197)	(-25)	(-421)	(-70)
Balance on goods and services	-507	-73	-1,610	-202	-2,250	-375

Source: Central Bank of Egypt.

Table 1.3: External Deficit Financing, 1952-72 (millions of US dollars)

	1952-58		1959-66		1967-72	
	Cumulated total	Yearly average	Cumulated total	Yearly average	Cumulated total	Yearly average
Balance on goods and services	-507	-73	-1,610	-202	-2,250	-375
Debt service	-53	-8	-448	-56	-1,496	-249
Foreign currency requirements	-560	-81	-2,058	-251	-3,746	-624
Supply of funds	73	11	1,636	204	3,564	594
Grants and other transfers	...	...	12	1	1,566	261
Loans	...	...	1,725	216	1,638	273
Loans from Comecon countries	(...)	(...)	(n.)	(n.)	(810)	(133)
Other inflows a	46	7	-108	14	225	42
Net monetary flows and errors and omissions	27	4	7	1	105	18
Change in reserves (convertible currency)	-487	-70	-422	-53	-182	-30

Note: a. includes short term commercial credit

Source: Central Bank of Egypt and World Bank.

grew. Egypt's resource requirements were satisfied by financial aid from the communist block countries (Egypt's main allies at the time) and wheat imports from the United States.

Then in 1967 the Egyptian economy suffered a serious blow when the Canal was closed. The losses on the invisible account were only partly compensated for by an increase in merchandise exports.

This export increase was made possible by a series of bilateral agreements between Egypt and the Comecon countries, from which Egypt received much financial assistance (see Table 1.4). On the other hand Egypt imported mainly from the West and this continued to worsen the external balance, in that, since only those exports not financed by the bilateral agreements brought about an increase in foreign reserves, Egyptian imports absorbed reserves faster than they were being added to. As a consequence, the 'foreign exchange gap' turned out to be higher than the balance of goods and services.

Prior to 1958 two agreements for development financing were reached with the Soviet Union to build a plant for the production of iron and steel. In 1958 Egypt signed an agreement of commercial cooperation with West Germany. These agreements, however, did not require any cash disbursement and as a result Egypt did not have any real debts until the end of 1958.

In the following period, which was characterised by an intense process of planned industrialisation, the amount of financial assistance that poured into Egypt was considerable, particularly on the part of the Soviet Union (see Table 1.4) and the United States. The short term credits only became relevant in 1964/5 and 1967/8 when the United States brought their financial assistance to an end.

Between 1967 and 1972 Western aid was minimal and this gap was filled by the Arab countries (in particular Saudi Arabia, Kuwait and Libya) which, following the Khartoum summit, 1967, assured Egypt that they would replace the revenues lost (by Egypt) as a result of the closure of the Suez Canal. The Soviet Union, however, continued to be Egypt's main source of financial assistance.

Table 1.4: Average Yearly Inflow of Loans (net), 1956-60/1971-75 (millions of US dollars)

	1956-60	1961-65	1966-70	1971-75
Medium and long term loans	71.5	77.2	81.2	424.5
Western countries (a)	45.0	16.0	21.1	46.0
Comecon countries	26.5	36.4	51.2	41.1
Arab countries	-	24.8	8.9	337.4
IBRD/IDA	6.2	2.5	-4.3	15.2
Suppliers' credits	20.0	32.2	22.1	64.6
Euromarket loans	-	-	-	45.2
Bank loans	2.8	14.3	5.0	215.8
Total	100.5	126.2	104.0	765.3
Note (a) Including US loans repayable in Egyptian pounds	16.8	76.7	-24.4	-15.1

Source: World Bank, Central Bank of Egypt and Egyptian Ministry of Planning.

From the early 1970s to the Camp David agreements (1979), the Egyptian economy entered a new, profound process of transformation which eventually led to its present-day configuration. It was in this period, in fact, that the decisions that would usher in the ODEP were taken. Moreover, with the Camp David peace agreements, Egypt regained the capacity to exploit its Sinai oil resources to the full as well as enjoying revenues from the reopened Suez Canal and the income from the tourism which returned once peace was restored. At the same time growing emigration produced a substantial flow of remittances.

The ODEP was institutionalised by Law 43 of October 1974 which dealt with the regulation of foreign investments and the setting-up of foreign firms in the country.

Dessouki (1981) notes that as early as 1970 Sadat had already taken a series of actions geared to promote the expansion of the private sector. In 1971 the Egyptian Central Bank contributed 500 million Kuwait dinars to the capital of the Arab Investment Guarantee Fund (instituted under the patronage of the Arab League) to guarantee private Arab investments against 'non-commercial risks'. Then, in order to improve the climate for private investment, a law was passed in May 1971 which abolished the government's power to appropriate private capital. The new constitution confirmed this stance. In July 1971 an agreement was signed with Great Britain for the reimbursement of properties confiscated in 1960.

Law 65 of September 1971 guaranteed foreign investments against confiscation and made them tax free for a period of five years. It also permitted the repatriation of profits and capital. In April of the following year a commercial treaty was signed by Egypt and the European Community, and an agreement was reached by Western governments, oil companies and Arab countries regarding the international financing of the Sumed project (an oil pipeline from Suez to the Mediterranean). In June diplomatic relations were re-established with West Germany and the government set up a fund to finance private sector imports. A new exchange market was also set up with a devalued rate with respect to the official rate in order to encourage tourism. And finally, properties sequestrated by the State were returned or reimbursed.

In 1973 this policy of progressive liberalisation was continued; tourists were able to buy duty free goods in foreign currency and private individuals were allowed to sell apartments for foreign currency and then use this currency to import building materials (this practice led to the so-called 'own exchange system'); a parallel money market was set up allowing commercial banks to operate in foreign currency (and this eventually led to today's two tier monetary system).

1975 saw the beginning of a series of consultations with the International Monetary Fund (IMF). This was to lead to the adoption of a stabilisation programme in order to assure the USA and Saudi Arabia, Egypt's two main creditors, of the country's will to accept the rules of the international market and so convince them to start a large programme of financial assistance.

In 1977 the Egyptian government, under pressure from the IMF, decided to eliminate most of the subsidies on subsistence consumption goods. Following this decision, however, rioting broke out, leading to more than seventy deaths (Dessouki 1981). This episode convinced the Western countries and the Arab states to concede funds to Egypt independently of the dismantling of the subsidy system. It also highlighted the constraints that might be met by any attempt to return directly to a free market economy.

This background helps us to understand the nature of the Egyptian economy today. It is an open economy but one in which the role of the State is still dominant, at least in two aspects: the determining weight of public industry and the 'welfare state' which is based on the subsidy system.

GROWTH, INFLATION, SAVINGS AND INVESTMENT

Since 1974, the year in which the ODEP was officially introduced, the Egyptian economy has grown rapidly and the structure of its interdependence with the international economy has undergone substantial modifications (see Table 1.5). The slowness with which national accounts data are elaborated, combined with their less-than-perfect reliability, prevents us from offering a fully up-to-date picture of the performance of the main macroeconomic indicators. A summary indication of the ODEP's impact is nevertheless offered by the data in Table 1.6 which gives an idea of the evolution of a number of macroeconomic aggregates from the start of the ODEP to 1980.

If we look at exports and imports as a share of GDP, a first approximation indicator of the economy's openness, we find that these shares doubled for exports and tripled for imports. Considering imports and exports together, Egypt emerges as the most foreign-trade-dependent economy of all the less developed countries (LDCs) with a population of more than 20 million; and this remains true, as the World Bank (1980) has noted, even if workers' remittances are not considered.

Another element that has characterised the opening of the economy, as was recalled above, is the substantial inflow of capital. In the six years from 1974 to 1979, the total foreign capital inflow (including direct investment) amounted to nearly $20 billion. This flow led to an increase in the ratio of foreign debt to GDP which hit 56.7 per cent at the end of 1979, thanks primarily to the grant component of the debt.

The rate of growth of GDP, as given in official figures, averaged 8 per cent over this period but probably the single element that best summarises the effect of the ODEP is the rise in the investment rate.

From 1975 to 1979 gross investment (including inventory accumulation) averaged 30 per cent of GDP. In large part private investment, both Egyptian and foreign, was responsible for this increase. This increment in the rate of accumulation is all the more surprising if we consider that between 1967 and 1973 gross investment was just barely enough to cover capital depreciation.

Much of this investment, it should be noted, concerns the accumulation of stocks, which decreased considerably during the interwar period. Moreover, in 1974 the closure of the traditional export markets of

Table 1.5: Impact of ODEP (Percentage Shares of GDP)

	(1972/73)	(1979/80)
Exports (goods and services)	14.6	43.8
Imports (goods and services)	21.0	53.0
Gross foreign capital inflow (including direct investment)	10.4	17.6
Stock of existing debt	38.0	58.0
Debt service (% of GDP)	2.4	8.2
(% of exports)	16.2	21.4
Investment	22.3	30.4
Private investment	5.2	9.4
Average GDP growth rate (1972-80)	8.0	

Source: World Bank.

Eastern Europe meant that stocks were increased by unsold products.

In any case, with the progressive introduction of the ODEP, the rate of Egyptian economic expansion was extraordinary. In fact, a number of studies suggest that the growth was even greater than is indicated by the official figures.

By an examination of the material available, we can highlight some central points which will allow us to draw an accurate picture of Egypt's major macroeconomic problems. In the following pages, we will examine each of these individually and in the last section of this chapter an attempt will be made to give an overall picture, with the intention of singling out the main problems that currently face the Egyptian economy.

According to some studies (Choucri and Eckhaus, 1979, ESU, 1981), both the real and the nominal income growth rates may have been higher than is indicated by official data which would mean a higher real growth rate for the economy as a whole.

This hypothesis is suggested by a comparison of national accounts data with other indicators, in particular those related to the expansion of liquidity. A comparison of these figures reveals, for example, that in the 1970s (see Table 1.7) liquidity grew much faster than GDP at current prices (and that, consequently, money velocity diminished).

As it is reasonable to suppose that the data on liquidity expansion are correct, we need to explain the use made of the greater liquidity injected into the system.

One possibility is that the growth of real income was greater than is recorded in official statistics. This is the thesis argued by Choucri and Eckhaus (1979) and admitted by the ESU (1981). Choucri and Eckhaus hold this hypothesis to be quite probable, in that it is apparently supported by the behaviour of such other indicators as electricity consumption, which usually follows the same trend as industrial production.

If this hypothesis were to be confirmed, the conclusion would have to be that the real growth of the Egyptian economy under the ODEP has been even higher than the already impressive levels recorded in official

Table 1.6: GDP, Overall Resources, Investment, 1974-79, Current Prices (millions of Egyptian pounds)

	1974	1975	1976	1977	1978	1979
GDP at market prices	4,339	5,218	6,727	8,283	9,671	12,409
Imports of goods and services, excluding factor services	1,616	2,154	2,287	2,770	3,626	5,804
Exports of goods and services, excluding factor services	890	1,053	1,498	1.876	2,130	3,905
Total resources	5,065	6,319	7,516	9,177	11,167	14,308
Consumption	4,090	4,578	5,606	6,743	8,085	10,496
Total investment	975	1,741	1,910	2,434	3,082	3,812
Fixed investment	685	1,282	1,471	1,873	2,666	3,402
Change in inventories	290	459	439	561	416	410
Percentage of GDP						
Total investment	22.5	33.4	28.4	29.4	31.9	30.7
Fixed investment	15.8	24.6	21.9	22.6	27.5	27.4
Change in inventories	6.7	8.8	6.5	6.8	4.4	3.3
Fixed investment/ Total resources	13.5	20.3	19.6	20.4	23.9	23.9

Source: World Bank.

Table 1.7: Expansion of Liquidity, 1970-79 (millions of Egyptian pounds)

	1970	1971	1972	1973	1974	1975	1976	1977	1978	1979	Average annual growth rate 70-79	73-79	78-79
Money Supply (M1)	783	846	989	1,205	1,053	1,863	2,239	2,942	3,547	4,324	20.9	23.7	21.9
Currency	525	559	631	777	948	1,156	1,388	1,749	2,184	2,627	19.6	22.5	20.2
Time deposits	258	287	358	428	555	707	851	1,193	1,363	1,697	23.3	25.7	24.5
Quasi-money	270	238	266	331	498	567	822	1,160	1,658	2,454	27.8	39.6	48.0
Liquidity (M2)	1,053	1,084	1,255	1,536	2,001	2,430	3,061	4,102	5,205	6,778	23.0	28.0	30.2
GDP at current prices at factor costs	2,793	2,958	3,196	3,515	4,154	5,064	6,164	7,400	9,008	11,936	17.5	22.0	32.5
GDP at constant (1975 prices at factor costs	3,826	4,051	4,220	4,220	4,548	5,061	5,521	5,907	6,532	7,065	7.0	8.1	8.2
Velocity of circulation	2.65	2.73	2.55	2.29	2.07	2.08	2.00	1.80	1.73	1.76	-4.6	-4.4	1.1

Source: Central Bank of Egypt.

Table 1.8: Consumer Price Index, Urban Population (June 1965 = 100)

	June 1976	Variation %	June 1977	Variation %	June 1978	Variation %	June 1979	Variation %	June 1980	Variation %	April 1981
General Index	167.0	13.5	185.7	11.2	207.8	11.9	220.4	6.1	274.4	24.5	305.2
Food and beverages	202.0	19.7	228.3	13.0	249.6	9.3	254.6	2.0	337.8	32.7	390.5
Housing	109.0	1.8	109.3	-	110.2	0.8	111.2	0.9	116.1	4.4	114.5
Furniture and other durables	135.7	12.2	146.3	7.8	179.5	22.7	187.7	4.6	187.8	0.1	201.4
Clothing	144.7	7.0	161.1	11.3	226.8	40.8	247.4	9.1	292.6	18.3	309.6
Transportation and communication	135.1	9.7	144.5	7.0	145.1	0.4	185.6	27.9	193.9	4.5	207.9
Entertainment and medicines	142.6	4.7	168.0	17.8	202.0	20.2	239.4	18.5	269.9	12.7	276.8
Personal	128.0	3.9	132.4	3.4	150.0	13.3	178.7	19.1	210.7	17.9	215.4

Source: CAPMAS.

data. For precisely this reason several analysts (ESU, 1981; US Embassy, 1982) have put forth the hypothesis that, partly as a result of the persistent international recession, the Egyptian growth rate over the next few years will be much lower than in the past, as it is inconceivable that such rapid growth as the 1970s witnessed could be sustained.

A second possibility is that inflation was higher than officially recorded (see Table 1.8). This possibility can certainly not be neglected, especially in view of the presence of subsidies (which will be discussed later on) that keep both retail and wholesale prices indices artificially low.

According to official data, the rate of variation in the GDP deflator was relatively modest (see Table 1.9), never exceeding 14 per cent in those years. But since the late 1970s, and in the first years of this decade, prices have soared.

In 1981 the monetary authorities followed a restrictive policy which succeeded in lowering the rate of inflation with respect to 1980. Recent estimates however suggest that in 1982 the inflationary process, especially as regards consumer price variation, has once again speed up.

Irrespective of the actual price movements, the substantial accumulation of liquidity, typified by the growing value of real money stocks, would seem to confirm that the inflationary potential of the Egyptian economy has been growing steadily and that it may soon be transformed into effective inflationary pressure causing rapidly and constantly rising prices. This, as a third hypothesis, would also explain the discrepancy between monetary expansion, income growth and price rises that emerge from the official data.

Moreover, the very structure of Egypt's money and credit markets generates an accumulation of repressed inflation. The still scanty though growing credit capacity, but primarily individual preferences, lead to money hoarding, while the influx of liquidity from abroad through channels not directly controlled by the authorities helps satisfy the high liquidity preference.

This inflationary potential represents a major constraint with regard, for instance, to restructuring

Table 1.9: GDP Deflator (1975 - 100)

1970	73
1971	73
1972	76
1973	79
1974	91
1975	100
1976	111.6
1977	125.2
1978	137.9
1979	168.9

Source: CAPMAS

Table 1.10: Real Monetary Balances (M2/GDP deflator)

1970	1971	1972	1973	1974	1975	1976	1977	1978	1979	Average yearly growth rates		
										1970/79	1973/79	1978/79
1,442	1,485	1,651	1,944	2,199	2,430	2,547	3,276	3,774	4,013	12.0	12.8m	6.3

Source: Central Bank of Egypt.

government expenditure and the system of subsidies which would obviously have to be increased if new inflationary pressures emerged. This potential, moreover, could further stimulate demands for income redistribution, which have been strong in recent years and whose accentuation could augment problems of political and social stability.

Finally, inasmuch as it is essentially a potential demand for non-subsistence consumer goods, which are mostly imported, this inflationary potential represents a threat to the balance of payments.

The inflationary potential thus risks aggravating the two main obstacles - in Egypt as in many LDCs - to continued growth; the foreign exchange gap and the savings gap.

A number of studies (e.g. World Bank, 1980; Kheir El Din, 1980) have concluded that of these two gaps the more important for the Egyptian economy is the gap between savings and investment.

The favourable trend in the balance of payments over the past few years seems in fact to confirm that the availability of foreign currency does not constitute a serious obstacle to Egyptian development (at least not in the short-medium term). However, the future evolution of this constraint will depend on the ability of the Egyptian economy to promote sufficient capital accumulation to provide the country with a productive structure capable of exporting a growing share of manufactured goods and primary products.

In other words, the central issue facing the Egyptian economy concerns the behaviour of future investments and the economy's ability to finance them. However, due to the still substantial presence of public enterprises in industry, the evolution of the savings gap depends mainly on the formation of public savings.

We have recalled that from the outset of the ODEP (see Table 1.6) the share of investments in the GDP has been growing, reaching a third of national product. Along with investment growth, however, there has been a quite remarkable growth in private consumption, which together with the growing government budget deficit has brought a current account deficit in the balance of payments that has been financed essentially by an inflow of public capital from abroad.

The growth of private consumption has been more and more marked in recent years. The causes are to be sought in various factors which, by encouraging individual consumption, have discouraged saving.

The growth of individual consumption is explainable as one of the effects of the progressive opening of the economy to the international market. As mentioned above, this has led to a rise in available liquidity. At least at first, the increased liquidity produced an increase in real wealth, thanks to relatively contained inflation (until recent years). The containment of inflation, in turn, was in large part due to the widespread practice of subsidies throughout the economy. (Subsidies cover not only subsistence goods, but also goods such as cars, gasoline, and electric power.) The increased level of real wealth, however, did not bring with it a substantial increase in voluntary savings; the accumulation of liquidity should, therefore, be considered a sort of 'temporary forced savings' waiting to be transformed into demand for consumer goods, mainly imports, as soon as supply constraints relax enough to permit it.

It should be added that the real wealth of the richest strata of the population has grown as a consequence of the rise in real estate values caused by the pressure of demand for housing from the constantly growing urban population.

In the face of this accumulation of wealth, the economy has not generated a mechanism for its allocation that would permit an adequate shift of resources from consumption to investment. This shortcoming can be traced mainly to the inadequate development of a financial and credit system capable of encouraging private saving, as well as to the still scanty ability of private and public industry to take advantage of the opportunities that may arise.

The problem of inflation is also crucial with regard to the inadequacy of aggregate savings. The amount of domestic, and in particular, public savings is in fact closely connected with the mechanism of price formation and with the relation between domestic and international prices.

During the 1960s, when there was de facto a planned economy, Egypt was a 'fixed price economy' and up to the mid-70s, that is, until the introduction of the ODEP, prices played no major allocative role. Resources were distributed administratively and the market played only a marginal role. Furthermore, both domestic and international inflation were quite moderate, and even if certain domestic prices happened to be 'out of line' with world prices, this produced no significant economic distortions.

The opening up of the Egyptian economy coincided with the explosion of worldwide inflation and the devaluation of the Egyptian pound, while the market began to take on a growing role. The result was an upward pressure on prices induced by attempts to re-adjust the relative prices which had been altered by inflation itself.

The upward surge of prices, in turn, put an upward pressure on government spending for subsidies, which as we have noted is one of the main features of the Egyptian 'welfare state'. In other words, the need to maintain the real income of the poorest part of the population, despite inflation, entailed an alteration of relative prices which seriously hurt the formation of public savings. Because of the presence of subsidies, inflation in Egypt, encouraging investment, tends to widen the savings gap (inasmuch as it lowers the state's propensity to save) and in this way inhibits the economy's growth capability.

The problem under discussion can now be formulated more explicitly. The main obstacle to the future growth of the Egyptian economy is the unsatisfactory performance of public finance, on the investment side and also, and primarily, on the savings side.

This phenomenon can be explained in various ways. One interpretation takes the aforementioned presence of a savings gap as the main obstacle to economic development, attributing its existence mainly to the inadequate formation of public savings with respect to expenditure.

A second aspect concerns the recently noted (Gemmel, 1981) fact that an increase in government expenditure's share of national income, regardless of how it is financed, entails lower growth capacity for the system. This thesis is based on the idea that the public sector in general has lower productivity than the private sector and that therefore its relative expansion lowers (or slows) the rise in the average productivity of the system.

This argument, derived from a model devised for the analysis of advanced economies, can only be partially valid for the Egyptian economy (Bacon and Eltis 1976), and specifically for that portion of public expenditure not connected with investment. The consumption component of Egyptian government expenditure is however certainly significant, especially if subsidies are considered.

This brings us to the final aspect of this question. The decisive weight of public enterprises in the Egyptian economy means that despite the growing role of private industry, public investment is still the central factor determining capital accumulation trends.

PUBLIC FINANCES AND THE QUESTION OF SUBSIDIES: THE ROOTS OF THE SAVINGS GAP

Thanks to its past history and despite the decision to institute the ODEP, the Egyptian administration still disposes of a vast array of economic policy instruments, the five year plan, the annual plan, the internal budget, the foreign exchange budget, the central bank, controls on trade flows, and so on, as well as local government agencies and ownership of a large part of industry and banking.

It is no simple matter to distinguish clearly among the tasks of the various agencies of government economic intervention. There are institutions that act as public enterprises, others that function as commercial companies. From the macroeconomic viewpoint, then, it is more useful to analyse the consolidated government budget. Still, it is necessary to distinguish among three main functions of the public sector: the administrative function, equivalent to the traditional role of the state as the supplier of services such as education, health etc.; the economic function performed by public enterprises; and the 'welfare state' function, centring mainly on the subsidy mechanism. What follows is an evaluation of public revenues and public spending.

Before proceeding, however, it is worth underscoring the importance of the interplay between public finance and the international market. On the revenue side, taxes on foreign trade represent about 60 per cent of indirect taxes and 26 per cent of total state revenues. On the expenditure side, it should be noted that some 90 per cent of the consumption subsidies are for imported goods. It follows that terms-of-trade policy has special importance for Egypt and that this policy should be evaluated with an eye to its interrelation with the various aspects of economic policy.

Table 1.11 shows the trend in public savings in the 1970s. Particularly noteworthy is the portion of consumption subsidies which turned government savings negative, while savings in the 'public' sector, i.e. by the public enterprises, remained positive and rising in those years.

Table 1.12, which compares public sector saving with public sector investments (expressed as percentage of GDP), shows the public sector's growing resource gap.

We can now turn our attention to a more detailed analysis of government revenues (see Table 1.13).

In the period under examination, indirect taxes accounted for over two-thirds of total revenues. Of them, tariff duties and the profits obtained thanks to the two-tier exchange system (see below) accounted for more than half. This implies that the growing international openness of the Egyptian economy could, from this viewpoint, provide a major increment in revenues. Much will depend on the success of the free zone policy in increasing trade.

Turning our attention now to direct taxes, it is worth noting that the largest share of direct taxation comes from the tax on industrial profits (which increased from 3.3 per cent of GDP in 1974 to 5.4 per cent in 1979). This increase was mainly thanks to the rapid growth of value added in the oil industries and the Suez Canal.

Also from the point of view of public finance

Table 1.11: Formation of Public Savings (millions of Egyptian pounds, current prices)

	1974	1975	1976	1977	1978	1979
1. Indirect taxes	552	784	996	1,530	1,563	1,841
2. Direct taxes on private income	92	97	122	136	135	147
3. Direct taxes on public sector income	105	159	223	324	478	596
4. Gross government revenues	749	1,040	1,341	1,990	2,176	2,584
5. Total government consumption	899	1,298	1,670	1,628	2,012	2,375
6. Gross government savings (excluding subsidies)	-150	-258	-329	362	164	209
7. Consumption subsidies	410	622	434	650	900	1,370
8. Net government savings	-560	-880	-763	-288	-736	-1,161
9. Net financial savings of public sector	287	317	449	496	773	1,118
Transferred profits	188	154	243	384	539	1,001
Self-financing	150	210	331	268	473	350
Other income	97	120	101	113	119	230
Deficit of public authorities	-87	-93	-119	-139	-185	-229
Interest on public debt	-61	-74	-107	-130	-173	-234
10. Public sector inventory accumulation	174	275	263	337	250	270
11. Social security surplus	245	253	295	353	381	456
12. Consolidated savings of public sector (8+9+10+11)	146	-35	244	898	668	683

Source: World Bank.

Table 1.12: Public Savings and Public Investment, 1974-79 (per cent of GDP)

	1974	1975	1976	1977	1978	1979
Public savings	3.3	-0.7	3.6	11.0	6.9	5.5
Public investment	18.2	26.3	21.3	22.2	25.4	23.0

Source: World Bank.

Table 1.13: Government Tax Revenues, 1974-79 (per cent of GDP)

	1974	1975	1976	1977	1978	1979
Indirect taxes	12.7	15.0	14.8	18.5	16.2	14.8
Excise duties and price differentials	4.5	4.4	4.2	4.1	3.8	4.5
Foreign trade taxes	5.3	7.7	8.0	11.8	9.5	7.3
Local government collections	1.5	1.8	1.3	1.3	1.5	1.3
Other indirect taxes	1.4	1.1	1.3	1.3	1.4	1.7
Direct taxes	4.6	4.9	5.1	5.6	6.3	6.0
Business profits tax	3.3	3.7	4.1	4.7	5.6	5.4
(petroleum and Suez)	(0.5)	(0.8)	(1.4)	(1.6)	(2.2)	(2.4)
Personal income tax	0.8	0.6	0.7	0.6	0.5	0.4
Property taxes	0.5	0.6	0.3	0.3	0.2	0.2

Source: World Bank.

Table 1.14: Government and Public Sector Expenditure, 1974-79 (per cent of GDP)

	1974	1975	1976	1977	1978	1979
Government consumption	20.7	24.9	24.8	19.6	20.8	19.1
(General public services)	(4.0)	(4.5)	(4.6)	(5.2)	(4.8)	(5.8)
(Defence) a	(7.8)	(11.3)	(11.2)	(7.2)	(7.3)	(5.6)
(Education, health and other services)	(8.9)	(9.1)	(9.0)	(7.2)	(8.7)	(7.7)
Consumer subsidies b	9.4	11.9	6.4	7.8	9.3	11.0
(Wheat and flour)	(4.2)	(5.0)	(2.6)	(1.8)	(3.0)	(5.1)
Public authority deficits	2.0	1.8	1.8	1.7	1.9	1.9
Interest on Public Debt	1.4	1.4	1.6	1.6	1.8	1.9
Public investment expenditure c	18.2	26.3	21.3	22.2	25.4	23.0

Notes: a. Includes emergency fund deficit.
b. Includes adjustments for arrears in 1978 and 1979
c. Includes public sector stock accumulation.

Source: World Bank.

therefore Egypt's great structural resources (oil, Suez Canal, tourism and emigrants' remittances) constitute a guarantee of at least minimum revenue, but at the same time they increase Egypt's dependency on external factors. These sources of government revenue are also the most efficient, the other sources being subject to high levels of evasion.

Personal income taxes (which account for less than one per cent of GDP) are almost irrelevant as regards determining the total yield.

The limited impact of direct taxation on the economy plus the fact that even the high income Egyptians benefit from the vast system of subsidies, lead to the conclusion that the Egyptian 'welfare state', besides being in effect universal, lacks the kind of redistributive fiscal measures required by such economic and social arrangements. This limited impact however is hardly justifiable after the 1974 implementation of the ODEP which favoured middle and high income classes (see Chapter 3).

Let us now briefly consider the expenditure side (excluding subsidies). The structure of Egyptian public expenditure can be summed up in just a few features (see Table 1.14). Current public expenditure absorbs a very high share of GDP (around 35 per cent) while the share going for public consumption (around 20 per cent) is close to average international levels. Investment spending has risen since the implementation of the ODEP, surpassing 20 per cent of GDP.

A significant portion of public consumption and of current government expenses in general goes for defence. This means that if current spending on general services and other items such as education and health is excluded, most of Egypt's current spending is the fruit of specific government choices in both foreign policy (defence) and domestic policy (subsidies). Since current expenditures represent the principal factor engendering the savings gap, the future closing of the gap will depend on two fundamental decisions: replacing the subsidy system as the cornerstone of the 'welfare state' and achieving a stable, lasting peace which makes it possible significantly to reduce defence spending.

It should not be forgotten, however, that expenditure on education too is at least to some extent welfare expenditure. This is due to the fact that even in the days before the ODEP the state encouraged easy access to higher education, and guaranteed graduates jobs in the public administration. (This has consequently become a reservoir of underemployed labour whose productivity is practically zero.) However, since the advent of the ODEP, the public administration has lost its attractiveness for the young graduates due to the increase in alternative employment opportunities offered by the development of the private firms (both domestic and foreign). The discussion is different however as regards public investments. In spite of the fact that the level of public sector investments is considerable and, therefore, such as to increase further the savings gap, they can and indeed must continue to play a central role in Egypt's industrialisation process. Their effectiveness therefore, must be considered from the macroeconomic point of view.

THE IMPACT OF SUBSIDIES ON THE EGYPTIAN ECONOMY

As will already be clear, subsidies play a crucial role in Egypt's public finance and in the Egyptian economy in general. The relative weight of subsidies (for consumer goods in particular) increased steadily throughout the 1970s (see Table 1.15). Since 1973 in fact expenditure on subsidies has increased sharply and constantly in concomitance with the big jumps in world prices, which, as will be remembered, strongly influence the level of subsidies. Apart from rice, all the major subsidised foodstuffs are largely or totally imported, and the import share for those not totally imported has been growing. Food subsidies take two forms: 'direct' subsidies, which appear under the 'cost of living subsidies' item of the government budget, i.e. subsidies for wheat, flour, etc.; and 'implicit' subsidies, which consist of the losses borne by the government owing to the difference between domestic production costs and the selling price to the consumer, as in the case of the rice subsidy.

The second category also includes subsidies on non-food items, such as electricity, gasoline, automobiles and so on. This second item does not appear in the government budget as a subsidy. Instead, it takes the form of losses for public enterprises and is thus to be considered a form of price administration.

The subsidised goods are supplied to the population through four different channels. The most important goods (such as bread) are available in unlimited quantities at the subsidised price, others, such as oil, sugar and tea, are only obtainable on the presentation of a ration ticket. However, they are supplied at regular intervals. Others yet, such as rice, are rationed but are supplied at irregular intervals depending on availability, and finally such goods as frozen meat and fish are sold on the principle of first come first served.

Table 1.16 shows the impact of subsidy expenditure on Egypt's fiscal balance and how it is financed.

Subsidy expenditure as a share of the overall budget deficit has grown steadily and now represents some 14 per cent of total public expenditure. This fact, along with other considerations, has sparked an intense and widespread debate among Egyptian politicians and scholars on the consequences of the subsidies for the Egyptian economy and on the necessity or desirability of eliminating them.

The subsidies play a variety of roles in the economy. They are important because of the role they play:

(a) in determining the distribution of income (and because they are essential for the maintenance of subsistence-level incomes for the bulk of the population),
(b) in determining the structure of relative prices and their allocative role,
(c) in determining the performance of the inflation process,
(d) as a determinant of the state's budget deficit and its financing (almost exclusively by liquidity creation),
(e) and because of the repercussions on the country's balance of payments.

Table 1.15: Cost of Living Subsidies, 1973 to 1979 (millions of Egyptian pounds)

	1973	1974	1975	1976	1977	1978	1979
1. General Authority for Supply Commodity (GASC)	115.5	337.2	449.3	352.4	407.2	434.7	995.7
2. Others	15.3	91.1	131.0	105.8	88.6	246.1	292.7
3. Total	130.8	428.3	580.3	458.2	495.8	680.8	1288.4
4. Percentage share of GASC (Item 1/Item 3)	88.3	78.7	77.4	76.9	82.1	63.9	77.3

Source: Egyptian Ministry of Finance.

Table 1.16: Cost of Living Subsidies, Budget Deficit and Current Government Expenditure (millions of Egyptian pounds)

	Cost of living subsidies (1)	Budget deficit (2)	Debt with CBE (3)	Net CBE loans (4)	Share of deficit financed by CBE debt (5)	Share of subsi- dies in deficit (½) (6)	Total government expenditure (7)
1973	130.8	534.0	1,514.5	195.9	36.7	24.5	-
1974	428.3	805.0	1,818.7	304.2	37.8	53.2	3,161.3
1975	580.3	1,388.0	2,832.9	1,014.2	73.1	41.8	4,717.4
1976	458.2	1,337.0	3,251.5	418.6	31.3	34.3	4,777.8
1977	495.8	1,269.0	3,593.4	341.9	26.9	39.1	5,402.0
1978	680.8	2,097.8	4,595.4	802.0	38.2	32.5	6,680.2
1979	1,288.4	2,680.1	n.a.	1,197.0	44.7	48.1	9,172.9

Source: Korayem, 1982.

Maintenance of the subsidy system is considered a necessity for sociopolitical, as well as income distribution, reasons. However, the damage this system does to the Egyptian economy is becoming more and more evident. As far as income distribution is concerned, the events of recent years indicate that the lot of the poorer strata has worsened perceptibly (see Chapter 3). Though the subsidies make it possible to keep living standards at a subsistence level, they cannot in and of themselves preserve unaltered, much less narrow, the spread between the highest and the lowest income groups. It should also be noted that the present subsidies system covers non-subsistence goods from which even, and in the case of subsidies for gasoline, automobiles and electricity only, the higher income groups benefit.

This brings us to the second aspect, namely the impact of subsidies on the relative price structure. As official sources themselves have noted (ESU, 1981), for many existing subsidies one should really speak of excessively low prices, which do not cover operating costs and give rise to a distorted cost structure for services (considered as production inputs). The present system of subsidies is thus a factor which contributes to a poor allocation of resources and is, therefore, a hindrance to greater productive efficiency and an impediment to gains in competitiveness for the industrial sector. A similar argument (see Papanek et al., 1982), perhaps even more general in scope, applies to the effect of subsidies on the terms of trade between agriculture and industry.

Keeping the prices of farm products much lower than the prevailing international market prices discourages farm production and encourages migration from the countryside to urban areas, with a whole series of easily imaginable negative consequences. In the long term, the maintenance of subsidies may increase the system's inflationary tendencies in that it does not permit sufficient growth of productivity, owing to its perverse effects on the allocation of resources. The inflationary impact of maintaining the current subsidy structure may become manifest in the short term too, however. Given a process of income redistribution in favour of the wealthier classes, produced by the inflationary mechanism itself, the subsidy system increases the real income of those classes (as recalled above, they are the sole beneficiaries of some subsidies) and increases demand pressure on luxury consumer goods.

Apart from the inflationary impact due to the alteration of relative prices and incomes, the present subsidy system also feeds the mechanism of inflation financing through expansion of the public deficit. As mentioned earlier, the deficit is financed almost entirely by expanding the money supply.

Taking all these considerations together then, the current system, conceived to protect the real living standards of the poor, risks aggravating their problems because of its inflationary potential which does nothing to help narrow the gap between the poor and the rich classes.

The question of subsidies has been examined by a considerable number of scholars and many hypotheses have been forwarded as to how it should be tackled. These may be divided into three distinct groups: those who favour a straightforward elimination of the subsidies; those who favour their elimination but also a simultaneous increase in the lowest wages; and those who favour a modification of the subsidy system.

Let us first of all consider the results of a World Bank simulation carried out with an econometric model (World Bank, 1978). The hypothesis under examination consists in the elimination of the subsidy system and the study of the short term (economic) effects.

Initially, as is only to be expected, removal of the subsidies would produce a price increase which, due to the low elasticity of substitution of the subsidised goods, would cause aggregate demand to fall. And, even if food imports were only to fall marginally, this would have a positive effect on the trade balance. It is demand for goods other than foodstuffs which would fall most significantly.

The price rise and the consequent fall in real wages would spark off a spiral of nominal wage increases, and this would increase inflationary pressures. An increase in aggregate demand would follow, and this would lead to new price rises. It is not possible to establish precisely what the net effect on aggregate demand would be, however, according to the World Bank, the relative fall in the demand for consumer goods would leave space for larger investments (income remaining constant). In the short term, an increase in investments would lead to an increase in the imports of intermediate goods but in the long term it would increase the country's productive capacity, thereby favouring exports.

It should be added that the net long term effect on the balance of payments (not considered by the World Bank study) should take into account the loss of competitiveness that would arise as a result of higher inflation, unless the exchange rate were devalued accordingly.

These results, however schematic, give us an idea of the likely macroeconomic impact of a removal of the subsidy system. A more articulate discussion of the problem and one which pays more attention to the role of subsidies as factor costs is provided by Papanek (1982). His study suggests that, as the experience of other countries shows, an elimination of subsidies on consumer goods would lead to a fall in real wages, even in the case in which nominal wages were allowed to increase, and this would render the operation both politically and socially unsustainable. Papanek, in pointing out the dangerous effects on the industrial accumulation process, notes that one of the major advantages of the subsidy system is that by maintaining labour costs at low levels, it encourages accumulation.

On the other hand, the idea of eliminating the subsidies and simultaneously increasing nominal wages in order to maintain real wage rates would, according to another study (Davis and Lapittus, 1980) lead to an increase of at least 40 per cent in all incomes, whereas the incomes of the poorest groups of the population would need to increase by more than 50 per cent to compensate fully for the loss of the subsidies. Additional pressures on prices would result from allowing farm prices to equal international prices, and labour costs would increase due to an increase in the prices of public sector products which, as noted above, are in fact a form of implicit subsidy. As regards resource allocation, an increase in the labour costs of less qualified labour would result in new investments being more capital intensive and this could lead to employment problems. Both of these studies stress the loss of competitiveness and the inevitable pressures on the exchange rate that would result from such a policy.

Another recent study (Korayem, 1982) reached a similar conclusion concerning the ineffectiveness of eliminating the subsidies and simultaneously increasing nominal wages. In spite of the fact that the wage increases foreseen by the Planning Ministry (the so-called 'social contract' proposals) are substantial, Korayem concludes that they are not sufficient to maintain the purchasing power of wages. This conclusion (which is based on an observation of both the high correlation between subsidies and the prices of subsidised goods, and the lower income groups' high propensity to consume these goods) leads to two more proposals in the subsidies debate: that primary goods (with the exception of foodstuffs) and services should be supplied at lower prices, and that the poorest groups should be guaranteed a supply of foodstuffs. The attraction of these two proposals consists essentially in the fact that they would imply lower costs for the government than does the present system.

A different proposal (Papanek et al., 1982), essentially concerned with the allocative effects of subsidies, foresees a distinction between consumer subsidies and producers' prices. Industrial firms would pay the full price (based on world prices) for their previously subsidised inputs and would receive the market price for their output. In the case in which this were to create unacceptable difficulties for consumers, the firms would receive a subsidy from the government to hold down consumer prices.

According to this hypothesis, explicit subsidies would increase considerably. However, they would be more than compensated for by the fall in implicit subsidies (that is, in below cost prices for public goods and services). For example, energy costs would increase and this could have important implications for the general price level - the proponents argue, however, that this could lead to two advantages. On the production side, it would encourage firms to look for a more efficient combination of factors of production. (Labour would become relatively cheaper with respect to capital and this would lead to the adoption of more labour intensive production processes. This, of course, is the opposite of what would happen if subsidies were eliminated and wages increased.) Also, the income accruing to the government from the higher tariffs would permit the government to finance higher subsidies to the consumers. In the meanwhile, the general efficiency of the public enterprises would increase. Another hypothesis, advanced by the ESU (1981), is concerned with minimising the negative effects of the subsidy system on resource allocation, with the constraint of maintaining the purchasing power of the wages of the poorest classes. It is suggested that the number of subsidised consumption goods be limited (for example to 15 goods) and that it be guaranteed that the prices of these goods be held constant for a certain number of years. At the same time the state distributive system should guarantee a sufficient supply of subsidised goods to avoid the danger of repressed inflation. The remaining subsidies should be eliminated gradually over a period of, say, three to five years, in order to avoid excessive impacts on inflation and the standard of living. It is noted (and this argument can be extended to other hypotheses) that the gradual reduction of the public deficit which would follow, would allow the authorities to slow down the process of monetary expansion and so weaken the inflationary pressures.

And finally, if luxury goods became relatively more expensive, the relative price changes between consumption goods would lead to a redistribution of income in favour of the poorest classes. This would reverse current trends of income redistribution.

Let us now conclude this brief survey by examining the results of two more studies, which, however, differ from those already mentioned, in that they consider the question of subsidies in a wider context, looking at it from a macroeconomic point of view. The first stresses the relationship between agriculture and industry and the second concentrates on the problem at the root of the subsidies issue: the need to guarantee the population a means of subsistence during the process of economic development.

The first of these studies (Dethier and Esfahani, 1981) considers the effects of the reallocation of resources which would follow various price and subsidisation policies. The authors show how the current subsidy system, by discouraging agricultural production, increases the country's dependency on imported food-stuffs. In this sense then the current subsidisation policy increases the burden of maintaining the population at a subsistence level. This study suggests a subsidisation policy which would lead to such terms of trade between agriculture and the rest of the economy, as to encourage production in this sector.

The second study (Boutros-Ghali and Taylor, 1980) is more concerned with considering the question of subsidies and basic needs in general within a wider macroeconomic context, in order to analyse the constraints imposed on the economy by the satisfaction of these basic needs.

The authors arrive at the conclusion that an optimal growth path could be attained, in spite of the various constraints, if the relative prices of agricultural products and capital goods were increased in such a way as to cause a reallocation of resources in favour of the agricultural sector. They also stress that if the flow of international aid is maintained it will be possible for the development process to avoid putting excessive pressure on the exchange rate.

A final point of a general nature which has been explicitly defined in a study by Thomas (1981) but which was also mentioned by many of the experts and politicians that we interviewed, concerns the obvious but nevertheless important fact that in the long term the most effective way to reduce the weight of subsidies will be to improve the domestic production of subsistence goods, either by increasing agricultural productivity or by increasing exploitable resources (through the reclamation of new expanses of land) so as to be able directly to influence production costs and reduce the need for subsidies.

LIQUIDITY CREATION, MONETARY POLICY AND THE CREDIT SYSTEM

Table 1.10 shows that total liquidity and its components increased more rapidly during the 1970s than did GDP at either constant or current prices. The money supply (M1) grew at an annual rate of almost 21 per cent from 1970 to 1979 whereas GDP at current prices grew at 17 per cent per annum and GDP at constant prices grew at 7 per cent per annum. Total liquidity (M2) increased by 23 per cent. Moreover, these rates accelerated in the second half of the decade as did both GDP growth and the inflation rate. The monetary expansion decelerated in 1981 (see Table 1.17) with respect to the preceding years due to restrictive measures taken by the Central Bank to control inflation (which effectively diminished in 1981). The three sources of liquidity creation in the economy are: the public sector deficit; the credit system; and the balance of payments. In considering each of these sources we will briefly analyse the underlying mechanisms, which are the credit system and the exchange market (the public sector deficit having already been considered). These considerations will allow us to comment on the Egyptian money market.

The Central Bank's financing of the public deficit is still the most important source of money supply in Egypt. But the government's debt to the Central Bank has grown much faster than M1. Consequently there is not a one to one relationship between the public deficit and the expansion of the money supply (M1). A significant exception is the share of government spending that goes to pay for imports, with the exception of wheat and flour imports.

In this latter case, in fact the money created to finance the deficit is used by the Central Bank to acquire foreign currency, which means that the funds are channelled abroad and the new liquidity is immediately destroyed with an equal reduction in reserves. In this sense, therefore, payment of subsidies has a deflationary impact on the economy.

As to the composition of liquidity and its evolution over the past two years (see Table 1.18), of particular noteworthiness is the recent increase in its foreign

Table 1.17: Growth of Money Supply 1970-81 (millions of Egyptian pounds)

	1970	1971	1972	1973	1974	1975	1976	1977	1978	1979	1980	1981
Money supply (M2)	1,053	1,084	1,255	1,536	2,001	2,430	3,061	4,102	5,205	6,778	9,016	12,798

Percentage growth rates (on yearly base)

1970-79	1973-79	1979-80	1980-81
23.0	28.0	-33.0	41.9

Source: Central Bank of Egypt

Table 1.18: Change in Liquidity by Source (millions of Egyptian pounds)

	Dec. 1979	June 1980	Percentage change	Absolute change
Balance of payments	-1,833	-1,101	66.5	732
Government	7,601	8,218	8.1	617
Public authorities	993	1,178	18.6	185
Public enterprises	1,384	1,240	11.5	-144
Private sector	1,000	1,329	32.9	329
Others	463	660	42.5	197
	9,608	11,524	19.9	1,916

Source: Central Bank of Egypt.

Table 1.19: Deposits in Foreign Currency (millions of Egyptian pounds)

	1978	1979	Percentage change
Time deposits			
in foreign currency	489	538	10.0
total	1,363	1,697	24.5
foreign currency deposits as percentage of total	35.8	31.1	-31.7
Savings deposits			
in foreign currency	275	688	150.0
total	1,658	2,454	48.0
foreign currency deposits as percentage of total	15.5	28.8	85.8
Liquidity			
in foreign currency	747	1,216	62.8
total	5,205	6,778	30.2
foreign currency deposits as percentage of total	14.3	17.9	25.2

Source: Central Bank of Egypt.

component, which had begun to decline in the late 1970s. Loans to the private sector have also assumed sizeable dimensions while those to the public sector, though substantial in absolute terms, show only a modest rate of increase.

These recent trends seem to confirm the growing role of the private sector and the foreign sector in the formation of liquidity and suggest that financial and currency policies will have to be progressively modified to take account of a tendentially less significant role, in relative terms, of the public sector in liquidity creation.

Indirect confirmation of this comes from the trend - accompanying the slower growth of the money supply towards steadily rising interest rates, as a tool to encourage private savings and to support the exchange rate policy (see Table 1.23).

However, the main problems for Egyptian decision makers in terms of monetary policy lie in the relationship between liquidity in domestic currency and liquidity in foreign currency.

From this standpoint, the Egyptian economy has some peculiar characteristics. Somewhat stretching the point, it might be said that there is more than one freely circulating currency within the economy. Along with the Egyptian pound we also find foreign currency, especially the dollar.

There are three main channels for the collection of foreign currency.

The 'Central Bank Pool' receives all currency earned through the export of cotton, rice and oil and through the operations of the Suez Canal and the Sumed oil pipe line. These revenues are used to pay for imports of seven commodities: wheat, flour, tea, sugar, food oils, pesticides, and fertilisers. They are also used for debt services on international loans and to pay for certain portions of investment goods that enjoy suppliers' credit.

The 'Commercial Bank Pool' receives the foreign currency earned from exports of products other than those mentioned above plus income from tourism. It also receives that portion of workers' remittances that is converted into Egyptian pounds in commercial banks at

Table 1.20: Savings of Egyptian Workers Abroad 1976-June 1980 Remittances and Own Exchange Imports (millions of Egyptian pounds and percentages)

	Remittances through authorized banks		'Own exchange' imports		
	Amount	%	Amount	%	Total amount
1976	238.1	60.6	155.7	39.5	393.8
1977	358.2	57.5	265.2	42.5	623.4
1978	644.5	52.3	587.2	47.7	1,231.7
1979	610.5	42.1	839.3	57.9	1,449.8
1978 a	277.8	51.7	259.8	48.3	537.6
1979 a	278.2	41.1	398.9	58.9	677.1
1980 a	335.0	36.7	579.4	63.3	914.4

Note: a. January-June.

Source: Central Bank of Egypt.

the unified exchange rate. The currency collected in this pool is made available to the tourist industry. Exporters must deposit their revenues within 90 days of receipt. The currency thus collected is reallocated by the monetary authorities through the foreign exchange budget. Public enterprises, government agencies, and ministries are supposed to procure foreign currency solely through this channel, at the fixed exchange rate. In reality, both public enterprises and many commercial banks deal in foreign currencies outside this channel at a higher exchange rate.

The 'Own Exchange Pool' receives mainly workers' remittances and the currency so gathered is used for various purposes. The most important ones are paying for imports purchased directly by Egyptian workers abroad and consumed by their purchasers or resold to other Egyptians for Egyptian pounds. These imports are directly controlled by the workers in possession of foreign currency and do not pass through the official banking system.

The main channel for the transfer of these funds is through Egyptian agents operating in the oil producing Arab countries who buy currency from Egyptian workers at a higher rate, and use the currency to pay for imports or deposit it in Egyptian banks.

This pool is also fed by the currency which tourists sell outside official channels. That this source has been expanding is confirmed by the growing discrepancy between tourist presence and officially recorded revenues from tourism.

Finally, a large number of foreigners living in Cairo pay their bills (rent, for instance) in foreign currency. This item too, though of modest proportions, has been growing in recent years. Thus, in the second half of the 1970s the US dollar began to be used for transactions inside Egypt, and also to be deposited in banks operating in Egyptian territory (Table 1.19). In this sense then, an increase in foreign currency deposits has an effect on liquidity similar to an increase in domestic currency deposits.

This creates delicate problems for the monetary authorities, in the control of both the money supply and the exchange markets. The presence of a two-tier money market has proved in recent years to be an extremely important source of liquidity for those businesses operating in Egypt which have to make international transactions. The two-tier market is not only the product of an instrument (the own exchange system) that encourages the inflow of foreign currency (in so far as it offers an incentive to residents to engage in activities that produce foreign-exchange revenues), it is also a relatively important condition for the short term preservation of a favourable business climate for international enterprises. Maintenance of the two-tier system is also essential if the state is to enjoy the benefits of workers' remittances, which would probably not be so substantial were there no parallel market (see Table 1.20).

However, to these positive aspects of the system we must counterpose the negative ones which make it urgent to find a way to put an end to the system. Without going in to technical details, two major negative aspects of the system deserve attention. One is the monetary authorities' loss of control over liquidity creation. Because foreign currency is used not only as a store of value but also in transactions, it has become a true parallel currency circulating within the economy, completely outside the monetary authorities' control, even if it depends partly on the behaviour of that part of the banking system which operates in foreign currency. Certainly this kind of situation does not promote integration of the 'domestic' and 'international' sectors of the economy.

The second negative consequence is on the exchange rate policy. Egypt belongs to what could be called the 'dollar zone' because it is in that currency that most foreign trade is denominated. The two-tier monetary market reinforces this feature and makes pegging of the currency to the dollar practically indispensable. The main problem is selecting the (official) exchange rate between the Egyptian pound and the dollar. The rate cannot be too low (undervalued) because for one thing it would create too wide a gap between the quotations of the official and the parallel markets, giving rise to speculative movements of capital 'inside' the economy, and for another it would discourage remittances as well as accentuating the imported component of inflation. On the other hand, the rate cannot be set too high (overvalued) because this would hurt Egyptian exports. Indeed, it has been suggested (ESU, 1981) that the existence of the four main sources of foreign exchange earnings (Canal, oil, tourism, remittances) already generates an overvalued rate for the pound.

We may now consider the characteristics of Egypt's credit system, a sector which more than others has undergone change in recent years, following the introduction of the ODEP and the subsequent demands which this has entailed. In fact the regulation of the sector was updated by Law 43 (1974) and by Law 32 of 1977 (Foda et al., 1982). The Central Bank issues regulations according to the normal procedures of monetary policy and its interventions in the banking sector, often on the insistence of the IMF, have become more incisive of late.

A particularly important role is played by the limit on credit expansion which the Central Bank imposed at 65 per cent of (Egyptian) sterling deposits. This regulation is the credit system's most important constraint on liquidity creation. A very narrow margin has been fixed (two percentage points over deposit rates) as regards interest rates on loans and this does not help to provide the flexibility needed by the sector in the face of the current phase of expansion.

Many of the current regulations have lost their importance because they were brought in during a period when the cultivation of certain agricultural products, such as cotton, which required particular methods of financing, occupied a central position in the economy. Moreover, according to a recent study (Foda et al., 1982) many of the banks do not consider the Central Bank as lender of last resort because it can only lend to the banking system against the guarantee of cotton and gold.

The banking sector (see Table 1.21) is made up of 59 banks (December 1981). Of these 24 are commercial banks, 4 of which are in the public sector, the remaining 20 being either Egyptian institutions or joint ventures. Other, non-commercial banks include the specialised public banks, investment banks and merchants banks as well as branches of foreign banks.

Actually, though, the problem of choosing an appropriate exchange rate is not as restrictive as it seems if a broader time horizon is considered. At present Egypt's export potential is limited, consequently, though devaluation would favour Egyptian exports, the advantages of devaluation would be greatly reduced because of limited supply capacity, while the economy would suffer the disadvantages in the form of imported inflation and higher prices for imports, not to mention the negative effects on remittances from abroad.

In the short term then, devaluation does not seem to be a feasible policy. However, it could become practicable in the medium to long term, when conditions are ripe for a reunification of the currency market thanks to a decline in the relative weight of remittances and an expansion of the export oriented sector whose growth would be further stimulated by devaluation. In other words, such an exchange rate policy is conceivable only if accompanied by appropriate monetary and industrial policies.

Finally, it should be noted that the Egyptian economy, like the economies of many other LDCs, can be considered in a state of 'financial repression' (Fry, 1980; McKinnon and Mathieson, 1981). This seems to be confirmed by the excessively low level of interest rates in the 1970s and by the inadequate formation of savings which is partly a result of the low rates. It is, however, a peculiar example of financial repression in that it coexists with a parallel system (the dollar system) which is spurring a rapid maturation of the Egyptian economy. The Egyptian government, in collaboration with the IMF, is currently seeking to resolve this problem. It is commonly held, however, that the double currency market can be done away with only if there is a gradual decline in the importance of workers' remittances.

In order to appreciate the numerous modifications made to the banking sector in recent years, it is useful to consider some quantitative data. The evolution of the banking sector's activities in recent years may be summarised as follows:

Deposits (see Table 1.22) increased by 153 per

Table 1.21: Banks Operating in Egypt as of 31 December 1973

	Number
Central Bank of Egypt	1
Public sector commercial banks:	(4)
National Bank of Egypt	1
Banque Misr	1
Bank of Alexandria	1
Banque du Caire	1
Public sector specialised banks:	(3)
Arab Land Bank	1
Credit Foncier Egyptien	1
Principal Bank for Development and Agricultural Credit	1
Multinational offshore banks:	(2)
Arab African International Bank	1
Arab International Bank	1

Banks Operating in Egypt as of 31 December 1981

	Number
Central Bank of Egypt	1
Commercial banks	
Public Sector	4
Private sector Egyptian owned	9
Private sector joint ventures	11
Public sector specialised banks	
Arab Land Bank	1
Credit Foncier Egyptien	1
Development Industrial Bank of Egypt	1
Principal Bank for Development and Agricultural Credit	1
Investment and merchant banks:	
Egyptian owned	3
Joint Ventures	6
Branches of foreign banks	19
Canal zone banks	1
Other institutions:	
Nasser Social Bank	1
Representative Offices of Foreign Banks	29
Multinational Offshore Bank	1

Table 1.22: The Banking Sector Breakdown of Deposits as of 31 December 1978-81 (millions of Egyptian pounds)

Year Sector	1978 LC	1978 FC	1978 Total	1979 LC	1979 FC	1979 Total	1980 LC	1980 FC	1980 Total	1981 LC	1981 FC	1981 Total
Government Deposits:												
Demand Deposits	116	11	127	148	22	170	177	10	187	246	14	260
Time and Savings Deposits	63	3	66	70	8	78	94	11	105	147	12	159
Earmarked Deposits	42	18	60	54	17	71	48	75	123	56	12	68
Sub Total	221	32	253	272	47	319	319	96	415	449	38	487
Public Sector:												
Demand Deposits	413	234	647	772	286	1,058	944	405	1,349	1,167	148	1,315
Time and Savings Deposits	235	53	288	323	130	453	592	137	729	993	230	1,223
Earmarked Deposits	247	346	593	292	342	634	336	242	578	358	337	695
Sub Total	895	633	1,528	1,387	758	2,145	1,872	784	2,656	2,518	715	3,233
Private Sector:												
Demand Deposits	718	293	1,011	835	287	1,122	1,028	348	1,376	1,295	457	1,752
Time and Savings Deposits	693	366	1,059	988	760	1,748	1,450	1,339	2,789	2,367	2,234	4,601
Earmarked Deposits	63	83	146	74	135	209	127	200	327	233	370	603
Sub Total	1,474	742	2,216	1,879	1,182	3,079	2,605	1,887	4,492	3,895	3,061	6,956
Others:												
Demand Deposits	61	32	93	48	21	69	52	10	62	31	9	40
Time and Savings Deposits	124	84	208	101	101	202	62	96	158	35	131	166
Earmarked Deposits	4	2	6	4	4	8	5	2	7	7	1	8
Sub Total	189	188	307	153	126	279	119	108	227	73	141	214
Total Deposits:												
Total Demand Deposits	1,308	570	1,878	1,803	616	2,419	2,201	773	2,974	2,739	628	3,367
Total Time and Savings Deposits	1,115	506	1,621	1,482	999	2,481	2,198	1,583	3,781	3,542	2,607	6,149
Total Earmarked Deposits	356	449	805	424	498	922	516	519	1,035	654	720	1,374
Grand Total	2,779	1,525	4,304	3,709	2,113	5,822	4,915	2,875	7,790	6,935	3,955	10,890

Note: LC = local currency, FC = foreign currency

Source: Foda et al., 1982.

Table 1.23: Interest Rate Structure, 1975-81

Sight Deposits	29 Dec 1975		28 Feb 1977		15 June 1978	28 Dec 1978	29 Mar 1979	27 Mar 1980	26 May 1980	1 Jan 1981	3 July 1981
	Individual	Institutional	Individual	Institutional							
7-15 days							4.0	4.5	4.5	5.0	5.0
15-30 days	2.0	2.0	3.0	2.5	4.0	5.0	5.0	5.5	5.5	6.0	6.0
1-3 months	3.0	2.5	4.0	3.0	4.5	5.5	5.5	6.0	6.5	7.5	7.5
3-6 months	4.0	3.0	5.0	4.0	5.5	6.0	6.0	7.0	7.5	8.5	8.5
6-12 months	4.0	3.0	5.5	4.5	6.0	6.5	6.5	7.5	8.0	9.0	9.5
1-2 years	5.0	4.0	6.0	5.0	6.5	7.0	7.0	8.0	9.0	9.5	10.0
2-5 years					7.0	7.5	7.5	8.5	9.5	10.5	10.5
3-5 years						8.0	8.0	9.0	10.0	11.0	11.0
5 years						8.5	8.5	9.5	10.5	11.5	11.5
Savings Deposits	4.0		5.0		5.0	6.0	6.0	7.0	8.0	8.5	8.5
Lending rates, min-max	7-8		8-9		9-11	10-12	10-12	11-13	12-14	13-15	13-15
Central Bank discount rate	6.0		7.0		8.0	9.0	9.0	10.0	11.0	12.0	12.0

Source: Central Bank of Egypt.

cent between December 1978 (4,034 million Egyptian pounds) and December 1981 (10,890 million Egyptian pounds) at an annual growth rate of 36.5 per cent. The increase in foreign currency deposits was particularly marked (159 per cent over the period with an average annual increase of 38 per cent) whereas the increase in pound deposits was of the order of 150 per cent, registering an average annual increase of 36 per cent.

Savings deposits also increased - as a percentage of total deposits - thanks to both rises in interest rates (see Table 1.23) and the fiscal exemption of interest income; these deposits increased from 38 per cent to 56 per cent of total deposits, between 1978 and 1981.

High interest rates on the international markets made their impact felt on the Egyptian (dollar) monetary system, and this explains both the absolute and percentage increments of foreign currency deposits which are also increased by the spreading of arbitrage deals which involve the holding of foreign currency deposits (which offer higher interest rates) and the lending of pounds with the guarantee of these same deposits.

Private sector deposits with the banking sector amounted to 6,956 million Egyptian pounds in December 1981 and currently account for 64 per cent of the total deposits of the banking sector.

Sterling deposits normally have a 12 months maturity, whereas foreign currency deposits usually have a 60 days maturity. The public banks and many private banks encourage depositors to lengthen the duration of their deposits by issuing new financial instruments (such as the 'Golden Certificate' offered by the Egyptian American bank).

Banking sector loans increased between 1978 and 1982 (see Table 1.24) passing from 2,493 million Egyptian pounds in December 1978 to 8,024 million Egyptian pounds in December 1981 and recording an overall growth rate of 222 per cent (48 per cent per annum). Of these, sterling credits increased from 2,268 million to 6,523 million Egyptian pounds, that is, an overall rate of 188 per cent (42 per cent per annum), while foreign currency credits rose from 245 million to 1507 million Egyptian pounds, that is, at an overall rate of 513 per cent (83 per cent per annum).

Table 1.24: Bank Loans to the Private and Public Sectors on 31 December, 1978-81
(millions of Egyptian pounds: LC = Local currency, FC = Foreign currency.

	1978 LC	1978 FC	1978 Total	1979 LC	1979 FC	1979 Total	1980 LC	1980 FC	1980 Total	1981 LC	1981 FC	1981 Total
Agriculture												
one year maturity	72.2	-	72.2	62.7	1.1	63.8	94.4	3.2	97.6	195.7	20.7	216.4
more than one year maturity	14.4	-	14.4	20.5	3.2	23.7	23.8	4.3	28.1	83.2	4.6	87.8
	85.6	-	86.6	83.2	4.3	87.5	118.2	7.5	125.7	278.9	25.3	304.2
Industry												
one year maturity	192.0	27.9	219.9	275.8	53.7	329.5	402.8	196.3	599.1	720.0	239.0	959.0
more than one year maturity	25.8	24.1	49.9	48.7	28.3	77.0	86.8	38.4	125.1	133.1	69.0	202.1
	217.8	52.0	269.8	324.5	82.0	406.5	489.5	234.7	724.2	853.1	308.0	1,161.1
Commerce												
one year maturity	136.8	116.5	253.3	257.1	243.8	500.9	471.3	373.6	844.9	1,055.9	835.5	1,891.4
more than one year maturity	4.1	7.5	11.6	8.6	19.1	27.7	15.7	27.6	43.3	19.1	52.0	71.1
	140.9	124.0	264.9	265.7	262.9	528.6	487.0	401.2	888.2	1,075.0	887.5	1,962.5
Services												
one year maturity	29.7	14.5	44.2	62.6	28.1	90.7	116.5	72.0	188.5	342.4	180.4	522.8
more than one year maturity	15.6	5.6	21.2	37.1	13.1	50.2	57.2	25.8	83.0	109.7	60.1	169.8
	45.3	20.1	65.4	99.7	41.2	140.9	173.7	97.8	271.5	452.1	240.5	692.6
Total private sector												
one year maturity	430.7	158.9	589.6	658.2	326.7	984.9	1,085.0	645.1	1,730.1	2,314.0	1,235.6	3,589.6
more than one year maturity	59.9	37.2	97.1	114.9	63.7	178.6	183.4	96.1	279.5	345.1	185.7	530.8
	490.6	196.1	686.7	773.1	390.4	1,163.5	1,268.4	741.2	2,009.5	2,659.1	1,461.3	4,120.4
Loans to public enterprises												
one year maturity	1,746.6	15.2	1,761.8	1,876.4	27.3	1,903.7	2,592.0	41.0	2,633.0	3,577.1	21.8	3,903.9
more than one year maturity	30.9	13.2	44.1	96.3	81.4	167.7	148.3	12.2	160.5	286.8	17.5	304.3
	1,777.5	28.4	1,805.9	1,962.7	108.7	2,071.4	2,071.4	53.2	2,793.5	3,863.9	39.3	3,903.2
Grand Total	2,268.1	224.5	2,492.6	2,735.8	499.1	3,234.9	4,008.7	794.4	4,803.1	6,523.0	1,500.6	8,023.6
A/C in percentage (1)	22	87	38	28	78	36	32	93	42	41	97	51

(1) Private sector as percentage of Total

Credits to the private sector grew both in absolute terms and as a percentage of the total, passing from 687 million to 420 million Egyptian pounds, that is at a rate of 500 per cent (82 per cent per annum); consequently the share of total credits that went to the private sector increased from 38 per cent to 51 per cent.

Long term credits were also increased, passing from 97 million to 531 million Egyptian pounds, that is at a rate of 447 per cent (76 per cent per annum). Of these, sterling credits rose 475 per cent (79 per cent per annum) whilst foreign currency credits rose 399 per cent (71 per cent per annum). Overall, however, the foreign currency component of total credits increased by 1,256 per cent (140 per cent per annum) between 1978 and 1981, the sterling component increased by 356 per cent (76 per cent per annum).

In spite of the fact that short term loans dominate the credit system, the practice of rolling-over short term credits is widespread and in some instances (see Foda, 1982) involves 50 per cent of all credits.

As noted above, the foreign component of liquidity is such in the Egyptian financial system as to be able to speak of a two-tier currency system. However, the system is asymmetrical in that, if current regulations render sterling operations relatively inflexible, there is greater freedom of movement for foreign currency operations. The banks use foreign currency mainly to finance investments in the foreign markets. Interbank loans are widespread but are not always made use of due to the already high liquidity. Recently (1982), because of the relative decline in oil revenues, the public banks followed a more conservative policy and contracted an initial loan of 200 million US dollars on the European Eurodollar markets. Future transactions in this field will be conditioned to a large extent by the state of the balance of payments.

The ability of the banks in managing their own liquid assets varies from case to case. In many institutions, in particular the joint ventures, the management of liquid assets has become a predominant activity.

Other sources of liquidity, besides the payments made to the sector by the Central Bank of Egypt, are of the access that some specialised firms have to international organisations (such as the International Development Association, the United States Agency for the International Development, OPEC and OAPEC, and the World Bank). In 1980 the Misr-Iran Development Bank obtained a 30 million dollar loan from the World Bank and was the first to introduce on the market deposit certificates with floating interest rates but to date no more similar initiatives have been taken. The Arab International Bank recently floated bonds for 25 million dollars at floating interest rates on the Euromarkets at a rate of 3/8 per cent above the Libor and a maturity of five years.

The National Bank of Egypt is set to follow with a similar initiative, however for a larger amount. The search for funds on the Euromarkets, in spite of the abundant liquidity in the domestic economy, is justified by the need to lengthen the average maturity of loans.

The financing of industrial development takes on a crucial role in a period such as this when conditions seem right for a significant increase in the importance of both the private sector and the public sector (see Clark, 1981).

From this point of view the credit institutions may be divided into three groups: the Development Industrial Bank (DIB), which constitutes one group in itself; a second group which includes the Misr-Iran Development Bank and the Arab Investment Bank (AIB) and the new banks approved under Law 43 of 1974; and the third group which is made up of the public commercial banks and the public insurance companies.

Much small business financing is done by the DIB as most of its older clients are small businessmen and because much of the foreign aid managed by the DIB is destined towards the small businessman. The Misr and the AIB on the other hand are investment banks which were approved under Law 43, and in which the Egyptian government holds a controlling majority. These banks are very active in the promotion of projects and in leading credit syndicates which also include foreign banks (this allows them to enjoy very favourable conditions on the international markets). The banks approved under Law 43 may be divided into three groups. The commercial banks can be wholly Egyptian or joint ventures with an Egyptian participation of at least 50 per cent; these banks can operate both in sterling and in foreign currency. The investment banks may be joint ventures with either a foreign or Arab majority holding but can only operate in foreign currency. The merchant banks are wholly Arab or foreign banks authorised to operate in Egypt but only in foreign currency. All of these banks make loans for both medium term and short term projects.

The public commercial banks on the other hand rarely take on investments which have more than one year maturity, and in any case they invest for the main part in government bonds.

In general, recent studies (Foda et al., 1982: Clark, 1981) have shown that the availability of funds meets the demand (and this opinion is also shared by the bankers). However, a lot depends on the structure of the firms, among which there are many family businesses which often rely on retained earnings and in the case of expansion prefer to issue shares (though still retaining control of the business) and rely on credit only as a last resort. However, such a method of financing might not be sufficient in a situation where the development of the economy necessitates an increase in the size of firms.

The impression of a substantial equilibrium in the credit market is coherent with the phenomenon (noted above) of the recent increase in liquidity. This should partly mitigate fears of inflationary pressures generated by monetary expansion, in so far as the increase in the money supply will at least partially finance investments.

This recent trend, however, highlights Egypt's lack of an adequate structure of interest rates. By increasing domestic interest rates, the Egyptian authorities could improve the balance of payments situation (and as a consequence, the exchange rate) and also combat domestic inflation. In the current situation, such an increase in interest rates would not (for the aforementioned reasons) dramatically affect the investment process. What does seem necessary, however, is a greater articulation of financial instruments supplied to businesses, especially to small firms. An improvement in the management of financial risks by both the banks and firms would be desirable in the current context, in which the economy is becoming increasingly open to both international trade and finance. Currently, most trade risks are borne by the state. However, due to the dual nature of the Egyptian monetary system, individual operators are gradually increasing their share of the burden. Clark (1981) has suggested that in the intermediate period funds should be set up with the help of the larger banks, as a guarantee to firms against trade risks.

THE BALANCE OF PAYMENTS

As was pointed out earlier, the policies implemented under the ODEP entailed a substantial opening of the Egyptian economy to the international market which was accompanied by a major shift in Egypt's foreign ties. Economic relations with the Comecon countries (which were essentially bilateral in nature thus producing little hard currency earnings) were eliminated step by step but rapidly, while integration with the Western market economies in both trade and financial relations grew steadily. Immediately after the end of the 1973 war, reconstruction and the growth of public expenditure swelled imports to unsustainable levels given the limited amount of exports, which still consisted mainly of cotton and a few agricultural products whose world prices, to boot, were falling in the second half of the 1970s. In this period the trade deficit was financed in large measure by Arab capital. But towards the end of the decade, subsequent to the peace treaty with Israel (1979), the situation changed radically.

Since the conclusion of the peace agreements which led to the reopening of the Suez Canal and full recovery of Sinai, Egypt's balance of payments has taken on a configuration that makes it one of the most solid of the LDCs. This strength derives mainly from the four sources of hard currency earnings mentioned above: oil, the Suez Canal, workers' remittances and tourism. The revenue from these items has risen rapidly in recent years making it possible to cover a large part of the trade deficit (see Table 1.25), even though there was an overall worsening of the situation in 1981. In addition, the massive influx of foreign capital, especially in the form of US development aid, has kept the country's foreign exchange reserves healthy.

As we can see, over the past few years imports have grown faster than exports. While the latter consist mainly of oil and cotton, the former (which have been growing at a rate ranging from 20 to 30 per cent a year) consist of goods essential to the very survival of the nation (foodstuffs and investment goods). The deterioration in the balance of trade that began to emerge in 1981 and 1982 prompted the government to impose some controls on luxury consumer goods in particular.

Recent trends have confirmed Egypt's dependency on imports and have identified the central problem that will characterise the external equilibrium of the Egyptian economy in future years. This may be explained as follows.

The Egyptian economy's strong capacity to finance imports currently depends (apart from capital flows) mainly on the performance of the four items discussed above. In a medium to long term perspective, however, it is reasonable to suppose that foreign exchange earnings from these four sources will be increasingly less able to cover import requirements, owing to two simultaneous effects; faster growth of import needs than of export capacity (excluding oil) because of the projected high rate of economic and population growth, and a slowing down of the rate of growth of revenues from the four major sources.

It is, however, difficult to predict the future trends of these four items, especially since they depend largely on factors extraneous to the behaviour of the Egyptian economy.

Workers' remittances are contingent on the job opportunities for Egyptians in other Arab countries. In other words, since the supply of Egyptian labour is definitely highly elastic, remittances depend mainly on the level of demand for labour in other countries. This problem will not be discussed in detail here but it

Table 1.25: Balance of Payments, Current Account (on settlement basis) (millions of US dollars)

	1974	1975	1976	1977	1978	1979	1980	1981
Balance of trade	-1,796	-2,755	-2,679	-2,521	-3,299	-4,163	-3,730	-4,830
Exports	1,671	1,566	1,609	1,992	1,984	2,512	3,850	4,040
(oil)	(104)	(164)	(268)	(600)	(688)	(1,347)	(2,500)	(2,820)
Imports	-3,467	-4,321	-4,288	-4,513	-5,283	-6,675	7,580	8,870
Service balance	169	285	1,083	1,261	2,026	2,559	3,040	2,370
Total Earnings	709	1,080	1,979	2,552	3,446	4,080	5,260	4,920
Freight	20	58	97	153	124	167	n.a.	n.a.
Suez Canal	-	85	311	428	514	589	660	888
Workers' remittances	189	365	755	896	1,761	2,214	2,700	2,200
Capital income	87	87	72	113	144	306	440	450
Tourism	265	332	464	728	702	601	780	590
Other	148	153	278	234	201	204	n.a.	n.a.
Total Payments	-540	-795	-894	-1,291	-1,420	-1,522	2,220	2,550
Freight	-23	-82	-79	-97	-75	-85	n.a.	n.a.
Capital income	-156	-189	-273	-319	-414	-428	n.a.	n.a.
Other commercial payments	-92	-166	-115	-126	-127	-109	n.a.	n.a.
Travel	-105	-105	-123	-172	-258	-247	n.a.	n.a.
Government transactions	-77	-102	-107	-167	-158	-192	n.a.	n.a.
Other	-87	-151	-197	-410	-387	-461	n.a.	n.a.
Current accounts balance	-1,627	-2,470	-1,596	-1,260	-1,273	-1,604	-680	-2,460

Source: Central Bank of Egypt.

Table 1.26: Simulation of Balance of Payments Trends 1981/2-1988/9 (millions of US dollars)

	Fiscal Year 1981/82	Fiscal Year 1982/83	Fiscal Year 1983/84	Fiscal Year 1984/85	Fiscal Year 1985/86	Fiscal Year 1986/87	Fiscal Year 1987/88	Fiscal Year 1988/89
Exports of goods and non factor services	9,119	10,352	11,804	13,507	15,491	17,654	19,889	22,215
Imports of goods and non factor services	-13,204	-15,189	-17,330	-19,685	-22,276	-25,106	-28,262	-31,887
Net factor service income	1,517	1,594	1,697	1,777	1,852	1,878	1,806	1,954
Current account balance	-2,568	-3,243	-3,829	-4,401	-4,933	-5,574	-6,567	-7,718
Amortisation payments	-1,662	-2,002	-2,223	2,330	-2,450	-2,597	-2,726	-2,868
Gross foreign exchange requirements	4,230	5,245	6,052	6,731	7,383	8,171	9,293	10,586
Expected multilateral capital inflows	4,677	5,378	5,987	6,588	7,227	7,889	8,559	9,334
Basic balance	477	133	-65	-143	-156	-282	-734	-1,252
Debt service ratio	21.3	22.4	22.0	21.0	20.0	19.7	20.0	19.5

Source: World Bank.

should be noted that remittances grew substantially until 1980 and then began to drop off in 1981 and 1982. This trend, which emerges from official balance of payments data, may be partially offset by an unregistered increase in the remittances that enter the country through unofficial channels which began to pick up after the Central Bank took actions to encourage it.

Income from tourism has also been declining in recent years. Apart from the possible negative impact of political instability, culminating in the assassination of President Sadat, the drop can probably be explained with the same argument put forward for workers' remittances. It is quite likely, in fact, that a large portion of the foreign currency from tourism has fled official channels because of the growth of the parallel market and the increasing divergence between the official and the parallel exchange rates. The tourist flow could increase substantially though, thanks to what seems to be constant improvement in the supply of tourist services, since Egypt's historic and artistic heritage is simply unique in the world.

Earnings from the Suez Canal have instead trended distinctively upwards in recent years. The future growth of revenues from this source depends mainly on the completion of works to modernise the waterway's structure and, of course, on future levels of international trade, which has been sharply restrained by the world recession.

The trend in oil earnings (which account for 70 per cent of overall earnings from raw material exports) has been remarkably upward in recent years but obviously it cannot fail to feel the effects of falling or stagnating oil prices. Future prospects are tied to forecasts for domestic production, a detailed discussion of which is provided elsewhere.

It is worth pointing out though that since 1979 earnings from sales of petroleum products have accounted for more than 50 per cent of Egypt's balance of trade income.

The rest of the country's export earnings come in large part from cotton while exports of other manufactured products account for only a minimal share. According to some observers, however (ESU, 1981; US

Embassy, 1982; World Bank, 1980), the latter should grow steadily in importance in future years.

Exports of industrial products have been declining in real terms since 1975. This trend can be attributed partly to rising domestic demand and partly to insufficient incentives for domestic industries to seek market outlets abroad. It is necessary that this trend be reversed, however, not only because the present sources of foreign exchange earnings will sooner or later be insufficient to cover import requirements but also to relieve, through the development of domestic industry and agriculture and the creation of new job opportunities, the pressure exerted by the swelling ranks of the Egyptian labour force. The dwindling of workers' remittances is in fact not only a direct balance of payments problem but also an indirect problem in the form of increasing pressure on the Egyptian labour market which can no longer be relieved by massive emigration (the decline in remittances is a sign that the Egyptian labour market is gradually being deprived of an important safety valve). This also implies an increase in the demand for imported goods.

It might be useful at this point, in order to give a more exact idea of the possible future evolution of the sources of Egypt's supply of foreign currency (net of capital flows) to consider the results of a World Bank study (World Bank, 1981). The study, which is concerned with the development prospects of the Egyptian economy, assumes that suitable policies are adopted to create incentives for industry and oil extraction, that monetary and financial management are improved (through a restructuring of the credit and exchange markets), and that exogenous variables (foreign investment, etc.) follow an 'intermediate' (neither too high nor too low) behaviour.

As may be seen from Table 1.26, Egypt's 'natural resources' should continue to account for a substantial share of currency earnings, even though their relative importance is falling slightly. In fact, as regards the four main items, we can expect to see a (relative) decline in the importance of oil revenues, the Suez Canal and workers' remittances. Earnings from tourism, however, should increase. On the other hand we can

Table 1.27: Capital Movements, 1974 to 1980 (millions of US dollars)

	1974	1975	1976	1977	1978	1979	1980
Unilateral transfers	42	90	87	63	54	88	n.a.
Autonomous capital (net)	156	495	1,091	1,205	1,528	2,181	n.a.
Direct investment	87	225	444	477	387	710	918
(Law No. 43 projects)	(5)	(18)	(48)	(80)	(146)	(179)	n.a.
(oil companies)	(82)	(207)	(396)	(397)	(241)	(531)	n.a.
Official aid flows	-21	210	490	803	1,028	1,034	953
(funding)	(140)	(361)	(598)	(931)	(1,202)	(1,208)	n.a.
(repayments)	(-161)	(-151)	(-108)	(-128)	(-174)	(-174)	n.a.
Private loans (net)	30	60	157	-73	113	437	460
Special aid and loans*	1,261	1,506	780	1,601	809	72	n.a.
Balance of non-monetary movements	-719	-425	508	1,350	976	769	n.a.
Errors and omissions	-874	-698	-1,184	-435	-504	-462	n.a.
Monetary movements (net)	1,053	1,123	676	-915	-472	-307	n.a.

* Includes defence aid.

Source: World Bank and Central Bank of Egypt.

expect no more than a modest increase in the export of manufactured products, although this in itself is worthy of note because (as noted above) during the 1970s the tendency was for these exports to decline in real terms.

Many observers suggest that the country's long term objective should be to develop export oriented industries (including an export oriented food processing industry) capable of becoming an additional source of foreign currency earnings and, above all, one that is more directly under Egyptian control than the current sources.

Egypt's existing capacity to earn foreign currency should therefore be considered a means for accumulating the resources needed to finance the development of an export oriented industrial base capable of bringing in enough foreign currency to make up for the progressive decline in earnings from the traditional sources.

Local industrial development will be financed by the inflow of private and official foreign capital, although it is evident that the latter will not continue indefinitely. In fact aid and grant loans inflows will gradually give way to market loans.

It should not be forgotten that, in spite of recent improvements, the current account on Egypt's balance of payments is still in deficit. Changes will need to be made regarding the composition of imports which, besides necessary goods and investment goods, include numerous luxury goods.

In terms of credit worthiness assessment, however, the Egyptian economy - analysed on the basis of its balance of payments structure - appears much more solid than most Third World economies. In 1981, for instance, official reserves rose 13 per cent over the previous year. Even at a time of pronounced international difficulties, Egypt's credit worthiness appears quite solid, as recent loans raised on the international market have shown.

AN OVERVIEW OF MACROECONOMICS AND FINANCE IN EGYPT

In the remaining pages of this chapter, we will attempt to provide an overall view of the Egyptian economy. In so doing we run the risk of oversimplifying many of the issues which we have already discussed at length. However, we feel that a summary of these issues might be useful at this point.

The growth of the Egyptian economy depends essentially on the growth of fixed investments. However, political and economic constraints determine to what extent it is possible to increase such investments. Two constraints in particular often obstruct the development process of an underdeveloped economy: the savings gap (i.e. a shortage of savings with respect to investments) and the foreign exchange gap (i.e. the trade deficit). Many observers agree that the first of these is the more relevant in the Egyptian context. In fact since signing the peace treaty with Israel Egypt has once again been able to count on four important sources of foreign currency:- oil, the Suez Canal, emigrants' remittances and tourism. Even though the earnings from these four items are not sufficient in themselves to cover all imports, together with the considerable flow of foreign (mainly American) aid, they guarantee funds to pay for import needs. This however holds true mainly for the short term, in that, with a given growth rate of domestic investments, the growth rate of manufactured exports (excluding oil) is determined, and in the short term this is limited by supply constraints.

In the long term productivity increases obtained through higher investment should increase export growth and in so doing lessen the external constraint. This would serve both to lower the Egyptian economy's dependency on foreign aid, and allow it to repay market loans (such as those recently obtained by several Egyptian banks on the Euromarkets).

A further element which might impede the attainment of external equilibrium is the share of imports of consumption goods over GDP.

The amount of luxury goods imported depends essentially on the low propensity to save of households (and on a widespread process of income redistribution in favour of the wealthier groups) whereas the amount of subsistence goods imported depends on the low propensity to save of the public administration. This is seen to be the case if one considers that a large part of current public expenditure goes to subsidise subsistence goods, many of which are imported.

This brings us to the central macroeconomic problem facing the Egyptian economy: the insufficient formation of both private and (above all) public savings. In fact various studies have shown that in the past the excessive growth of public consumption considerably lowered the possibilities of income expansion in Egypt, in that it subtracted resources from productive investments. This is equally true of the current situation.

In other words, the Egyptian economy faces an additional trade-off with respect to other developing countries. In order to increase investment in Egypt, it is not only necessary to contain private consumption but, given the above, it is also necessary to contain public consumption.

Any attempt by the authorities to fix a target for investments (and for the savings to finance them) could lead to conflict between private and public consumption, and given the nature of the public subsidies designed to help the poorer classes, this could lead to a redistribution of income, which, if not properly controlled, could lead - as in 1977 when subsidies on consumption goods were eliminated - to serious social disturbances.

Naturally, different compositions of aggregate demand (investment, public consumption and private consumption) make for different balance of payments constraints both in the short term (because the marginal propensity to import varies) and in the long term (because the amount of investments has a direct effect on the amount of exportable output).

Given the crucial role of subsidies on public expenditure, and their inverse relation with savings, the main trade-off is between short term social benefits (directly proportional to the expenditure on subsidies) and long term development possibilities (directly proportional to investment expenditure).

The existence of a savings gap has other implications for the Egyptian economy. One of these is the problem of financing the public deficit. Given that Egypt has an underdeveloped capital market and that the economy suffers from persistent bouts of financial repression (interest rates are held at artificially low levels) (McKinnon and Mathieson, 1981; Fry, 1980) the public deficit can only be financed (given the amount of net foreign capital inflows) by the creation of liquidity. This policy has often been followed in recent years, resulting in a considerable expansion of the money supply.

In an economy such as Egypt's, characterised by a growing openness to Western markets and by an inadequate domestic productive capacity, such a practice runs the risk of building up inflationary pressures and pressure on the balance of payments. Both of these outcomes adversely affect the exchange rate (let alone the persistence of more than one parity) and cause serious problems for the monetary authorities in the short term. The Egyptian monetary market is further complicated by its 'dual' nature: it permits an (almost) free circulation of both the dollar and the pound sterling.

This brings us to another central aspect of the Egyptian economy: the terms of trade policy. Here too, the authorities are faced with a trade-off: in this case between making Egyptian exports more competitive, by way of currency devaluation and therefore a worsening of the terms of trade, and the defence of a higher exchange rate. In spite of the fact that some observers favour the first option and claim that the current official Egyptian pound exchange rate is overvalued, there are many arguments which suggest against devaluing in order to increase competitiveness.

One of these reasons is that the low growth of Egyptian exports is due more to limits on the supply side (and therefore to the low rate of capital accumulation) than to factors on the demand side which might be affected by a devaluation. A second reason is that the worsening of the terms of trade would have the immediate effect of increasing the cost of those imports necessary to increase Egypt's productive capacity.

A third, and possibly more important, reason, is

that a devaluation could set the Egyptian economy off on a vicious circle such as the following. The devaluation would increase the cost of imported consumption goods, including those necessary for subsistence, and this would increase the public debt by increasing the burden of subsidies. This would inevitably lead to an acceleration of the monetary expansion which (as noted above) would adversely affect the balance of payments to the point of necessitating another devaluation.

It is clear from the above that public expenditure plays a crucial role in the Egyptian economy. With total public expenditure remaining constant, any possibilities of increasing development will depend on a greater share of public expenditure going to investment projects, as private investment is not yet in a position to take on the role of main engine of the economy.

Not all of the economically viable development opportunities are feasible from a political point of view, at least in the short-medium term, due to the difficulties associated with cutting expenditure on public consumption and subsidies.

The problem facing the Egyptian economy is that it must grow in such a manner as to be able to profit from the increasing opening of the economy and therefore attract foreign capital and private investment, but also in such a manner as to avoid causing problems of income redistribution which could arise either due to market mechanisms (inflation) or due to the workings of public finance.

The need to improve the organisation of the fiscal system constitutes another important problem. The system is highly regressive and is based for the most part on indirect taxes. It also suffers due to the high propensity to evade of the Egyptian taxpayers, and any attempts to increase the total yield by increasing tax rates would be just as likely to lead to higher levels of evasion.

Two more (political) factors will affect Egypt's long term position. First of all, the prospects for peace in the region will determine the choices which will dictate military expenditure. Secondly a possible reconciliation with the other Arab states could restore the flow of financial aid from these countries, which was interrupted following the Camp David agreements. This point will be considered at greater length in Chapter 3.

Chapter Two

THE STRUCTURE OF THE EGYPTIAN ECONOMY

INTRODUCTION

So far we have considered the broad economic and financial situation in Egypt and in this second chapter we will examine the structure and the structural evolution of the Egyptian economy.

The Egyptian economy is in many ways paradoxical. The two main examples of this concern Egypt's relative position in the context of the Arab world and the contrast between Egypt's short term and long term economic outlooks.

Egypt is a poor country in comparison with the rest of the Arab world. According to World Bank figures for 1979 the annual per capita income was 480 dollars: well below that of Morocco (740) and Tunisia (1,120) and at the other end of the scale from Kuwait, the richest of the Arab countries, with its annual income of 17,000 dollars per head. However, if we consider other important indicators, such as labour participation rates, literacy levels, and the wealth of skilled labour, then Egypt's position with respect to the other Arab countries changes dramatically. Thus with a rate estimated at 33.5 per cent for recent years Egypt's labour participation rate is higher than that of any other Arab country. In the other Arab countries this rate is below 30 per cent, and in a few, such as Kuwait, it is below 20 per cent.

In Egypt 44 per cent of the population is literate and this places it in eighth position among the Arab countries, after Lebanon, Kuwait, Jordan, Tunisia,

Syria, Somalia and Libya. However, in Egypt 14 per cent of 20-24 year olds attend university. This is higher than in the other Arab countries, with only Kuwait at 13 per cent coming close: then follow Iraq 9 per cent, Saudi Arabia, Jordan and Libya 7 per cent, Tunisia 5 per cent and Morocco 4 per cent.

It should also be noted that Egypt accounts for roughly 40 per cent of the population of the Arab East, and 36 per cent of the total Arab population in its widest possible definition (including Somalia). In 1979 the population of Egypt was estimated at roughly 39 millions. In that same year, the population of the Arab East (Asiatic Arab countries, Egypt and Sudan) was roughly 95 millions, and that of the whole Arab world was of the order of 152 millions.

Finally, in terms of economic structure (and in particular in the industrial sector) Egypt is the most advanced of all the Arab countries, being the only one of these to have a long industrial tradition, and a diversified industrial structure which has successfully passed the import substitution phase and is now in a position to become an exporter of manufactured goods. The percentage of GDP accounted for by the manufacturing sector is higher in Egypt (28 per cent) than in the other Arab countries, and it is on a par with Brazil and Singapore and higher than in Korea. Morocco is the next best Arab country with its manufacturing sector accounting for 17 per cent of GDP (1). More will be said on this when we discuss Egypt's industrial sector.

In short, Egypt is, and will remain, the industrial centre of the Arab world.

The divergence between the short term and long term economic outlooks may be explained by the fact that in the short term the Egyptian economy faces many serious problems whereas in the long term it will benefit from numerous assets around which it will be able to develop.

When studying Egypt's numerous current problems observers often tend to ignore the many positive results achieved in the past few years, just as they ignore the positive structural circumstances that brought them about. In fact when considering the short term future of the Egyptian economy, both foreign and Egyptian analysts tend to be pessimistic and depict a situation bordering on catastrophe. However, when one looks to the long term it is difficult not to be optimistic about the prospects for the Egyptian economy.

If we compare the structural assets of Egypt with those of other developing countries it is difficult to find another country which has so many clear and well defined investment opportunities and long term growth possibilities as does Egypt. It is the variety and combination of its assets and the overall balance of its economy which set Egypt apart from the rest. Future success however will depend on many factors and it is just as possible that the country's great potential may never materialise. We have already seen in the first chapter how little the Egyptian economy has developed and the investment problems brought about by the savings gap.

At a time when the industrialised countries, and as a consequence the developing countries as well, are plagued by economic diseases which baffle the analyst, and against which no economic policy seems to be effective, the Egyptian economy finds itself in the peculiar position of facing serious but conceptually simple problems. The amount of literature and the extent of general agreement on some of them is impressive.

While in most countries the main problem concerns what should be done, in Egypt everyone agrees that there are many obvious things to be done and any disagreement which does exist concerns the order of priority. The danger is not so much that of adopting a damaging policy, but that of not adopting any policy at all.

Another important factor which has had a bearing on the recent ups and downs of the Egyptian economy is that of the country's far-reaching historical roots. The fact that Egypt has such a long contemporary history as an economic and political unit also sets it aside in sharp contrast from the rest of the Arab world.

The contemporary history of Egypt as a unified state with a territorial definition substantially coinciding with today's, dates back to the rule of Muhammed Ali (1805-49). Independent of the Ottoman

Empire of which he was formally a subject, Muhammed Ali brought cotton farming to Egypt and experimented with state controlled industrialisation.

Since most of Egypt's problems are of a structural nature one might almost say that the problems of today are those of always, in spite of the fact that over the past two centuries almost every potential policy alternative has been applied, ranging from the state industrialisation of Muhammed Ali to the modernisation of the country's infrastructure carried out under the Khedives, from the pure liberalism under British guardianship to the protectionist measures of the nationalist middle classes who backed the Wafd, from Nasser's socialism to Sadat's ODEP. Policies are arrived at by a process of trial and error and in Egypt much has been tried and many mistakes have already been discounted. In this sense, it is the failures rather than the successes of past policies which limit the choice of today's politicians and narrow the otherwise wide range of possible policy options.

The historical roots of modern day Egypt also help to explain Egypt's position in relation to the rest of the Arab world, both as regards the level of development in the country (which depends on physical and human capital accumulated over time, and not just on current earnings) and also as regards its political identity. In fact, although Egypt is politically pan-Arab, it also has a highly developed national conscience, which does not exist to the same extent in any of the other Arab countries.

The discussion in the following pages will consider what we have called the obvious assets of the Egyptian economy and will be organised under the following headings: agricultural potential, hydrocarbons, human capital and migration, the Suez Canal, tourism, and the desert. Then we will discuss the dangers which threaten the realisation of the country's potential. We will then conclude this chapter with an examination of the problems and potential of Egypt's industrial sector.

THE OBVIOUS ASSETS OF THE EGYPTIAN ECONOMY

Agricultural Potential

Egypt has an advantage over almost all the other Arab countries in that it has the potential to increase its agricultural production by a significant amount. As will be noted below, this is only partly due to the benefits to be gained by increasing the cultivated area by reclaiming parts of the desert. The main increases will come from higher unit outputs.

This point, which is generally overlooked by non-specialist literature, is of vital importance. Agriculture in Egypt accounts for roughly 20 per cent of GDP, about 7.7 per cent of exports (in 1980) and employs 44 per cent of the workforce. These ratios have been falling over time (2), and moreover, in recent years the agricultural sector unlike the industrial sector has shown little vitality, with annual production increases in real terms below 2 per cent. Such figures have caused many to conclude (erroneously) that the agricultural sector is stagnant (3).

In Egypt, as in many other countries, independence is synonymous with industrialisation, and one can hardly dispute the political choice that was made in the past against the notion (fostered by the British colonial authorities) that Egypt has an agricultural vocation.

However, the agricultural sector in Egypt is not and should not be considered as a declining one: it has the potential for consistent and rapid growth.

In the past agricultural development has been interpreted narrowly to mean the extension of cultivated areas and it has often been noted that these areas have grown less quickly than has the population. From this it is concluded that Egypt is overpopulated (4). This approach however ignores the fact that although in most other countries the extension of cultivated areas grew even less than in Egypt while the population in some cases grew even more, they continued to increase agricultural production by adoption of new and more advanced technologies.

And finally, as unit output in Egyptian agriculture is already fairly high (especially compared to those of the other developing countries), many feel that the possibility of further increases is limited. However, as has been shown by many of the specialist writers on this subject, none of the above conclusions should be considered as final. As our intention in this chapter is to illustrate the agricultural potential of the country rather than suggest which policies should be followed, we will omit any discussion of priorities and will limit ourselves to listing the potential areas of growth.

The main policy followed by Egyptian governments to increase agricultural production has been that of reclaiming and irrigating new expanses of land. One must of course remember that Egypt is a desert country, and with the exception of a narrow stretch of Mediterranean coastline west of Alexandria it is almost without rainfall, therefore almost all cultivated land needs to be irrigated by the Nile. Beyond the Nile Valley the only cultivable areas are the oases which are to be found in some of the larger depressionary regions (Kharga, Dakhla, Farafra, Bahariya and Siwa: the first two of these together are known as the New Valley). (See Figure 2.1.)

The regulation of the Nile waters and the upkeep of the irrigation system have historically been central objectives for Egyptian governments, upon which has depended the economic prosperity of the country.

Throughout modern Egyptian history the area of cultivated land has increased rapidly; rising from 2 million feddans in 1821 to 5 million feddans in 1912 (1 feddan equals 0.42 hectares). There were little or no additions to this until the construction of the Aswan Dam and now the current area of cultivated land is roughly 6 million feddans.

However, the improvement of the irrigation system brought about an expansion of the areas which offer more than one crop per year, and on the eve of the Second World War the total cropped area had reached about 8.5 million feddans. Since then it has continued to grow, reaching 11,125 million feddans in 1975.

The government efforts to expand the cultivated area have often been criticised as being irrational and too costly, and by now it is a widespread opinion that the remaining areas worth reclaiming are few.

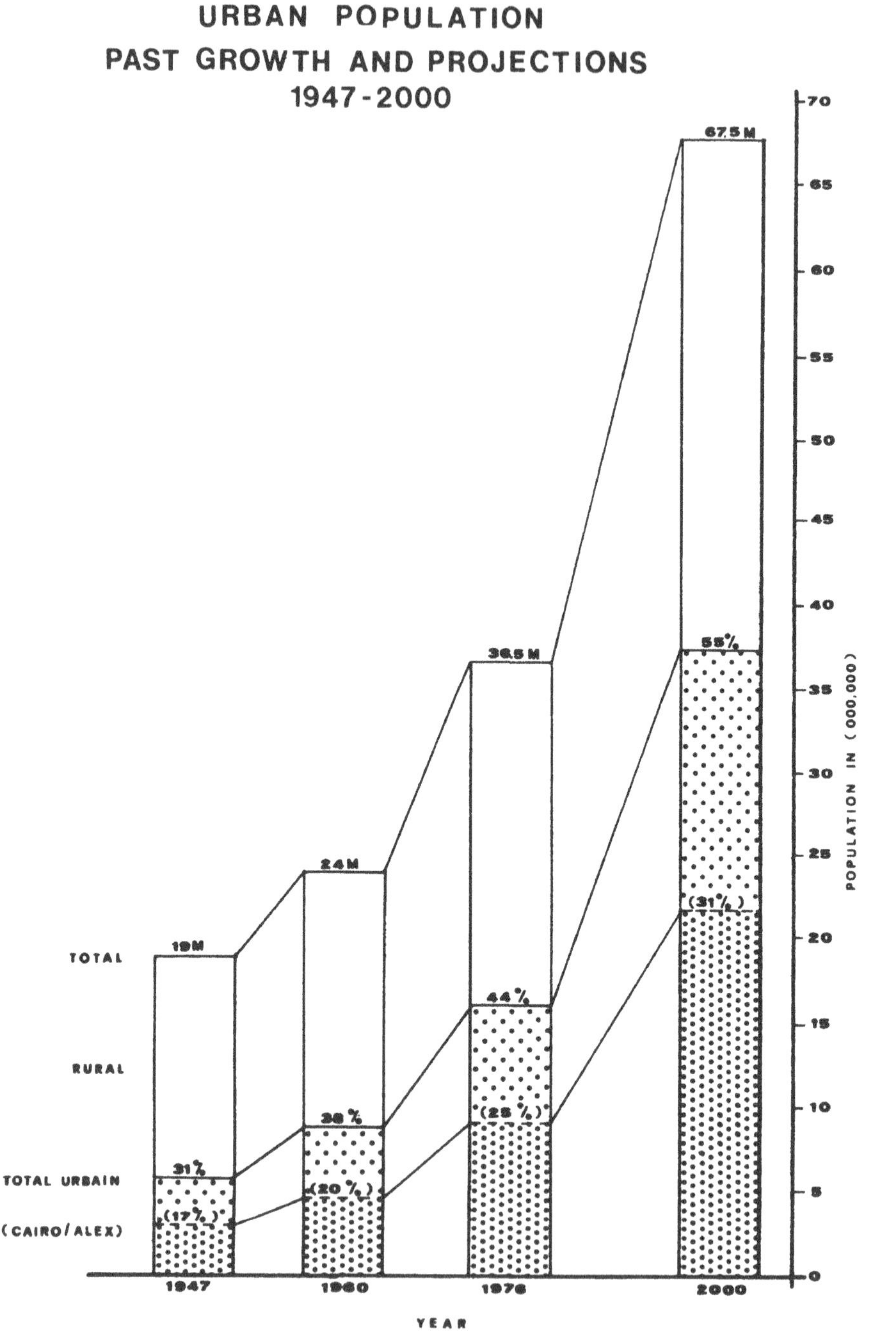
URBAN POPULATION
PAST GROWTH AND PROJECTIONS
1947-2000
TOTAL
RURAL
TOTAL URBAIN
(CAIRO/ALEX)
19M
31%
(17%)
24M
38%
(20%)
36.5M
44%
(25%)
67.5M
55%
(31%)
1947
1960
1976
2000
YEAR
POPULATION IN (000,000)
0
5
10
15
20
25
30
35
40
45
50
55
60
65
70

Fig. 2.1

Table 2.1: Land Reclamation: Schedule of Implementation of the Land Reclamation Programme 1978-99 a (in '000 fedans gross area)

Year	East Delta	Middle Delta	West Delta	Middle Egypt	Upper Egypt	New Valley	Total
1978	16.0	-	7.0	-	-	-	23
1979	21.0	7.0	20.0	5.0	23.3	4.5	80.8
1980	26.0	14.0	13.0	12.0	31.8	6.0	102.8
1981	33.0	20.4	24.0	19.0	20.0	16.0	132.4
1982	38.5	11.5	34.0	17.0	17.0	22.5	140.5
1983	52.0	8.0	39.0	12.5	16.4	28.5	156.4
1984	75.0	15.0	39.0	17.5	10.0	68.5	225.0
1985	95.0	15.0	35.0	15.0	10.0	68.5	238.5
1986	105.0	10.0	40.0	16.7	10.0	67.5	249.2
1987	115.0	10.0	40.0	5.0	10.0	64.5	244.5
1988	105.0	10.0	40.0		5.0	46.0	206.0
1989	105.0	10.0	19.0		5.0	38.5	177.5
1990	110.0	10.0	5.0			17.0	142.0
1991	110.0	10.0					120.0
1992	110.0	10.0					120.0
1993	40.0	7.5					47.5
1994	40.0						40.0
1995	40.0						40.0
1996	40.0						40.0
1997	45.0						45.0
1998	55.0						55.0
1999	72.0						72.0
Total	1,448.5	168.4	355	119.7	158.5	448	2,698.1

Note a. Excluding 120,000 feddans that will be irrigated from Greater Cairo sewage.

Source: Ministry of Agriculture, 1981.

Land reclamation remains however one of the government's priorities, partly because of bureaucratic inertia and partly because of the fact that the investment alternatives favoured by the critics naturally pertain more to private initiative rather than to state intervention. In a recent document, the government stated that further plans have been made to reclaim 2.8 million feddans of land (Ministry of Agriculture, 1981), about half of which is to be found on the eastern side of the delta, along the Canal and on the Mediterranean coast of Sinai. Most of the programme should be completed by 1990 (see Table 2.1.)

However, the expansion of the cultivated areas is neither the only nor the main policy which will lead to an increase in the output of Egypt's agricultural sector. The best prospects for growth seem to come from what is normally called vertical expansion, by which we do not mean more intense farming (for the level of intensity is already high), but rather the use of more advanced technology especially as regards drainage, the use of fertilisers, and the introduction of a wide variety of crops. A recent report concludes that 'the potential for further increasing the production of the areas already cultivated is enormous' (Ministry of Agriculture, USAID, 1982: 6). Although yields in Egypt are high by international standards (see Table 2.2), the figures 'do not take into consideration the unique nature of the Egyptian agricultural sector. In no other country is the agricultural system so dependent on irrigation. In no other country is the cultivated area so well served by high quality water. This unique situation is further favoured by the rich and deep alluvial soils which characterize the whole Nile Valley and Delta. Finally no country can boast better climatic conditions for agricultural production.' (Ibid.)

The conclusion is drawn that the Egyptian agricultural yields should rather be compared to those of the irrigated territories in the United States (see Table 2.3) and that they could become 'considerably higher than the current or potential irrigated yields in the US because the overall environment for crop production is generally superior in Egypt to average irrigated conditions in the US' (Ministry of Agriculture, USAID,

Table 2.2: Comparison of Egyptian and World Yields of 13 Field Crops on the Basis of 3-year (1978/80) Averages

Crop	World Yield tons/ha	Egyptian Yield tons/ha	Egyptian Yield as % of World Yield
Maize	3.126	3.884	124
Barley	1.977	2.682	136
Onion (winter)	12.431	26.517	213
Sugarcane	56.533	82.681	146
Wheat	1.906	3.241	170
Broad beans	1.001	2.190	219
Flax (fibre)	0.417	1.000	240
(seed)	0.468	1.219	260
Rice	2.723	5.643	207
Groundnuts	0.964	1.683	175
Lentils	0.611	1.046	171
Sesame	0.294	0.898	305
Potatoes	12.294	15.295	107
Tomatoes	20.955	17.262	82

Source: Ministry of Agriculture - USAID, 1982.

Table 2.3: Comparison of Average US and Egyptian Crop Yields Under Irrigated Conditions

Crop	Average Yields (MT/ha) Egypt	US
Maize	4.0	9.6
Sorghum	3.8	6.5
Rice	5.6	5.5
Barley	2.7	5.7
Soybeans	1.1	3.4
Sesame	0.8	2.0
Groundnuts	2.4	3.4

Source: Ministry of Agriculture - USAID, 1982.

1982: 90).

If Egyptian agriculture can look forward to such a rosy future, why have past results been so disappointing? The reasons are to be found in the government's agricultural policies, which, while on the one hand trying to make income distribution more equal within the sector, at the same time squeezed the agricultural sector to provide funds to finance the industrialisation effort.

This income redistribution policy principally consisted in the agrarian reform launched by Nasser in September 1952, only six weeks after his coming to power.

Nasser's reform, which limited the largest farm units to 200 feddans and redistributed any land in excess of this, is generally considered to have been one of his major successes. The net effect of it was to punish the major landowners rather than the owners of medium sized farm units, whose social and political role actually grew as a result of the reform (Mabro, 1974: 72; Binder, 1978) and who are now in a position to radically change the Egyptian agricultural sector.

Along with the agrarian reform Nasser also brought in a series of controls, on prices, on the marketing of agricultural produce, and on the allocation of lands to certain types of farming. By way of monopolising the cotton market and intervening in the markets of the other key products such as wheat, the government held agricultural prices at artificially low levels (see Table 2.4). This policy lightened the burden on public expenditure by cutting subsidies on subsistence goods, and generated a profit to the benefit of the State treasury.

In the long term however this policy has had three important consequences:

- it has caused an exodus from the agricultural sector;
- it has discouraged investments in the agricultural sector (5);
- it has increased the extent of non-controlled as opposed to controlled farming.

As regards this third point there has been an increase in horticultural farming and the farming of berseem (6) to the detriment of the main crops: cotton, wheat and sugar cane. Rice planting and production

Table 2.4: Government Procurement Prices as Compared with Free Market Prices, 1967-68

Crop	Average prices for compulsory purchases (Egyptian pounds) (1)	Average prices for free retentions (Egyptian pounds) (2)	Price differential (2)/(1) % (3)
Wheat (per ardab)	4	5.1	127
Rice (per dariba)	20	40	200
Onions (per ton)	11	16.5	150

Source: Abdel Fadil, 1975: 87.

Table 2.5: Crop Area Index, Major Crops 1950-76

Period	Cotton	Maize	Rice	Wheat	Fruit	Vege-tables	Short Season Clover	Long Season Clover
1950-54	100	100	100	100	100	100	100	100
1955-59	101	105	126	95	121	152	105	110
1960-64	99	98	154	88	156	211	107	118
1965-69	96	86	199	80	221	258	102	143
1970-72	88	87	220	83	264	280	102	143
1973-75	83	100	199	85	289	316	98	169
1976	73	100	212	88				

Source: World Bank and Ministry of Agriculture

have also increased (see Table 2.5).

This point is important for it suggests another possible strategy for developing the Egyptian agricultural sector: a shift in the relative importance of crops farmed.

If Egypt chose to fully integrate itself with the world market it could considerably increase the value of its agricultural produce by abandoning the cultivation of certain crops in favour of others (7). As far as cotton, rice and all horticultural produce are concerned Egypt enjoys a clear comparative advantage (8). On the other hand there should be a reduction in the cultivation of less suited crops such as wheat, maize, sugar cane and berseem (the latter could easily be substituted be it as regards animal feeding be it as regards fertility regeneration).

The main obstacle to this transformation is to be found at the political level. In Egypt there exists the widespread opinion that an excessive dependence on imports of essential foodstuffs could undermine the country's security. Egypt's preoccupation with national security - which surfaces as well for other issues, such as emigration, - has led to irrational behaviour on the part of the authorities.

In spite of the fact that current policies do not guarantee national security, as Egypt is already largely dependent on imported foodstuffs, and for all that there exist many other ways of guarding against sudden interruptions of supplies and erratic price fluctuations, most Egyptian economists continue to see food security as a priority objective (9). This is indeed strange in a world where economic interdependence is such that no country can be said to enjoy full economic security.

The key to solving many of the problems of Egypt's agricultural sector might be to allow domestic prices to tend towards international prices. Another possibility might be to move from a price policy which punishes the agricultural sector to one which favours it (such as exists within the EEC and generally in most industrial countries). Empirical research has shown conclusively that Egyptian farmers and landowners respond quickly to changes in food prices.

According to some recent estimates such a policy

might be able not only to contain the gap between domestic consumption and production of foodstuffs which is currently growing, but even to reverse it before the year 2000. Three possible scenarios have been projected for Egypt's agricultural balance (Ministry of Agriculture, USAID, 1982: 205-12). A first scenario (see Figure 2.2) is based on the hypothesis that unit yields continue to grow at the same rate as over the past twenty years. This would lead to a rapidly growing agricultural deficit, which would reach 4 billion dollars (1980 prices) by the end of this century. A second scenario (see Figure 2.3) is based on the assumption that unit yields will increase at a rate of 60 per cent until 1990 and at a rate of 100 per cent for the following ten years, with no change in the crops produced. The result in this case would be to avoid the deficit increase associated with the first policy. A third possibility (see Figure 2.4) is based on the hypothesis that an effort is made to increase productivity in the cultivated areas, by making a series of price adjustments and by cutting the consumption subsidies in order to cut down on waste, without however affecting the population's diet. It also hypothesises a change in the balance of crops produced with a greater emphasis going to production for export.

Obviously these projections should not be treated as forecasts but rather as simple illustrations of the fact that Egypt has great unexploited agricultural potential. However, they are realistic to the extent that any measures which would need to be taken in order to achieve them are well within the bounds of possibility.

Finally, in this context one must consider the prospects of agricultural cooperation between Egypt and Sudan. This cooperation will centre around the construction of several important waterworks in Sudan (the main one being the Jonglei Canal), which will make larger amounts of water from the Nile available to increase irrigation in both countries. The realisation of these plans would allow the cultivation of wheat, sugarcane and other field crops and livestock farming, using highly capital intensive methods, in large areas of the Sudan where conditions are far better than in Egypt. The Egyptian authorities hope for the success of this

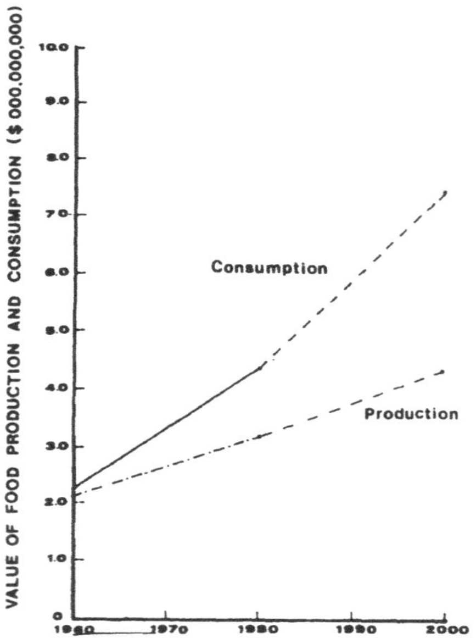

FIG. 2.2
THE VALUE OF FOOD PRODUCED AND CONSUMED IN EGYPT FROM 1960 – 1980 WITH PROJECTIONS TO 2000 A.D., ASSUMING A CONTINUATION OF THE PRESENT RATE OF INCREASE IN PRODUCTION (REFERRED TO AS "LOW" IN TEXIT).

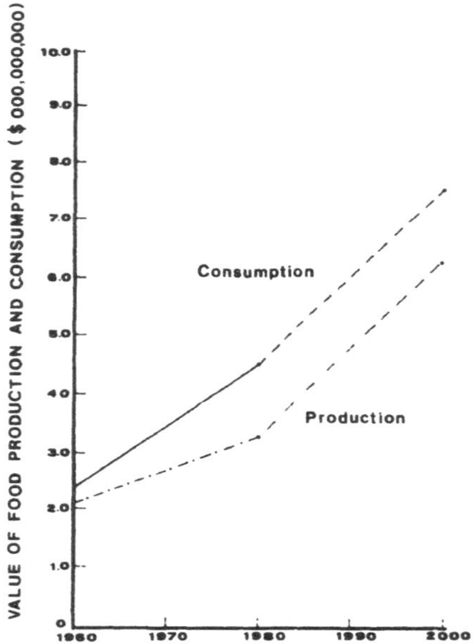

FIG. 3
THE VALUE OF FOOD PRODUCED AND CONSUMED IN EGYPT FROM 1960 – 1980 WITH PROJECTIONS TO 2000 A.D., ASSUMING AN INCREASE IN OUTPUT OF APPROXIMATELY 100 PERCENT OVER 1980 LEVELS (REFERRED TO AS "HIGH" PRODUCTION LEVELS IN TEXT).

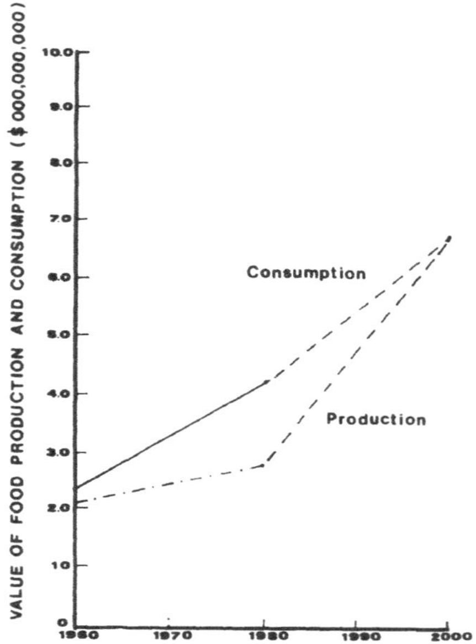

FIG. 2.4
THE VALUE OF FOOD PRODUCED AND CONSUMED IN EGYPT FROM 1960 – 1980 WITH PROJECTIONS TO 2000 A.D., ASSUMING PRODUCTIVITY INCREASES SET FORTH IN FIGURE 3, SOME SHIFTS TO HIGHER VALUED CROPS FOR EXPORT, AND SOME REDUCTION IN PER CAPITA CONSUMPTION LEVELS BELOW THOSE PROJECTED IN FIGURE 3.

cooperation which would involve Egyptian labour and capital in the exploitation of newly reclaimed territories in Sudan. Successful cooperation would allow Egypt to satisfy her food needs with imports from Sudan, and although as regards the balance of payments Egypt would not gain anything by importing wheat from Sudan as opposed to from the United States, successful cooperation with Sudan would relax fears about national food security and this might help to overcome the obstacles which have blocked the road to agricultural specialisation in Egypt.

Hydrocarbons

Although production in recent years has been increasing Egypt remains a relatively minor producer of oil and gas. Although it was born in the early years of the century, the Egyptian oil industry has been slow to develop. This has obviously been due not only to geological conditions, but to technical and political factors as well. However as these problems were gradually solved during the course of the seventies production levels rose, contributing greatly to the improvement of the balance of payments with respect to that of the previous decade.

In the fiscal year July 1981-June 1982 Egypt's production of hydrocarbons was 34.5 million tons (700,000 b/d). Relative to the previous year the output of crude oil increased from 30.6 million tons (613,000 b/d) to 32.1 million tons (643,000 b/d) while the production of gas and condensates also increased marginally from 2.2 to 2.3 million tons.

These production increases alone however do not tell the whole story, rather they must be seen in relation to the outlook for the future. Just as with the agricultural sector most of the economic literature on Egypt's oil industry is rather pessimistic in nature, constantly wondering what will happen when the oil finishes and exports cease. On the other hand many specialists writing on the subject are far more optimistic, and believe that Egypt will not run out of oil for several decades to come.

Crude reserves (i.e. known and commercially proven deposits) totalled 401 million tons in 1981, and therefore even in the absence of any further discovery Egypt would be able to maintain its production level for a further eleven and a half years.

This last hypothesis however is only of academic interest for there is much exploration going on and by the end of 1982 some very important discoveries had been made; in particular, along with further discoveries in the oil-rich provinces of Sinai and the Gulf of Suez, significant new discoveries had been made by AGIP off-shore in the Mediterranean (the el-Tina deposit) (Luciani, 1982: 8), and by Shell in the Western Desert (the Badr-el-Din deposit) (PIW, 1981/1982: 9). The latter discovery by Shell was considered to be of particular importance because it has increased the understanding of the geological structure of a region which had often attracted oil companies only to disappoint them later.

The Egyptian government has stated that production will reach the level of one million barrels a day by 1985, however the same forecast was made during the 1970s without ever being reached. Caution is therefore warranted as is suggested by the prudent attitude shown by the EGPC (Egyptian General Petroleum Company). The government's optimism however is even greater for later years and the Energy Minister recently announced that production will increase throughout the five year plan (1982-87) by 85 per cent to a total of 63 million tons (MEES, 8/XI/1982: 115).

As regards the market price for crude oil Egypt does not face the same problems that other Arab countries do. Not being a member of OPEC Egypt enjoys freedom of movement with regard to prices and raises or lowers them according to the market (see Table 2.6).

But if the outlook for the oil industry is bright, the outlook for the production of natural gas is even more so. The policy of the Egyptian government with regard to natural gas is to give priority to local utilisation and to the establishment of a National Reserve of 345 billion cu.m.; (Rustici, 1982: 3); once the National Reserve is secured an export scheme will be considered and the various foreign companies operating in the country will be allowed to pool their gas reserves to feed into a combined liquefaction complex. In the meantime the production of gas is deliberately held at low levels.

There is currently a programme of gas installation (major industrial and urban domestic areas) being carried out, but to date consumption levels have remained below that of new discoveries. Known reserves in 1982 were of the order of 260 billion cu.m., so therefore the objective of 345 billion cu.m. is not far off.

As regards the future, in spite of the many uncertainties that inevitably abound, the estimates of the country's gas deposits are most encouraging. According to the vice-president of Agip, Marcello Colitti, 'Egypt's total recoverable gas reserves could amount by the end of the century to a total of about 1,050 billion cu.m.' (Colitti, 1982: 15-16). Other commentators have put forward estimates not too far removed from this. Working under the assumption that domestic gas consumption will increase rapidly (taking the gas contribution to total Egyptian energy consumption from the 10 per cent of 1980 to 75 per cent in the year 2000) the vice-president of Agip has suggested that Egypt begin to export liquefied gas (LNG) at the level of 3 billion cu.m. in later years (Colitti, 1982: 19). The Egyptian government is keen on the idea of exporting gas but not until the National Reserve is obtained (El Ayouti, 1982: 6).

Gas exports would be of great assistance to Egypt's balance of payments, but local industries too will benefit much from its availability. Independently of its price, the very fact that gas will be available will allow Egyptian industry to adopt technologies which are more advanced and competitive than those based on alternative sources of energy. Needless to say this advantage would be further increased if the gas were sold at less than the international market price.

The latter is common practice in most Arab countries even if the economic rationale behind it is doubtful, and it is probable that it will be followed in Egypt where the authorities have a history of maintaining artificially low hydrocarbon prices. Currently domestic hydrocarbon prices in Egypt are roughly one quarter of the international market prices; the Egyptian consumer thereby enjoys an enormous hidden subsidy, which in 1981/2 cost the authorities 2.7

Table 2.6: Egyptian Crude Oil Price Variations in 1982 (dollars per barrel)

	Date on which variation came into force						
Crude (degree API)	1 Dec.	1 Nov.	1 Sept.	1 June	1 March	1 Feb.	1 Jan.
Suez Blend (33°)	31.75	32.60	32.60	32.60	32.00	33.00	34.00
Bellayim (26°)	28.75	29.00	28.60	28.50	28.00	28.65	30.50
Ras Gharib ($21-21.5^{o}$)	26.25	26.75	26.50	26.50	26.00	26.65	27.80

Source: MEES, 6 December 1982.

billion dollars in lost receipts (MEES, 15/XI/1982: A10).

A closing of the gap between domestic and international prices would increase the government's and/or the EGPC's receipts and would allow them to follow a more aggressive investment policy along the lines of that followed by ENI in Italy with the proceeds from the sales of methane. This price policy should not be seen simply as one of the Egyptian government's many mistakes, but it is surely another unexploited potential resource which, along with the others, helps to brighten the economic outlook of the country.

A second consequence of the artificially low prices regards the figures for GDP, which was underestimated by 10 per cent in 1979 (ESU, 1981: 14-16), and by even more in later years due to the price differential having widened. Obviously enough if any adjustment policy regarded only price levels it would have its effect exclusively on the nominal value of GDP; however, in the case in which share of oil production which is exported increased (due to an increase in domestic prices for other reasons) there would follow a real increase in available resources.

Human Capital and Migration

Egypt is the most populous of all the Arab countries, with a population of over 45 million in October 1982, after an increase of 1 million in the preceding ten month period. The size, quality and rapid growth of the population are factors which have both aided and obstructed economic development in Egypt. In this section we will limit our discussion to the ways in which this growing pool of human capital has aided Egypt's economic development. How it has obstructed the development process will be discussed further below.

Not only does Egypt have a large population but its accumulation of human capital is also considerable; Egypt having rates of literacy, schooling and labour participation which are high relative to those in the rest of the Arab world. Also important in this context is the fact that Egyptian labour has been traditionally wage earning in both the agricultural and the growing industrial sectors (10). Recent research has shown that female participation rates too have risen over the years

(11). This combination of circumstances puts Egypt in a category of its own in the context of the Arab world, in sharp differentiation from the largest oil producing countries. The plain fact is that within the Arab world Egypt has the largest pool of professionals, technicians, skilled labour and unskilled labour, and it is hardly likely to lose this pole position because the situation elsewhere is not improving very rapidly despite the oil revenue (or, more precisely, due to the oil revenue, which by offering easy income opportunities discourages many in these other countries from furthering their education (12). This wealth of human capital is one of the fundamental strengths of the Egyptian economy, both in the short and in the long term.

In the short run, the sudden availability of large amounts of oil money in other countries in the Arab region, coupled with a shift in policy and active encouragement on the part of the government, has led to an unprecedented flow of migrant workers leaving the country (Dessouki, 1978). Unfortunately the phenomenon of inter-Arab migration has not as yet been thoroughly researched and the most recent figures capable of offering an overall vision are those printed in Table 2.7. Since 1975 however the number of Egyptians migrating to other Arab states has increased greatly. The various estimates of the number of Egyptian emigrants working abroad vary between 500,000 and one million (Hansen and Radwan, 1982: 81-9). These estimates include only those actually working abroad: if families and dependents were also included the figures would exceed 1.5 million. (In the third chapter of this book we estimate the number of Egyptians working abroad at roughly 2 million).

Migration has become the most important transmission factor for oil revenue throughout the whole Arab region, along with official transfers which have become far less significant for Egypt since the signing of peace with Israel. Migrants' remittances reached almost $3 billion in 1980, equal to some 70 per cent of total exports. However, while this figure includes declared remittances, be they in Egyptian or foreign currency or be they in the form of duty free imported goods, it does not include emigrants' foreign currency deposits in Egyptian banks, nor does it include deposits in foreign banks nor any undeclared currency or goods brought back into the country. Suffice it to say that with all probability the inflow of income into the Egyptian economy is very much greater than $3 billion per year. A critic of Egyptian migration policy has acknowledged that: 'Proponents of the open door policy may well argue that Nasser's Egypt waged battles and spilled blood for the Suez Canal and the Aswan Dam, yet the silent outcome of one measure of the open door policy brings to Egypt much more hard currency' (Ibrahim, 1982: 71).

Migration in most cases is temporary. Egyptians working in other Arab countries enjoy a much higher income than they would in Egypt but at the same time suffer political and economic discrimination in their host countries. The host governments do not wish to see their immigrant populations stabilise and assimilate, and accordingly the immigrants remain on the margin of society. The fact that the average length of stay is increasing does not in any way contradict the prevailing short term nature of emigration.

This is an important point, for if the emigrants realise that sooner or later they will "go back home" they will tend to see Egypt as where their real interests lie and will consequently direct most of their savings in that direction.

Although existing surveys show that the lower echelons of the migrant community spend most of their newly found wealth on conspicuous consumption, a growing amount of this wealth is being directed towards investment expenditure (see Table 2.8) (13).

Most emigrants spend a high percentage of their initial earnings on various consumer durables (typically Japanese made electronic gadgets). This behaviour is typical of their low income background, but may also be explained by the fact that the domestic industrial sector lags far behind the new, more exacting demands of the market-place. This phenomenon should slowly but surely disappear as domestic manufacturers improve their supply and as the migrants decide to return home permanently and improve their conditions in Egypt. They will then tend to spend their income on real or finan-

Table 2.7: Inter-Arab Labour Migration in 1975 (After the Oil Price Boom of 1973/4)

Labour Importing Countries / Labour Exporting Countries	Egypt %	Yemen %	Jordan-Palestine %	Democratic Yemen %	Syria %	Lebanon %
Saudi Arabia	95,000 (23.9)	280,000 (96.6)	175,000 (66.1)	55,000 (78)	15,000 (21)	20,000 (40)
Libya	229,500 (57.8)	-	14,150 (5.3)	-	13,000 (19)	5,700 (12)
Kuwait	37,588 (9.4)	2,757 (1.0)	47,653 (18.0)	8,658 (12)	16,547 (23)	7,200 (15)
United Arab Emirates	12,500 (3.1)	4,500 (1.6)	14,500 (5.5)	4,500 (6)	4,500 (6)	3,000 (6)
Jordan (East Bank)	5,300 (1.3)	-	-	-	20,000 (28)	500 (1)
Iraq	7,000 (1.8)	-	5,000 (1.9)	-	-	1,100 (2)
Qatar	2,850 (0.7)	1,250 (0.4)	6,000 (2.3)	1,250 (2)	750 (1)	129 (0.2)
Oman	4,600 (1.2)	100 (0.0)	1,600 (0.6)	100 (0.0)	400 (0.6)	-
Bahrain	1,237 (0.3)	1,212 (0.4)	641 (0.2)	1,222 (2)	68 (0.1)	
Yemen	2,000 (0.5)	-	200 (0.1)	-	150 (0.2)	
Total	397,543 (100.0)	290,128 (100.0)	264,717 (100.0)	70,630 (100.0)	70,415 (100.0)	49,600 (100.0)
%	(30.7)	(22.4)	(20.4)	(5.5)	(5.4)	(3.8)

Labour Exporting Countries / Labour Importing Countries	Sudan %	Tunisia %	Oman %	Iraq %	Somalia %	Algeria Morocco %	TOTAL
Saudi Arabia	35,000 (76)	-	17,500 (46)	2,000 (10)	5,000 (76)	-	699,900
Libya	7,000 (15)	38,500 (99.6)	-	-	-	2,500 (98)	310,350
Kuwait	873 (2)	79 (0.1)	3,660 (10)	18,000 (78)	247 (4)	47 (2)	43,280
United Arab Emirates	1,500 (3)	-	14,000 (36)	500 (2)	1,000 (15)	-	62,000
Jordan (East Bank)	-	-	-	-	-	-	32,800
Iraq	200 (0.4)	-	-	-	-	-	15,200
Qatar	700 (1)	-	1,870 (5)	-	-	-	14,870
Oman	500 (1)	100 (0.3)	-	-	300 (5)	-	8,800
Bahrain	400 (1)	-	1,383 (4)	126 (4)	-	-	6,200
Yemen	-	-	-	-	-	-	2,350
Total	45,873 (100.0)	38,649 (100.0)	38,413 (100.0)	20,625 (100.0)	6,547 (100.0)	2,547 (100.0)	1,295,750
%	(3.5)	(3.0)	(3.0)	(1.6)	(0.5)	(0.2)	(100.0)

Source: Birks and Sinclair, 1980: 134-5.

cial investments.

The latter phenomenon in fact is already under way in the Egyptian countryside where the building industry is booming, and it is to be expected that Egyptian return migrants will invest in small self run enterprises both in the countryside and in the city. Thanks to large scale migration a process of primitive accumulation of unprecedented scope is under way in Egypt. If one considers that in 1981 23 percent of all rural families in Egypt received remittances from family members (Hansen and Radwan, 1982: 101) one may understand how widespread the phenomenon is and how great its potential. Another consequence of the high levels of emigration has been the diminution of the previous excess labour supply and this has brought about high wage increases in many important sectors (14). In particular agricultural wages have risen dramatically in recent years bringing about a major improvement in farm-workers' conditions (15).

On the other hand the 'capturing' of the savings of the higher echelons of the migrant community, and their channelling towards domestic investment should prove to be more difficult. It would entail a significant diversification and deepening of the Egyptian financial system to offer an attractive alternative to the financial opportunities of Bahrein or Beirut or the main European financial centres. However, in spite of there being more lucrative opportunities elsewhere, it seems that many of these Egyptian nationals living abroad are willing to invest in Egypt.

Migration has been blamed for a number of Egypt's current economic ills. The most serious claim is that emigration is depriving the country of its best workers, causing shortages in some sectors (Ibrahim, 1982: 73-86). The most oft-cited example is that of the construction industry where wages rose considerably and projects were delayed due to the shortage of skilled workers.

While this negative effect of emigration on the Egyptian economy should not be underestimated, we feel that the fast growth in population (and therefore labour supply) renders it only of short term interest. It should also be noted that labour mobility has increased in Egypt, as has reaction to wage differentials, be they

Table 2.8: Declared Remittances: Financial and Duty-free Imports, 1977 and 1980 a (millions of Egyptian pounds)

Form of remittance	1977	1980
Financial		
Transfers to E£ accounts	279.9	641.8
Cash, US$ bills, etc.	104.4	176.5
Total, financial	384.3	818.3
Duty-free imports		
Electrical equipment	18.6	64.8
Means of transport	60.0	240.4
Materials for artisans	33.6	234.0
Spare parts	52.1	133.2
Food	32.6	127.1
Other household goods	18.2	22.6
Metal products	18.4	117.8
Cosmetics	1.1	1.4
Textiles	6.2	10.8
Commodities for... b	7.9	58.6
Other	16.5	59.7
Total, duty-free imports	265.2	1,070.4
Total remittances declared	649.5	1,888.7

Notes: a. Undeclared remittances with transfers to US$ accounts and other foreign exchange accounts in Egypt excluded.
b. Illegible Source: Central Bank of Egypt, information supplied to the ILO mission.

Source: Hansen and Radwan, 1982: 240.

geographic or sectorial (16). It has been shown by a recent ILO study that although the high levels of emigration have caused problems the number of employees working in the construction industry has actually risen (17).

There is also reason to believe that labour mobility, which is often blocked by financial constraints, will increase as a consequence of funds made available from migration, and channelled within family structures and ties.

There has been much controversy over future levels of emigration and the effect of emigrants' remittances on the balance of payments. Many of the opinions put forward are, we feel, overly pessimistic.

It is felt by many that net emigration will soon begin to taper off, eventually reaching zero (i.e. the number of those leaving the country will be equalled by those returning) (18). Although this must inevitably occur sooner or later, it is by no means certain that it will in fact occur soon.

Those who believe that net emigration will soon reach zero base their argument on the fact that the job situation in the other Arab countries is becoming increasingly tight, due to infrastructure programmes having been completed.

In political circles, many have voiced the fear that Egypt has become too dependent on emigrants' remittances and that this weakness might be exploited by the other Arab states to put pressure on the Egyptian government.

Hansen and Radwan (1982: 167) go so far as to hypothesise what would happen if all Egyptian emigrants were suddenly forced to return home (19). We feel however that this exercise is purely academic. Just as Egypt is dependent on emigrants' remittances so too are the other Arab countries dependent on Egyptian labour. In fact neither Egypt's rift with the other Arab countries nor the armed conflict between Egypt and Libya in 1977 had any real effect on migration. To suggest that all Egyptian migrants might suddenly be sent home is to border on the absurd and in fact the whole argument that net emigration will soon drop to zero is totally unfounded.

It is not true that all the main oil producing

countries have already completed their infrastructure programmes. In Iraq for instance, extensive reconstruction will be needed at the end of hostilities with Iran, and there still remains much work to be done in some of the other Gulf states. The fact that many airports and roads have already been built does not mean that there is nothing else to be done, and in any case it is wrong to assume that all Egyptian migrants will be tied to the construction industry. Migration will continue as long as wage rates in the other Arab states are so much higher than in Egypt and it will not be until these wage differentials have been narrowed that we can expect net emigration figures to approach zero.

It should also be noted that not all Egyptian migrants head for the Gulf countries. Migration to the Gulf countries seriously depleted the domestic supply of labour in Syria, Lebanon and Jordan, and replacement migration to the latter originating in Egypt is already important. In fact Egypt has become the 'labour supplier of last resort' for the whole Arab world, which on the whole suffers from a shortage of manpower, and it is probable that Egyptian migration will continue to increase right through the 1980s (20).

It must not be forgotten however that although it will continue for some while to play a crucial role in the domestic labour market and the balance of payments, migration remains a temporary phenomenon. To date, migrants have not been able to settle in their host countries, and this situation is unlikely to change. The population of the main oil producing countries will thus remain relatively small and this will have an adverse effect on the growth of their industrial sectors. While this 'limit to growth' has not yet been felt in any of the Gulf countries or Libya, it will become more obvious in the future. The possibilities for making a quick fortune will disappear, and an increasing number of families will come to depend more upon past investments than on current income. Although those who lived through the 1970s boom will probably settle in their respective countries, their children (many of whom will have studied abroad and will benefit from capital accumulated within the family) will be more likely to head for countries where the economic outlook for the future is brighter.

Egypt's traditional role as a major centre of the Arab world corresponds to deeply rooted structural factors which are not likely to change in the near future. Although residents of the rich Arab countries can bring the benefits of high technology and afford air conditioning, desalinated water and fast travel by air, it is not difficult to imagine that when the oil finally runs out these countries will no longer attract migrants and indeed will find it increasingly difficult to maintain their native populations. The traditional centres of the Arab world should benefit from this expected turn in the shape of capital and financial inflows. Such a tendency is already apparent in the rush on luxury apartments in Cairo and Alexandria, and in the long term should bode well for the financing of Egyptian development.

The Suez Canal

The Suez Canal is a very important asset from two points of view: on the one hand it contributes to the balance of payments and on the other hand it is a centre which will attract internationally oriented industries.

The reopening of the Canal and the plans made for its future development were of great symbolic value in the context of Sadat's peace offensive toward Israel. Once again the Canal was 'centre-stage', just as it had been the symbol of the Khedivial period, the immediate raison d'etre of British rule, and finally the object of Nasser's revolt against foreign domination.

Throughout the years in which the Canal was closed because of the Israeli occupation of the Sinai, it appeared that it might not be so important after all, and that its role in international trade was bound to decline. This was felt to be the case because in that period very large and ultra-large crude carriers were being built in great numbers, allowing the transportation of huge quantities of crude from the Gulf to the European and American markets by circumnavigating the African continent. However since the Canal has been reopened, and even more so since the first enlargement in 1980, it has become clear that the supertankers are not seriously threatening the role of the Canal: in fact, the opposite may be true, that is, that the reopening of the Canal has contributed to rendering these supertankers both economically and technically obsolete.

The renewed importance of the Canal is based on numerous economic and political factors. The latter are pushing the Arab oil producing countries to reduce as far as possible their dependence on export outlets on the Gulf, and establish alternative loading terminals on the Red Sea or the Mediterranean. The East-West Saudi pipeline which became operative in 1981 is a major step in this direction and an Iraqi pipeline may follow. On the basis of these trends and other assumptions it has been estimated that the traffic across the Canal may well reach a figure of 2.7 million barrels per day by 1985. This conclusion is reached under the assumption that the Sumed pipeline (which runs from the Gulf of Suez to the Mediterranean) will be utilised at full capacity after the planned additions are completed (Luciani, 1982). Recent studies have shown the benefits to be gained by using the Canal to transport oil headed for European destinations (21).

A further widening and deepening of the Canal is currently under discussion. At present the Canal can take fully laden tankers of up to 150,000 tons and 375,000 tons in ballast. After further deepening, the Canal would be able to take fully laden tankers of up to 260,000 tons which today can only transit if half laden. The economic rationale of further deepening the Canal has been questioned in some quarters, but the project is strongly backed by the Japanese interests which carried out the first enlargement and to which this second would also be entrusted.

The expectation that the Canal may also become an important locational attraction for internationally oriented industries in the long run is well founded. At the same time it is not surprising that so far results have been rather disappointing.

The reasons why the Canal is not attracting a lot of industrial interest at present are two-fold. Firstly the Canal is evidently not yet sufficiently equipped and developed. Secondly it is more likely to attract industries which are presently suffering an international crisis of over-production, and in which there is very little fresh investment. Any planned industrialisation of the Canal should provide for the creation of a series of free zones. One of these free zones has already been created at Port Said, another at Port Tewfick and there are plans to create another at Adabiya, near Suez. Feasibility studies carried out by foreign experts (Reynolds, Smith and Hills Inc., 1979; USAID, 1980) were optimistic about the future of these free zones but to date most of the plans approved have concerned warehousing, rather than industrial transformation.

The truth of the situation is that Egypt's port facilities are insufficient to handle even the domestic needs of the country - let alone to attract entrepot trade. Large expansion schemes are under way both in Alexandria itself and nearby in El Dikheila, as well as in Port Said and Suez.

According to the World Bank (World Bank, 1982) however, total planned port capacity in Egypt will reach the level required to bear the projected traffic no earlier than 1987, and if the planned capacity is not further increased it will already be insufficient by 1988.

Thus, it is very unlikely that the Canal will be perceived by the international business community as being an attractive location for export oriented industrial projects before the 1990s, and even then large scale investment will be necessary to realise the Canal's potential.

The Canal's long term outlook however is brighter. It will be able to attract oil related industries and industries with a high energy consumption and finally industries involved in the manufacture of final products which are costly to transport over long distances, and for which the Canal zone could easily become an excellent base from which to serve the whole regional market.

Considering the advantage that the Canal holds over its main potential rivals (from Malta to Bahrein) as regards skilled labour supply and other services, it is difficult to imagine that the Canal will not develop and become one of the main industrial centres of the whole region within the next thirty years or so.

Tourism

Although it is commonly underestimated, the growth potential for tourism in Egypt is considerable. This potential for growth has three sides to it:

(a) Egypt attracts tourists from the other Arab countries because Cairo and Alexandria with their cosmopolitan atmosphere are the two main urban centres in the whole region, and because Egypt is traditionally the political and cultural centre of the Arab world. Also in its favour is the fact that the climate in the Gulf countries is intolerable for at least two months of the year.

(b) Egypt attracts tourists from all over the world, for in terms of archaeological and historical heritage, no other country in the Mediterranean, except Italy and Greece, has richer assets. Worldwide, one should perhaps add China, no more. As in Italy (though not Greece), Egypt's artistic heritage stretched almost without interruption from 2500 B.C. to the present day, transcending the Roman civilisation, the early Christian period and the various stages of Islamic history. So far only a small percentage of the total heritage has been exploited: in fact in Cairo itself most of the Islamic monuments, some of which are of extraordinary beauty, are in ruins or not easily accessible.

(c) The natural setting of the country is also a potentially important tourist attraction. The most promising assets are the Red Sea coast and the Sinai coast, which offer more than a thousand kilometres of almost entirely undeveloped coastline (there exist only two or three hotels), which with its excellent climate, rich marine life and coral reef is the perfect setting for year-round beach oriented tourism.

To date the growth of tourism in Egypt has been confined to the second of the three dimensions just mentioned. The first dimension suffered a blow following the worsening of relations between Sadat and the rest of the Arab world. This however is felt to be no more than a short-term effect, and indeed Cairo registered high levels of Arab tourism in 1982.

The growth of culturally inspired tourism has long

been blocked by the restricted availability of accomodation. All recent efforts at development in this sector have accordingly concentrated on improving facilities in the traditional tourist centres: Cairo and the more famous tourist centres on the Nile, such as Luxor and Aswan, are surrounded by new and often enormous hotels and many other equally large scale hotels are under construction. A study carried out by the World Bank (World Bank, 1978: III, 126) showed that in the mid-70s the Egyptian hotel industry was among the most profitable in the world, registering a gross income of 45.6 per cent of the turnover. By increasing their presence in the area the large hotel companies have shown that they foresee a bright future for the area (22).

Although new projects to develop beach oriented tourism (especially on the Sinai coast, the west coast of the Red Sea and to a lesser extent on the Mediterranean) are under way or are at the planning stage, it is only to be expected that relatively little attention will be paid to this aspect of tourism so long as the boom of cultural tourism continues.

And further, the existence of bottlenecks in the building industry, in managerial capacity and in the availability of skilled labour, along with the limited transport network make it unlikely that the tourist sector will grow any faster than at present.

However, it seems reasonable to believe that the present rate of growth will be maintained over the next decades, first of all by further developing tourism in the main cultural centres, then by gradually developing the less well known areas of historical interest. This process will then be continued by higher investment in up-market seaside resorts, and then finally - by which time communications will have improved - by providing for mass tourism at lower prices.

It is impossible to predict just how long this process will take to unfold, for the general economic situation, which strongly influences demand, could change radically.

The Desert

Although almost always regarded as a negative element, the fact that the desert occupies around 96 per cent of

Egypt brings with it some advantages.

Apart from oil there are large deposits of manganese and phosphates and the desert is also the source of various materials used in the construction industry (it also provides materials for the manufacture of ceramics and glass etc.). Discoveries could still be made for much is still to be learned about the geology of the desert (Mabro, 1974: 40-1).

The oases could be extended by land reclamation projects and much attention has been given to the possibility of turning this land over to the cultivation of non-traditional crops (which would serve as animal feed) using the abundant sources of brackish water where sweet water is not available.

The desert offers the potential for the creation of new urban settlements which would leave the fertile areas for agricultural use and would help to reduce congestion in the major cities.

Some 'new' cities are already being built in the desert but the more general plan is that the existing cities (with the exception of the Delta centres) will expand towards the desert rather than along the Nile.

The desert also offers the possibility of developing alternative or additional energy sources to the hydropower of the Nile waters and to hydrocarbons. Nuclear power stations could be situated far from towns and cities, thereby minimising the opposition which has blocked the development of this energy source in the United States and most West European countries. The desert would also be an ideal location for the development of solar energy.

The desert is, lastly, an important tourist attraction and potentially important residential area as is shown by the rapid growth of such desert areas as Arizona, Nevada and New Mexico in the United States.

The above however are still only possibilities and it is difficult to know just how feasible they really are. In fact the economic benefits from the desert will remain limited for many years to come.

OBSTACLES TO DEVELOPMENT: THE DEMOGRAPHIC EVOLUTION OF EGYPT

Population Growth

If the Egyptian economy can count on all the aforementioned assets, why do so many observers have doubts about its future growth?

Political mistakes might cause delays or entail less than optimal results, but surely with so many positive features high growth and development cannot be far off.

Unfortunately the situation is not quite so simple as it seems, due mainly to the rapid population growth and its various consequences.

To explain the nature of the problem we will first of all consider the main demographic trends. It will be noted that the Egyptian population has grown rapidly over the years and that in fact growth rates have been accelerating. This fact has an important bearing on the performance of the economy and especially on the labour market. One of the most difficult questions facing Egyptian policymakers is whether the country can expect excesses or shortages of manpower in the long term. This point is of major importance for on it will depend decisions concerning the optimal capital intensity of new investments and which sectors of industry should be favoured.

We will also consider the pressure that these demographic trends are putting on the country's infrastructure. The rapid population growth has shown that the existing infrastructure is far less than adequate, and in fact enormous public expenditure programmes will be necessary to provide even a basic level of infrastructure for the year 2000.

Finally in this section we will see how the population increase has had a determining effect on the allocation of resources. It has tended to increase the amount going to consumption in both the public and private sectors and also the quotas going to investments in the construction industry and infrastructure. However, the quotas going to productive investments have fallen as a result, and in spite of what was said in the first chapter about the savings gap, massive investments will be necessary to exploit the country's many assets.

In fact there is a distinct possibility that Egypt will fall into a trap whereby the population will be such as to use up all available resources leaving no margin for productive investments or leaving such a small margin that per capita income would remain constant or even fall.

According to the most recent estimates, Egypt's population is growing at an annual rate of 2.7 per cent, that is at the rate of one million inhabitants every ten months. The fact that other Arab countries have even higher population growth rates (23), does not change the magnitude of the problems currently facing Egypt.

Better health facilities and improved hygiene have caused mortality rates to fall and although family planning information has been made available Egypt, unlike almost all other countries, has seen birth rates oscillate rather than fall.

The period before the 1970s saw a clear decline in birth rates and in fact during the period 1952-72 this decline was even more marked than that of mortality rates, falling from 45.2 per thousand to 34.4 per thousand. Thus in 1972 a population increase of two per cent was recorded - hardly cause for concern. However, birth rates have grown steadily since 1972 reaching 38.8 per thousand by 1978 (CAPMAS, 1981: 16). Falling mortality rates and rising birth rates can only lead to a rapidly growing population and by 1980 the birth rate had increased again to 42.4 per thousand (Saleh, 1982), the same as 1964.

The first results for 1981 seem to indicate a fall in the birth rates, however the exact magnitude of the fall is not yet known.

How then can this major turnabout from falling to rising birth rates be explained? There are three possible explanations, and each one projects a different scenario for the future.

The first is purely statistical, and underlines that the birth rate is a composite measure which reflects both fertility (that is the average number of children for each mother) and the age composition of the population. With a rapidly growing population it would be possible for birth rates to increase even if fertility remains constant, until the age structure of the population changed and reached a new dynamic equilibrium.

In Egypt however data on the level of fertility are only available through the censuses, the last of which was carried out in 1976, and no more recent figures are available. In any case it would remain to be explained why fertility rates were falling rapidly pre-1970, and then the pattern changed.

The second explanation concerns the end of the war with Israel. It is suggested that the end of hostilities in 1973 brought about greater optimism and hope for the future, which led to a baby boom similar to that experienced in the United States and Europe around 1950 (World Bank, 1978: II,7). If this explanation were correct we might have expected the phenomenon to deflate fairly quickly, however as the years have passed and the phenomenon has continued this explanation has lost credibility.

Recently, new explanations have been put forward. In particular it has been suggested that the rise in birth rates can be explained by the increasing value of child labour in the agricultural sector, in relation both to the introduction of increasingly labour intensive farming, and to the migration of male adults to other Arab States. A comparative analysis of data for several provinces proved the existence of a correlation between birth rate trends, child labour income, and the evolution of the crops farmed; however, there was little statistical support for a correlation between birth rates and adult migration (Saleh, 1982). This explanation, though, is no more conclusive than the others. If it were it could pose serious problems for the Egyptian economy, for it would suggest a perverse correlation between certain consequences of economic progress and the birth rate.

As we have seen, the dramatic change in birth trends cannot be easily explained. This must be recalled in discussing the different projections of the Egyptian population for the year 2000 (see Table 2.9) and the various consequences for economic development that these will entail. Estimates of Egypt's population for the year

Table 2.9: Population Projections 1980, 1990 and 2000

		Population ('000)			Annual growth rate (%)	
		1980	1990	2000	1980-1990	1990-2000
CAPMAS (1980)		42,289	54,290	68,018	2.53	2.28
UN (1979)	Low	41,870	51,777	61,943	2.15	1.81
	High	42,120	53,811	67,493	2.48	2.29
World Bank (1980)	Low	39,948	48,232	54,881	1.90	1.30
	High	39,948	50,667	63,342	2.41	2.26

Source: Hansen and Radwan, 1982: 51.

Table 2.10: Population Projections and Indirect Growth Rates to the Year 2000

Category	1975	1980	1985	1990	1995	2000
Total Population (thousands)	37,772	42,069	46,472	50,908	55,251	59,374
Aged 6-11	5,883	6,348	6,644	6,877	7,085	7,169
Aged 12-64	23,843	27,229	30,852	34,575	38,302	42,000
Aged 65 and over	1,282	1,516	1,793	2,123	2,512	2,981
Population growth rate (per cent)						
Aged 6-11	-	1.5	0.9	0.7	0.6	0.2
Aged 12-64	-	2.7	2.5	2.3	2.0	1.8
Aged 65 and over	-	3.4	3.4	3.4	3.4	3.4
Fertility rate		4.6	4.1	3.6	3.2	2.9
Net reproduction rate		1.7	1.6	1.4	1.3	1.2
Birth rate (per thousand)	-	34.2	31.4	28.7	26.0	23.3
Death rate (per thousand)	-	12.7	11.4	10.4	9.6	8.9
Natural rate increase (per thousand)	-	21.5	20.0	18.3	16.4	14.4

Source: World Bank.

2000 range from a minimum of 54 millions to a maximum of 68 millions. If we consider that current population growth rates are higher than any of those on which the estimates are based, including that of CAPMAS, there is reason to believe that the highest estimate will be the most realistic.

Another important point to note is that, over the next twenty years or so, not only will the total population change but so will its composition (see Table 2.10). Even though it is almost certainly off the mark, in that it underestimates the relative weight of the younger age group, the World Bank's projection clearly predicts that the total population increase will consist mainly of an increase of the population of working age (those in the 12-64 age bracket). On the one hand this underlines the problem that Egypt will face of creating jobs for the many who will enter the market each year. On the other hand it also foresees a positive situation whereby labour participation rates should increase and the average number of dependents per worker should fall, favouring an acceleration of accumulation. However, everything depends on the assumptions made about the fertility rate. If this does not fall as rapidly as the World Bank's projection suggests the 6-11 age group, which the World Bank study estimates will remain constant, will actually continue to grow rapidly (24). This would not only increase the average number of dependants per worker but would also increase the burden on the school system and on Egypt's infrastructure in general. Not only would possibility of accelerating private accumulation be negatively affected but the burden on public expenditure and public services would increase considerably.

In conclusion, Egypt's rapidly growing population may prevent the country from being able to exploit its numerous assets. If in fact the fertility rate is the determining factor of the rapid increase of the Egyptian population the relative weight of the very young (6-11 year olds) will continue to rise. This would seriously hinder economic development in the country. If on the other hand the cause of the recent population growth trend has been the particularly high number of potentially child-bearing women and/or other transitory phenomena such as the aforementioned baby boom, conditions relatively more favourable to economic development will be brought about.

Whatever its size and dimensions, the increase in the labour force and the need to provide employment to the new entrants will have far-reaching consequences for the future of the Egyptian economy. We will now consider this point in greater detail.

Employment and Labour Force Growth

We will first consider the employment problem for the period up to 1985 - for which the demographic trends are known - then we will turn our attention to the 1990s.

According to the 1980-84 development plan (Hansen and Radwan, 1982: 175-83), the labour force will register an annual increase of 450,000 new units over the five years. The plan further assumes that net migration will be roughly 170,000 per year. Therefore for unemployment figures to remain constant, 280,000 jobs will need to be created in the domestic economy each year. However, it is further assumed that each year 455,000 new jobs will be created and this would allow the unemployment level to fall by 170,000 per year, and therefore by 850,000 units over the five years. Since at the beginning of the period the official number of unemployed was 375,000 the plan implicitly foresees the 1985 situation as being one of acute labour shortages. This scenario is based on the assumption that productivity increases by a yearly average of 6.3 per cent, slightly below the record for 1975-80. The plan also assumes that public sector employment will record an annual increase of 175,000.

Bearing in mind these assumptions we may now consider the alternative employment scenarios proposed by the ILO (see Table 2.11). Assuming a 6.3 per cent increase in productivity (see top half of table) and constant government employment the employment level would remain constant. However if we assume the same productivity increase and an increase in public sector employment of 175,000 per year, but zero net emigration, then the unemployment level would fall slightly. As was seen in the last section, we believe that it is unrealistic to assume that a significant number of emigrants will return to Egypt, as is assumed in the other ILO scenarios. It is however more useful to assume that the public sector will shed some of its excess labour, as this is one option which is open to the government and could become relevant, especially if productivity increases turn out to be less than forecast. In fact if we assume (see lower half of table) a lower (and, in the opinion of Hansen and Radwan, more realistic) productivity increase the model forecasts that unemployment levels will fall dramatically, and that an acute shortage of labour will arise. In such a situation the public sector could easily free itself of much of its excess labour. Overall then these figures suggest that over the next few years the Egyptian labour market should be able to avoid running into intractable disequilibria. It should be added that the assumption concerning the creation of new jobs is based on an annual productivity growth in the industrial sector of around 10 per cent; which is the rate actually recorded in the past few years.

These conclusions however differ from those reached by a Boston University research team led by Gustav Papanek (1982: 43-9). Papanek believes that 'Egypt may well face a time bomb in the prospect of rapidly rising unemployment and underemployment'.

Papanek's quantitative estimates however do not differ much from those we have already considered (see Table 2.12). He claims that in 1985 the total number of new entrants to the labour market will be between 400 thousand and 465 thousand (he rightly considers the lower figure to be 'pessimistic' for it would imply greater hidden unemployment). His 'pessimistic' scenario also assumes a net return of migrants. As we have already argued this assumption seems to be inconsistent with the evidence. His 'intermediate' scenario assumes zero net emigration; it also assumes a considerable exodus from the agricultural sector, whereas both the five-year plan and the ILO study foresee a modest employment increase in this sector (+1 per cent). Papanek shares the widespread opinion that Egypt's agricultural sector has no future, and indeed sees an exodus from this sector as being desirable. We have

Table 2.11: Employment Alternatives Under the 1980-84 Plan (thousands)

Indicator	Plan	Plan, but constant government employment	Plan, but zero net emigration	Plan, but zero net emigration and constant government employment	Plan, but stock of emigrants and excess government employment reduced to half	Plan, but all emigrants return and all excess government employment removed	Plan, but all emigrants return
Labour productivity: + 6.3% annually							
Labour force	450	450	450	450	450	450	450
Net emigration	-170	-170	0	0	+100	+200	+200
Domestic labour supply	+280	+280	+450	+450	+550	+650	+650
Employment	-455	-280	-455	-280	-180	-80	-455
Unemployment	-175	0	-5	+170	+370	+570	+195
Rate of unemployment, 1984 a. (%)	-4.2	3.4	3.0	10.0	17.4	24.3	10.2
Labour productivity: + 2% annually							
Labour force	450	450	450	450	450	450	450
Net emigration	-170	-170	0	0	+100	+200	+200
Domestic labour supply	+280	+280	+450	+450	+550	+650	+650
Employment	-982	-807	-982	-807	-707	-607	-982
Unemployment	-702	-527	-532	-357	-157	+43	-332
Rate of unemployment, 1984 a. (%)	-27.1	-19.5	-18.4	-11.3	-3.1	4.5	-9.5

Note: a. We assume that the labour force in 1984 is 12,250,000 before emigration. Source: Estimates made by the mission.

Source: Hansen-Radwan, 1982: 182

already criticised this opinion; at any rate the data clearly show that emigration has caused labour shortages in the countryside; thus one may visualise decreasing employment in agriculture in connection with an assumption of continuing net emigration; but if net emigration becomes negative it is hard to see why employment in agriculture should fall. Papanek's assumptions for the 'intermediate' scenario thus seems to be rather incoherent. His 'optimistic' outlook on the other hand seems to be acceptable.

Papanek's goal is to estimate the number of jobs that will need to be created in the industrial sector, because his thesis is that industrialisation policies must be revised in favour of more labour intensive projects. His estimates of the number of jobs that will need to be created in industry vary from a maximum of 370,000 in the intermediate scenario to a minimum of 260,000 in the optimistic scenario. Both of these figures are considerably higher than the 75,000 new jobs per year up to 1985, estimated by the authors of the five-year plan and Hansen and Radwan. The difference between the estimates is entirely due to Papanek's residual method of calculating the demand for new entrants in the industrial sector. Not only does he see a bleak outlook for agriculture, but also for the building and construction industry, which he feels will create fewer jobs in the future because 'it (has) absorbed a fifth of the new labour force in 1979 but cannot continue to expand at this rate' (25). But why can it not? Shortage of skilled labour is often cited as the major obstacle to faster growth in construction.

Our purpose here is not so much to deepen the discussion from a normative point of view, but rather to note that the possible outlooks (even in the short term) for the Egyptian economy are many and varied. This is due to the fact that many of the variables move along a fast growth path, and even small changes in the assumptions build up to major differences in relatively short time horizons. Thus the model is highly sensitive to changes in the assumptions.

However, the high reactivity of the variables also implies that there will be many possibilities to correct worrying trends. This will lead to results which may

Table 2.12: Labour Force Estimates, 1979 and 1985 (orders of magnitude per year in '000)

	Total (1979)	Estimated Increased 1979	Projected Inter-mediate	Increase, Pessi-mistic	Mid-1980s Optimistic
1. Increase in labour force					
a. Males employed in Egypt	(8,930)	110	345	445	210
b. Females employed in Egypt (excluding agriculture)	(540)	40	70	40	90
c. Migrants (net)	(1,400)	145	0	-100	150
d. Unemployed	(460)	85	15	15	15
e. Total	11,330	380	430	400	465
2. Additional Employment required in Egypt (1a + 1b)		150	415	485	300
3. Source of additional employment in Egypt					
a. Agriculture	(4,000)	-80	-60	0	-80
b. Construction	(450)	79	35	25	60
c. Tourism	(70)	15	10	5	20
d. Government	(2,500)	90	0	50	0
e. Trade, service etc.	(1,000)	-20	60	55	40
	8,020	75	45	135	40
f. Required employment in manufacturing (and mining)	(1,555)	70	370	350	260
4. Investment required in manufacturing - per job (in thousands of Egyptian pounds)		(15.5)	(8)	(15.5)	(8)
Total (in millions of Egyptian Pounds)		(1,100)	(3,000)	(5,400)	(2,000)

Source: Papanek, 1982.

well be far from the optimum, still it is difficult to see Egypt in the mid-80s suffering from a substantial disequilibrium between supply and demand in the labour market.

To the contrary in fact it seems probable that the Egyptian economy will be able to absorb a fair share of the large pool of hidden unemployment, especially in the public sector.

Needless to say, the farther the time horizon the more difficult forecasting becomes. However, broadly speaking it is likely that the need to create new jobs will constitute a source of worry for the authorities for some time to come. Hansen and Radwan note: 'We already know that Egypt is bound to experience an acceleration in new entrants around the year 1990' due to the high birth rate in the 70s. However, exactly when these new entrants will enter the labour market will depend on many variables, such as the raising of the school leaving age. In 1981 a law was passed which raised the years of compulsory education by three, from six to nine years, and it is to be assumed that implementation of this law will gradually become more widespread.

In this context we might also consider the question of the size of Egypt's armed forces and the duration of the draft. Egypt's armed forces are currently made up of 452,000 men, 255,000 of whom are conscripts. Military service lasts three years, (IISS, 1982: 54). Any variation in the number of soldiers, in the duration of service and/or in the economic use made of the armed forces could have a significant effect on the equilibrium of the labour market.

In 1982 it was suggested that the armed forces (or rather a part of them) be employed as a peacetime army involved in civilian infrastructure projects. This new scheme which has since been put into practice allows the armed forces to bid for public contracts and compete with private firms. Income gained in this way is held by the military authorities and spent on improving and modernising military equipment and installations.

This has had the effect of achieving two objectives: on the one hand it reduces, ceteris paribus, the burden on the public budget of maintaining an efficient army, and on the other hand it occupies an army which has always had a major role to play in the country's affairs.

Although the peacetime army was not principally thought of as an instrument to intervene in the labour market it will certainly help to create new jobs. A recent World Bank study suggested that Egypt 'create a special service Corps. These Corps would accommodate both the graduates currently guaranteed public employment as well as unskilled labor...administrative responsibility might be shouldered by the Engineering Corps of the Armed Forces' (World Bank, 1982a: 18).

If the Egyptian economy were ever to suffer from an excess labour supply (a situation which could only come about in the long term) this kind of intervention into the labour market would be of great value, for there exist many potential large scale projects which could be carried out by this means, and successful completion of these projects would contribute significantly to the economic potential of the country.

Notwithstanding the rapid population growth there is no reason to fear that unemployment will rise to such levels as to threaten political stability or to force the authorities to increase welfare spending to the extent that investment would be crowded out. There does however exist the danger (taking a 'pessimistic' view of things) that the public sector will continue to be overstaffed and therefore relatively less able to promote economic development. Taking a more optimistic view however, there exists the possibility that hidden unemployment in the public sector will be reduced by employing fewer new people and making better use of those already employed. In conclusion, difficult though it may be, we feel that the interaction between the population growth and employment opportunities can be managed successfully by the political leaders.

The Pressure on Infrastructure

However, the effects of population growth on the labour force and on employment are only one side of the coin; a second and even more obvious consequence of the rapid population growth is the pressure it has put on the country's infrastructure. This pressure is ever present in daily life, affecting everything from telephones to urban transportation, from railways to the road network, from drainage to running water, and housing conditions first and foremost. The task of bringing existing facilities back to a minimum standard of efficiency and adding to them fast enough to keep pace with the rising population will be immense.

Housing is a particularly difficult problem in Egypt and the situation has been worsened by migration towards the main urban centres (Cairo and Alexandria). A rough but credible estimate put Cairo's population at around ten million at the end of 1982.

That housing is a major problem is shown by the fact that the number of those living in tents on rooftops (where a large variety of domestic animals are also often raised) or in the cemetery (the City of the Dead) was put at above one million (Fadil, 1981). A majority of families live in a single room.

In the past the government tried to alleviate the problem by creating large popular housing schemes in the existing cities, and more recently it has attempted to launch altogether new towns, independent from the already existing urban centres. The programme to reconstruct the Canal zone plays a central role in the government's policy, and it is hoped that it will become a third great urban centre alongside Cairo and Alexandria. It is by no means sure however that current initiatives will be sufficient to keep pace with the population growth.

A team of Egyptian and American consultants looked into the matter and their forecast for the future was somewhat pessimistic (Padco Inc. et al., 1982); they did however base their judgement on some rather pessimistic assumptions (26). The study criticised some of the government's policies as being far too costly and put forward what might be called a 'defensive strategy', designed to eliminate only the most obvious problems by the end of this century. It is argued that, in spite of everything, Cairo and Alexandria still offer the best existing urban infrastructure, and that to improve and add to existing centres costs less than starting from scratch. The new towns strategy is rated too costly. Rather, it is suggested that greater emphasis

Table 2.13: Urban Population Distribution

	Preferred Strategy 2000 Population (000's)	Annual Population Growth Rate (1985-2000)	Trend 2000 Population	Population Growth Rate (1985-2000)
Cairo Metropolitan Region	16,500	3.60	16,368	3.54
Alexandria Metropolitan Region	5,500	4.03	4,495	2.64
Canal	2,089	4.48	2,289	4.62
Delta	6,952	2.23	8,014	3.20
North Upper Egypt	1,811	2.53	1,830	2.60
South Upper Egypt	3,748	3.69	3,629	3.47
Remote Areas: Sinai, Red Sea Coast Western Desert, Northwest Coast	400	3.16	375	2.71
Total	37,000	3.37	37,000	3.37

Source: Padco Inc., 1982

Table 2.14: Investment Expenditure (by Zone of the Preferred Strategy for Urban Growth, 1986-2000

Zone	Total Cost (in millions of Egyptian pounds)	Share of Investment %
Cairo	23,370	53.0
Alexandria	8,243	18.7
Delta	3,703	8.4
North Upper Egypt	1,232	2.8
South Upper Egypt	3,254	7.4
Canal	3,704	8.4
Remote	588	1.3
Total	44,094	100

Source: Padco Inc., 1982.

should be put on the 'satellite towns' which surround the main centres, even though schemes presently under construction are faulted for adopting too high a standard (this thesis implies that in the year 2000 the average Egyptian should be offered an average of considerably less than two rooms per family). The study also argues against plans to develop the rural towns, as new housing would occupy and use up arable land. It does, however, mention three urban centres in northern Egypt which could easily be developed: Aswan, Qena and Assiut. These are the main elements of what is called the 'preferred strategy', the implications of which in terms of urban population distribution are illustrated in Tables 2.13 and 2.14.

Demographic Growth and Allocation of Resources

This discussion of the pressures on infrastructure brings us to a very important connection between demographic growth and the allocation of resources, and that is that although Egypt has great potential for economic development a large part of the population is still very poor and lives in miserable conditions. The higher the population growth, the larger is, ceteris paribus, the share of current income that must be allocated to investment in order to reach a given rate of growth in per capita income. The problem is whether or not it will be politically feasible to impose a heavy investment burden on an extremely poor population.

This is the problem of the savings gap, analysed in the first chapter of this book. But the political implications of the savings gap may not be fully understood if sufficient stress is not laid on the levels of poverty to be found in Egypt. We have already mentioned some of the conditions to be found in the cities: the situation in the countryside is summed up in Table 2.15, which measures poverty adopting the threshold method. The number of families and individuals receiving an income considered to be below the poverty line fell between the end of the 1950s and the mid-1960s. However, since then this number has risen dramatically. The fact that almost six million people (and this figure only considers the rural population) live below the poverty line, in a country with a

Table 2.15: An Estimate of the Rural Poor in Egypt, 1958/59, 1964/65, 1974/75 and 1977

Item	1958/59	1964/65	1974/75	1977
Household income corresponding to poverty line (Egyptian pounds)	93	125	270	327
Total population ('000)	25,832	30,139	36,417	
Rural population ('000)	15,968	17,754	20,830	
No. of rural families ('000)	3,224	3,345	4,166	
Rural families below poverty line				
Percentage	35.0	26.8	44.0	35.3
Number ('000)	1,161	903	1,833	
Rural population below poverty line				
Percentage	22.5	17.0	28.0	
Number ('000)	3,593	3,018	5,832	

Source: Hansen and Radwan, 1982: 99.

(1975) population of less than 37 millions, gives an idea of the problem.

And lastly it should be noted that rapid population growth influences not only the absolute amount but also the destination of investment expenditures.

It is not difficult to grasp how political pressure in favour of a rapid improvement in the standard of living, the huge demands for investment in infrastructure, public services and housing, and under some hypotheses also the need to offer public sector employment to specific categories of new entrants into the labour force, can combine to generate a situation in which there are no longer sufficient resources to invest in the productive sectors, and in particular in industry.

INDUSTRIAL GROWTH: PROSPECTS AND OBSTACLES

The Egyptian economy is thus on a razor edge. On the one hand it might enter the vicious circle characterised by high wages and growing investments and be in a position to exploit the country's great structural resources. On the other hand it might fall into a vicious circle characterised by a rapidly growing population, and become too involved with its immediate problems to be able to devote sufficient resources and political energies for ensuring its long term growth.

The final outcome will depend on many factors, but above all it will depend on the performance of the industrial sector. Industry alone can offer employment, is capable of rapid productivity increases, and can generate the export flows which in turn will attract foreign capital.

In the following pages we will discuss Egypt's industrial sector and industrialisation policies. Initially we will look back on Egypt's industrial growth over the past few decades, and discuss how industrialisation policies have changed. We will then attempt to explain the significance of Sadat's Open Door Economic Policy (ODEP). We further look at the role of the public sector and consider to what extent Egypt's public industries are efficient and competitive at the international level.

We will also examine the role played by private sector industries and note the importance of foreign investment. Finally we will briefly summarise the debate among academics on industrialisation policy options, in order to give the reader a feeling of potential future trends in Egyptian industrial growth.

Industrial Development in Egypt

Although industrialisation efforts had already begun in Egypt early in the 19th century, it is only since 1945 that production levels in industry have increased systematically, if with some fluctuations, and that the industrial sector has increased its share of GDP by a significant amount (see Table 2.16).

Since the Second World War there have been two major slowdowns, in 1964-8 and in 1971-3, and these were of major importance in determining Sadat's political and economic turnabout. In spite of the many hesitations and difficulties that limit the effectiveness of Egypt's current industrial policy, industrial growth has been quite satisfactory since the launching of the ODEP. In 1979 the value of industrial output (measured at 1975 prices) rose by more than 10 per cent, whilst the 1975-9 average was over 7 per cent (ESU, 1981). It is difficult to chart the current progress of Egypt's industrial sector because of lack of data, but recent trends may be seen in Table 2.17. The relative weight of basic consumption goods (foodstuffs, textiles) has fallen rapidly, whereas the importance of intermediate and semi-finished products has risen. Consumer durables and investment goods are also increasing in importance.

Industrialisation Policies

Attention is often drawn to the seemingly sudden changes made to Egypt's industrialisation policies and in particular to the changes in one direction under Nasser (emphasis on planning and public ownership) and in the opposite direction by Sadat's open door policy. However, there has been greater continuity in actual decision making than one is led to think by the rhetoric accompanying any policy shift.

Nasser's period was characterised by the great emphasis on industrialisation, and although during this period the public sector was in some cases enlarged at the expense of private ownership, through a series of nationalisations, the main focus of government action was the creation from scratch of a heavy industry sector, a feat that private industry had never dared and could not have managed. Today some of Nasser's great industrialisation projects, such as the Helwan steelworks, may appear inefficient, but it is to them that Egypt owes its position as the most industrially advanced country of the Arab world. In Egypt as in many other countries the private and public sectors are mutually dependent and the incessant political debate over which should be given priority, although often characterised by rigid ideological contraposition, in practice only marginally affects equilibria between the two.

But if Nasser's dirigisme endowed Egypt with the needed industrial base, it predictably soon led to inefficiency and bureaucratic paralysis. This policy put an ever increasing burden on the state's finances, leaving no other option but to squeeze income out of agriculture and neglect investment in infrastructure, and causing growing problems.

It is against this background that Sadat's ODEP must be understood. The open door policy certainly does not imply the liquidation of the public sector. Such a turn would in essence be unthinkable. The public sector is still quantitatively much more important than the private sector and this situation is unlikely to change (although some degree of statistical reclassification might generate the contrary impression (27)).

The main changes brought in by the open door policy were introduced with Law 43 of 1974 as modified by Law 32 of 1977. Law 43 was meant specifically to stimulate foreign investment, but thanks to the later modifications it became the general legal framework for encouragement of the private industrial sector as well as for the reform of public industry (28).

The law provides that all potential foreign investors must submit their plans for approval by the General Authority for Investments and Free Zones, which is apparently inclined to grant approval most liberally (29) and confer the various benefits and privileges on

Table 2.16: Contribution of Industry to GDP at Constant Prices (in millions of Egyptian Pounds)

Year	Industry in GDP	Index	Annual Rate of Increase %
	(at constant 1954 prices)		
1945	91	100.0	-
1946	92	101.1	1.1
1947	101	111.0	9.8
1948	113	124.2	11.9
1949	126	138.5	11.5
1950	133	146.1	5.6
1951	132	145.0	-0.8
1952	132	145.0	0
1953	134	147.2	1.5
1954	146	160.4	8.9
1952/3	140	100.0	-
1953/4	143	102.1	2.1
1954/5	152	108.6	6.3
1955/6	163	116.4	7.2
1956/7	174	124.3	6.7
1957/8	190	135.7	9.2
1958/9	202	144.3	6.3
1959/60	213	152.1	5.4
	(at constant 1959/60 factor costs)		
1959/60	256.3	100.0	-
1960/1	285.6	111.4	11.4
1961/2	309.9	120.9	8.5
1962/3	329.2	128.4	6.2
1963/4	369.6	144.2	12.3
1964/5	385.0	150.2	4.1
1965/6	394.3	153.8	2.4
1966/7	397.1	154.9	0.7
1967/8	378.4	147.6	-4.8
1968/9	415.6	162.1	9.8
1969/70	442.4	172.6	6.4
	(at constant 1969/70 factor costs)		
1969/70	542.0	100.0	-
1970/1	600.2	110.7	10.7
1971/2	615.9	113.6	2.6
1972	615.4	113.5	-
	(at constant 1972 factor costs)		
1972	589.3	100.0	-
1973	602.6	102.2	2.2
1974	638.3	108.3	5.9
1975	773.6	121.2	(11.9)

Source: World Bank 1978: III, 67.

Table 2.17: Composition of Gross Value-added by Categories of Industries, 1947, 1966/7, 1969/70, and 1975 (in Percentages)

Category	1947	1966/7	1969/70	1975
A (basic consumer goods)	79.8	55.0	51.6	49.7
B (intermediate industries)	19.7	38.2	40.6	40.6
C (consumer durables/equipment)	0.5	6.8	7.4	9.3

Source: World Bank, 1978: III, 71.

which more will be said shortly. Projects involving foreign equity capital (be it Arab or other) should generally be in the form of a joint venture, with an Egyptian partner, who can be either an individual or a firm (public or private). Law 32 has extended the provisions of Law 43 to cover all-Egyptian firms. Furthermore, independent of who is the main shareholder, a private/public joint venture is considered a private concern which may bid for benefits and privileges under Law 43. This has allowed public enterprises the opportunity to undertake new investment projects as joint ventures. Further, it is now possible for a public firm to incorporate an existing plant separately and then turn it into a joint venture in connection with its modernisation. In this way a process of progressive 'privatisation' of public enterprises is now possible (Hansen and Radwan, 1982: 217).

The projects approved under the conditions provided for by Law 43 need not undergo the many legal restrictions which are normally applied to private investments. This allows enterprises operating under Law 43 a high level of managerial independence in decision making. They can for instance hire labour without relying on the public employment agency, decide whether or not to distribute a share of profit to the workers, and allow (or deny) worker participation in the decision-making process. They also enjoy complete freedom as regards the composition of the board of directors, and are allowed to import and export without a licence.

Projects approved under Law 43 also benefit from substantial financial incentives. Profits are tax free for a period of five years, which may be extended in special cases.

Interest paid on loans contracted abroad is exempted from income tax and the same applies to distributed profits not in excess of 5 per cent, for an indefinite period. The General Authority also has the power to waive customs duties on certain imports such as machinery or construction materials.

The law includes provisions for the banking sector. Commercial banks can enter into joint ventures dealing in either national or foreign currency as long as the Egyptian partner has at least a 50 per cent share in the venture. Investment banks may also be organised as joint ventures; they are restricted to dealing in foreign currency, but are authorised to finance foreign trade as well as investments. Finally, branches of foreign banks are allowed to operate, on condition that they deal exclusively in foreign currency.

The law also provides for the setting up of free zones which enjoy all the usual privileges, and guarantees against both nationalisation and expropriation.

The Role of the Public Sector

The exact size of the public sector in Egypt is a point of some controversy. It is difficult to know what should be included as part of the public sector. It has been estimated by an Egyptian government source that the public sector generates 64 per cent of industrial production, of which 50 per cent is accounted for by public concerns under the control of the Ministry of Industry and 14 per cent is attributable to the public economic agencies (30). The remaining 36 per cent, generated in the private sector may be split between private firms under the control of the Ministry of Industry (21 per cent) and cooperatives and artisans (15 per cent). However, an American scholar (Jones, 1981: 14-III) estimated that the public sector generates 31.4 per cent of GDP (see Table 2.18). We cannot compare these two estimates as they deal with different aggregates, however Jones's estimate is lower than others with which it may be compared. Nonetheless even this estimate suggests that the public sector plays a more important role in the Egyptian economy than in other comparable LDCs.

The Egyptian public sector suffers the same problems as public sectors the world over. There is an excessive level of bureaucratic control and little space is left for decentralised initiative. Managers are badly paid and lack motivation, and are subjected to excessive political interference, particularly with respect to decisions on hiring and firing, and industrial relations have been made complex by legislation which strongly favours workers' rights. However in spite of all this the literature on the subject is unanimous in acknowledging that alongside the many problems there exist many well administered public enterprises and more are in a position to achieve considerable improvement.

Public enterprises are also frequently made to suffer artificially low sale prices imposed on them for political reasons, and this often makes even well run concerns run at a loss. The result of this is that supply often lags behind domestic demand as successful producers cannot accumulate funds to invest and increase capacity, and the gap must be filled by higher priced imports. In such cases the domestic product is often difficult to find on the shelves, but still the message of the market does not get through to the firm.

Many observers have commented on the level of efficiency to be found in the public sector. Amongst the most recent is the following:

> The available efficiency evaluations present a mixed picture. On the one hand there is evidence of competent top managers doing a highly creditable job given the constraints imposed by macroeconomic conditions, inherited technology and ministerial constraints on decision making. On the other hand, there is also considerable evidence of actions which could considerably improve efficiency and which are within the discretionary realm of managers, but have not been taken. (Jones, 1981: II 34-II, 35).

In other words the situation is by no means desperate, though it could be improved upon.

Hansen and Radwan (1981: 209) note that 'There is no reason why Egyptian public enterprises should not be able to compete with private domestic firms and foreign firms'. Table 2.19 shows the increases in output, employment and real fixed capital of public enterprises operating in four major industries over the period 1972-8. Also printed are estimates of the annual rate of increase in labour productivity and capital productivity (measured on output value at constant prices except in the case of spinning and weaving). Labour productivity increased in all four industries and capital productivity increased in all but the sugar industry.

Moreover, many other important industries in which

Table 2.18: An Estimate of Public and Private Value-added by Industry, 1977 (millions of Egyptian pounds)

	Public	Private	Total	Public Enterprise Share (%)
Agriculture	57.7	1,979.9	2,037.6	2.8
Petroleum	124.5	343.3	467.8	26.6
Manufacturing and other mining	774.1	345.5	1,119.6	69.1
Electricity	83.1	0.0	83.1	100.0
Construction	251.0	106.5	357.5	70.2
Transportation and comm.	200.0	121.6	321.6	62.2
Suez Canal	169.2	0.0	169.2	100.0
Trade and finance	581.9	606.3	1,188.2	49.0
Housing	12.0	231.5	243.5	4.9
Public utilities	23.1	0.0	23.1	100.0
Other services	1,067.5	321.2	1,388.7	3.2
Total: GDP at factor cost	3,344.1	4,055.8	7,399.9	31.4

Source: Jones, 1981.

Table 2.19: Output, Input Productivity in Major Industries of Public Enterprises, 1972-79 (percentages)

	Imdustry				
	Spinning and weaving	Chemical	Food		Metal manu-facturing
			Including sugar	Excluding sugar	
Increase 1972-78					
Output index	20.5	-	8.4	-	-
Output value at constant price	- [b]	75	10.7	111.5	77
Numbers employed	14.8	45.3	3.3	73.3	33.2
Capital stock, deflated value	16	49	20	17	67
Annual compound rate of increase [c]					
Labour productivity	0.8	3.2	1.2	12.7	5.9
Capital productivity	0.6	2.7	-1.3	10.4	1.2

- = zero value.

Notes: a. 1973-78, excluding aluminium which began producing during the period.

b. Negligible, but not included, due to obvious inconsistencies in estimate.

c. Measured on output value at constant prices except for spinning and weaving.

Source: Hansen and Radwan, 1982: 210.

the public sector plays a major role appear to be competitive at the international level.

Public sector efficiency has also been analysed with the use of more rigorous techniques, such as calculating the value added by public sector firms using international prices (Handoussa) (31) (see Table 2.20). The table shows two sets of figures for each company: the 'Domestic Resource Cost' (DRC) and the 'Effective Rate of Protection' (ERP). The DRC explains the relationship between the costs and benefits of an industrial activity with respect to the trade balance. The currency saved (in the case of import substitution in which domestic goods are substituted for imports) or earned (in the case in which goods are exported) constitutes the benefit, which is measured as the difference between the value of the output at international prices and the value of inputs purchased abroad. The value of domestic inputs (calculated at international prices) constitutes the cost. The DRC is defined as the ratio between costs (numerator) and benefits (denominator), and therefore the activity is socially advantageous whenever the DRC falls between 0 and 1 (32).

The ERP on the other hand is determined by the following equation:

$$ERP = \frac{\text{value added at domestic prices}}{\text{value added at international prices}} - 1$$

It follows then that an ERP value greater than zero or smaller than -1 means that the activity benefits from effective tariff protection, whereas on the other hand an ERP value between 0 and -1 means that the activity is penalised (33).

As may be seen from the figures, Handoussa's conclusion is that the Egyptian public sector benefits at the most from a modest level of protection, and in many cases the activities are actually discouraged. At the same time all the activities, with the exception of aluminium production, have a positive effect on the balance of trade.

Some important limitations of this methodology

Table 2.20: Handoussa's DRC & ERP Measures for Public Sector Companies

Sector: Company/product	ERP	DRC (Egyptian Pounds per dollar)
Food		
Food canning	0.3	0.54
Food canning (Edfina)	0.15	0.55
Biscuits (Biscomisr)	0.06	0.38
Vegetable oil (Alexandria Oil and Soap)	-0.92	0.07
Alexandria Confectionery	-0.20	0.42
Egyptian Starch and Glucose	-0.50	0.19
Food flavour	-0.58	0.28
Beverages		
Soft drinks (Sico)	-0.53	0.24
Tobacco		
Tobacco	-0.97	0.43
Spinning & Weaving		
Cotton spinning (Misr/Shebin El Kom)	0.92	0.70
Carpets (Arab Carpets)	0.14	0.56
Final wear		
Cotton knitwear (Cairo Clothing/Tricona)	0.01	0.70
Cotton underwear (Nasr Clothing/Kabo)	-0.04	0.44
Chemicals		
Nitrogen fertiliser (Kima)	-0.72	0.51
Nonmetalic products		
Cement enterprise no. 1	-0.79	0.44
2	-0.84	0.48
3	-0.72	0.42
4	-0.71	0.40
Basic metals		
Aluminium (National Metal Industries)	0.69	1.32

Source: Kheir El Din and Lucas, 1981.

should be noted at this point. The above calculations are based on production activities actually carried out at the time of the study: therefore no implications can be drawn for production activities which were not under way (and which might yield positive results). Furthermore, the level of efficiency in a given sector is judged on the basis of technology presently used in that sector, and the adoption of new technology could increase the level of efficiency. Therefore, it need not always be the case that no further investment should be made in a sector which currently registers a DRC reading greater than one or less than zero.

This is well illustrated by the case of the aluminium plant at Naga Hammadi. The production of aluminium needs large inputs of electric energy, and the plant in Egypt was built shortly after the completion of the Aswan Dam, when Egypt had an excess supply of electrical energy. Now the electricity is produced by oil-fired thermic plants and the international oil price has risen greatly over the years. The DRC calculation for the aluminium plant is based on an energy cost which is very much higher than that actually paid by the plant, and higher than that which could reasonably be foreseen when the plant was built. The high DRC therefore is not a symptom of public sector efficiency but rather the outcome of an investment decision which ex post appears to have been mistaken (34) because of the unpredictable increase in energy prices in the 1970s.

Proposals have long been under discussion to reform public sector legislation, increasing the discretional power of the managers, and shielding them from direct political interference. However, scholarly opinions have differed over this suggestion: some feel that giving a greater margin of discretional power managers in the pubic sector will not necessarily lead to better results unless the price system is reformed and appropriate procedures are adopted for the allocation of investment funds.

The existence of a lively debate on this point should not lead us to forget that in fact a reform is already under way thanks to Law 43 and subsequent modifications. In fact, the authorities themselves are currently urging public enterprises to give priority to investments which will modernise existing plants, and to revise new investment projects so that they may be organised as joint ventures. This means that the most efficient firms in the public sector (those with the most enterprising managers) will no longer come under the legal obligations imposed on public enterprises and will pass to the private sector. At the end of this process only desperately obsolete plants and firms with very poor management will remain in the public sector. If the former were closed down and new more enterprising managers were introduced into the latter, one can almost imagine a situation where all public enterprises would have evolved from operating companies into holdings controlling joint ventures that belong to the private sector. It is unlikely that this extreme situation will ever arise, however it does serve to illustrate the direction in which the system is moving.

The Private Sector and Foreign Investment

Far less is known about private industry in Egypt than about enterprises in the public sector, however recent research projects a very positive image: 'The private sector enters the Eighties with a great deal of momentum. Its share in production, although still modest, has been growing and its rising development share implies continuing output growth in the future' (Clark, 1981: 2).

The study is based on a series of 46 interviews with managers in the private sector. It was seen that one third of them were increasing production and sales at the rate of 20 per cent to 30 per cent per year and half of them at even higher rates. How competitive a firm is depends mainly on the quality of its product, and a 'significant' number of these firms were involved in exporting their products (35).

The most dynamic firms in the private sector are those which were affected by the provisions laid down in Law 43. Attempts were made to assess the effectiveness of this law very soon after it had been passed, and up till 1980 most opinions were negative: many projects had been approved but very few had been realised, and these were all to be found in banking and tourism. However as time goes by assessments appear to grow more favourable.

Thus, in his study Clark observes that Law 43 has allowed the rapid growth of a pipeline of projects which, though approved, are not yet at the production stage and notes that 'it is significant that the flow of projects from the pipeline to the productive stage has speeded up of late'.

He further holds that 'In view of the size of the present pipeline, and the recent trend in projects entering production, it seems evident that the value of Law 43 investment coming into production will continue to increase rapidly during the next few years.' (Clark, 1981: 7). Clark's analysis is based on the figures in Tables 2.21 and 2.22.

Table 2.23 shows that most of the capital invested in the wake of Law 43 up to December 1981 was in fact of Egyptian origin. Non-Arab investors contributed a total of 165 million Egyptian pounds.

It is interesting to note that Clark (1981: 9) has shown that Egyptian public enterprises are partners in roughly one fifth of the non-banking projects approved. This shows that Law 43, which it was originally hoped would stimulate foreign investment, has in fact had the dual effect of promoting private domestic investment and 'privatising' public enterprises. So far it has not really increased foreign investment.

The Debate on Industrialisation Policies

There is great controversy over which industrialisation policies should be followed in Egypt and it is important to understand just how varied the options are. It will be seen that dramatic changes are very unlikely.

There is almost unanimous agreement in the literature on the fact that Egypt will have to develop industrial exports and pass from a phase in which the emphasis was on import substitution to one in which the accent is on exports. (36).

However, in order to reach this objective various strategies have been suggested, with notable differences between them.

Many feel that the open door policy has had a negative effect on the economy and underline the fact that it has not succeeded in attracting the expected

Table 2.21: Proportions of Projects in Production, Under Execution, and Only Approved, as of 31 December 1978 and 31 December 1980 (Authorised Capital Plus Loans, and Per Cent of Sector Total) (in thousands of Egyptian pounds and percentages)

	31 Dec. 1978 Production	%	31 Dec. 1978 Execution	%	31 Dec. 1978 Only Approved	%	31 Dec. 1980 Production	%	31 Dec. 1980 Execution	%	31 Dec. 1980 Only Approved	%
Inland												
Tourism	83,768	15	327,313	57	159,201	28	78,939	10	447,231	58	244,809	32
Transport	7,665	13	26,582	44	26,189	43	71,016	82	597	1	14,705	17
Agriculture	36,731	15	165,026	66	49,462	20	134,617	39	78,118	23	132,949	38
Manufacturing	64,080	6	614,071	59	369,686	35	276,927	13	877,288	42	929,180	45
Housing	124,346	51	82,572	34	36,330	15	65,757	16	298,656	72	50,694	12
Services	12,747	5	86,241	35	148,351	60	71,382	16	124,010	27	260,202	57
Non-financial total	329,337	14	1,302,075	54	789,219	33	698,638	17	1,825,900	44	1,632,539	39
Banks	90,467	70	32,000	24	7,000	24	227,300	46	32,400	7	237,000	48
Investment companies	53,200	27	98,976	51	42,350	22	324,569	49	121,087	18	215,665	33
Petrol/mining	6,289	67	1,329	14	1,760	19	15,722	15	19,454	18	70,308	67
Inland total	479,293	17	1,434,380	52	840,329	31	1,266,229	23	1,998,841	37	2,155,512	40
Free Zones												
Agriculture	54	100	-	-	-	-	n.a.		n.a.		n.a.	
Manufacturing	27,687	8	34,334	10	272,592	81						
Storage	103,896	59	55,243	31	16,658	10						
Services	92,914	68	9,343	7	35,179	26						
Non-finalcial total	224,551	35	99,920	15	324,429	50						
Banks	6,250	100	-	-	-	-						
Petrol/mining	37,012	88	2,391	6	2,838	7						
Free zone total	267,813	38	101,311	15	327,267	47	350,615	26	751,559	55	268,352	20
Inland + Free Zones												
Non-financial total	553,338	18	1,401,294	46	1,113,899	36						
Grand total	747,106	22	1,535,691	45	1,167,596	34	1,616,844	24	2,750,400	40	2,423,864	36

Source: Clark, 1981.

Table 2.22: Manufacturing Projects (by Industry) In Production, Under Execution, and Only Approved, as of 31 December 1978 and 31 December 1980 (Authorised Capital Plus Loans, and Per Cent of Sector Total) (in thousands of Egyptian pounds and percentages)

	31 Dec. 1978						31 Dec. 1980					
	Production	%	Execution	%	Only Approved	%	Production	%	Execution	%	Only Approved	%
Inland												
Manufacturing	64,080	6	614,071	59	369,686	35	276,927	13	877,288	42	929,180	45
Textiles	6,091	2	284,983	97	4,023	1	22,614	7	292,614	85	30,953	9
Foods	5,451	8	25,639	38	36,181	54	63,731	23	70,114	25	141,547	51
Chemicals	26,519	24	49,957	44	35,961	32	76,942	28	122,551	45	72,342	27
Engineering	5,175	2	20,024	7	256,909	91	30,741	8	107,319	28	250,429	64
Building materials	754	0.3	199,838	90	21,147	10	35,072	5	249,789	36	409,939	59
Metals	19,137	53	15,672	43	1,399	4	33,805	72	11,822	25	1,285	3
Pharmaceuticals	240	1	5,779	35	10,712	64	4,521	14	6,534	20	21,495	66
Wood	713	4	12,179	75	3,354	21	9,501	35	16,545	61	1,290	5
Free Zones												
Manufacturing	27,687	8	34,334	10	272,592	81	n.a.		n.a.		n.a.	
Textiles	11,708	16	14,210	19	48,440	65						
Foods	5,953	49	78	1	6,093	50						
Chemicals	9,399	33	6,701	24	12,299	43						
Engineering	452	2	3,782	13	24,510	85						
Building materials	-	-	822	1	152,537	99						
Metals	175	1	3,141	10	26,720	89						
Pharmaceuticals	-	-	5,600	74	1,993	26						

Source: Clark, 1981.

Table 2.23 Per Cent Distribution of the Capital Assets of the Inland Projects That Started Production by Types of Activity and Nationality of Investors up to 31 Dec. 1981 (in thousands of Egyptian pounds)

	Total Capital		Nationality						
	Value	Per cent	Egyptian	Arab	European	American	Other countries	not specified	Per cent share in capital
1. Investment	337,869	100.0	64.5	27.0	3.1	.3	3.5	1.6	30.9
2. Banks	281,100	100.0	75.0	3.9	8.6	4.6	6.7	1.2	25.7
3. Tourism	54,482	100.0	62.2	20.8	13.6	.1	3.3	-	5.0
4. Housing	14,868	100.0	68.7	31.3	-	-	-	-	1.4
5. Transport and communications	32,594	100.0	53.2	18.0	18.1	-	10.7	-	3.0
6. Agriculture and animal husbandry	77,428	100.0	78.1	10.3	6.0	-	1.7	3.9	7.1
7. Contracts	42,806	100.0	66.4	10.5	18.6	.3	4.2	-	3.9
8. Technical consultancy	7,385	100.0	63.4	2.8	17.0	7.8	9.0	-	.7
9. Services	14,385	100.0	80.8	1.6	10.5	5.3	1.8	-	1.3
10. Spinning and weaving	28,357	100.0	53.6	25.0	3.6	13.3	1.9	2.6	2.6
11. Food	43,736	100.0	74.4	11.1	13.3	-	1.2	-	4.0
12. Chemical	56,383	100.0	65.2	22.9	5.5	6.2	.2	-	5.2
13. Wood	9,147	100.0	60.4	27.1	11.9	.6	-	-	.8
14. Engineering	20,339	100.0	50.2	19.6	30.0	.2	-	-	1.9
15. Construction and fireclay	22,759	100.0	63.3	30.5	6.2	-	-	-	2.1
16. Metal	27,240	100.0	49.0	38.4	9.9	.8	1.9	-	2.5
17. Pharmacological	3,443	100.0	2.1	-	4.9	93.0	-	-	.3
18. Mining	1,250	100.0	83.0	13.9	3.1	-	-	-	.1
19. Petroleum	14,334	100.0	14.6	-	85.4	-	-	-	1.3
20. Health and hospitals	2,494	100.0	88.8	11.2	-	-	-	-	.2
Total	1,092,399	100.0	66.7	17.0	8.9	2.4	3.8	1.2	100.0

Source: CAPMAS, 1982.

amount of foreign investment (37). They also stress that it risks subordinating national development to the logic of international capitalism and the interests of multinational corporations and that it stimulates non-productive and speculative investment. Others take the opposite view and suggest that Egypt should follow the example of certain countries in East and South-east Asia and base her development policies around private enterprises and export-led growth.

The latter suggestion, which is characteristic of Gustav Papanek's Boston University team (Papanek et al., 1982), merits further attention as it represents one of the extremes in the debate. It will be recalled that Papanek and his team base their analysis on the number of jobs that will need to be created by the industrial sector. They suggest that while the public sector has only a fair outlook, the private sector has an exciting growth potential. The Boston University team also attempted to estimate the comparative advantage for the main import substituting industries, such as steel and motor vehicles. The results of this study (which are somewhat less than convincing on a technical level) show that these industries have a negative comparative advantage. On the other hand the export potential of other industries is deemed very bright.

On the basis of the various contributions to the Boston University project Papanek (1982: 3) concludes that 'Egypt could take advantage of the vacuum created by higher wages in East Asia and Latin America and follow the pattern of rapid industrialisation, pioneered by Japan and followed by Korea, Taiwan, Brazil and others'. He suggests that this will be possible thanks tc the following positive factors:

(a) Labour costs are relatively low in Egypt: 'an industrial worker's hourly wage is equal roughly to a quarter of that in Hong Kong ... Productivity is generally low but in 1976 labour costs per unit of output in the textile industry were equal to half or less than half of those in Europe';
(b) there is a great potential supply of female labour;
(c) proximity to both Arab and European markets;
(d) foreign currency is available to purchase primary

materials and machinery;

(e) 'a labour force with more education and a longer industrial tradition than many low wage countries'.

Although Papanek's conclusions may be criticised in many ways (38), they are still interesting, both as regards his opinion on the potential of Egypt's industrial sector and as regards his proposals. In fact in most cases the policy options proposed by Papanek do not necessarily contradict possible alternative strategies; on the contrary, they complement them in that they are no different from the policies in support of employment and exports which are widely adopted by industrial countries. The one issue on which Papanek's approach flatly conflicts with most alternatives is exchange rate policy. He believes that Egypt's exchange rate is maintained at artificially high levels by factors which will soon cease to be important such as oil revenue and emigrants' remittances. Consequently, Egyptian industry is seen as suffering from the 'Dutch disease' (an overvalued currency). The decline in present sources of foreign currency should be anticipated by promoting industrial exports and adopting an aggressive exchange rate policy.

However, this approach would have considerable negative effects. Due to the rigidity of food imports, if the subsidy system were not modified a devaluation would not lead to an increase in the domestic prices of food imports, but rather to an increase in public expenditure; as was seen in Chapter 1, ceteris paribus, this would further reduce the resources available for public investments, and would increase inflationary pressures. The matter of subsidies has become a political problem: it is known that they are gradually being phased out, but the process needs to be slow, for any sudden cut could lead to public disorder and political tension; a falling exchange rate would only lengthen the time span needed to completely phase out the subsidies. This might not, in itself, be reason enough to resist devaluation while the balance of payments is running at a large deficit: but to devalue before such an action becomes absolutely necessary in order to increase the competitiveness of Egyptian industry seems less than wise. Further, judging from the data reported by the same team at Boston University, Egyptian industry is faced by a far greater number of export opportunities than it is currently able to exploit. Thus if oil revenues and emigrants' remittances were to continue to increase, even if at lower rates than in the past, the logic of an aggressive exchange rate policy would be doubtful. Under such conditions, forcing down the exchange rate implies a mercantilistic approach and would lead Egypt to increase its international reserves.

If on one hand Papanek is correct when he suggests that Egypt should avoid borrowing from the private international markets, it is difficult to understand why he believes that Egypt should follow such a policy as would discourage official concessional aid as well. In fact it is difficult to understand how a country which accumulates reserves could continue to bid for vast aid flows. In other words, an aggressive exchange rate policy would only make sense if currency inflows from other sources were in fact to decline, and industrial exports were to grow just enough to compensate for this fall. Unless this happens Egypt will have no great need to boost exports.

A further weakness in Papanek's analysis is that he ignores the regional dimension. Although he makes the point that proximity of the Arab markets is a positive factor for the development of Egyptian exports, he does not consider the fact that these markets require different products from those required in Europe and from those which pulled the export-led growth experienced by some countries in the Far East. In other words, should Egypt try to become a Hong Kong of the world economy or a Germany of the Arab world? If the latter is chosen, Egypt should continue to focus on basic and heavy industry. While this priority need not be indiscriminate (because some industries such as petrochemicals and steel are in the process of being developed in the other Arab countries), attention may be focussed on the manufacture of electrical machinery, transport vehicles and other machines, i.e. industries that Papanek and his team feel should be neglected.

A further approach which is often put forward in

the debate, leading to indications which differ from those of the Arab regional integration scenario, underlines the need to preserve national security. In brief, just as with agricultural production and food security, many feel that Egypt cannot run the risk of depending on imports for supplies of essential intermediate products, for reasons which are more political than economic in character. This approach suggests that more emphasis be put on 'balanced growth' and dependence on international trade be minimised.

In practical life it is unlikely that any of these approaches will be followed to the exclusion of the others. A return to protectionist policies, in order to follow an industrialisation strategy based on import substitution, has become impossible because of emigration and the importance of remittances. One can also rule out the possibility of Egypt adopting an aggressive exchange rate policy, while it is more likely that other measures will be taken to boost exports.

NOTES

1. For a categorisation of the rate of industrial development in the Arab countries which illustrates Egypt's pre-eminence see Muntasser (1982: 110-1). He notes that:

> Analytically, Arab states can be divided into three groups. First are those states that are still in their first development phase and engaged in primary production (agriculture and extracting industries). All oil-rich countries come into this category: Saudi Arabia, the Gulf States and Libya, in addition to other agricultural states such as Sudan, North and South Yemen, and Mauritania. Second are the states where industrialisation is of recent date and industries are at the early stages of import substitution. This group comprises the remaining Arab states, with the exception of Egypt. Two types of countries fall into this group: (i) countries which export oil but do not rely on it exclusively (namely Iraq and Algeria) and (ii) the Arab Mashriq states (Syria, Jordan, Lebanon)

and the remaining Maghreb countries (Tunisia and Morocco). The third category comprises only Egypt, whose industrialisation process, which started with import substitution, began at a much earlier period and has now come to an end.

2. In 1960 agriculture accounted for 30 per cent of GDP, more than 80 per cent of exports and employed 58 per cent of the workforce.

3. For example, Muntasser writes: 'As regards Egypt, its greatest source of development is the industrial sector because the agricultural sector has long since exhausted its capacity to expand and its annual growth rate does not exceed 1.1 per cent' (1982: 115). This may have been true for 1978-9 but was certainly not true for the five year period from 1975 to 1979.

4. S.E. Ibrahim notes that 'although the agricultural sector is still Egypt's major employer, the total area of arable land has increased by only 20 per cent over the last hundred years ... The population on the other hand has quadrupled ... This is another indication of overpopulation in Egypt.' (1982: 64-5).

5. The statistics on investment allocation show that a considerable emphasis was put on the agricultural sector for the whole period during which the Aswan Dam was being built, as the latter was considered as pertaining to the agricultural sector. However, after the completion of the Dam investment in the sector fell rapidly, and by the late 70s it had fallen to around 7 per cent of total fixed investments. This figure however reflects neither the current importance nor the potential of the agricultural sector.

6. Berseem (clover) is used for animal feeding, and its cultivation is one of the steps in Egyptian crop rotation. It is important in that it increases the fertility of the land, which is reduced by the cultivation of cotton. The increased cultivation of berseem reflects the growing importance of livestock farming in Egypt, which has been brought about by the increased consumption of meat (stimulated by subsidised prices) and by the fact that for the main part drawing power is still provided by draught animals rather than tractors in the Egyptian countryside. Cattle breeding

(unlike the breeding of white meat animals) is not rational in the Egyptian context and the role of the draught animals could easily be filled by machines. And finally, chemical fertilisers, rather than berseem, could be used to fertilise the land.

7. 'It was argued that ... a shift of cropping patterns from the more traditional field crops to horticulture will not only contribute to a closing of the food gap ... but it can also contribute foreign exchange earnings ... A mere 200,000 feddans devoted to horticulture could earn as much foreign exchange as six million feddans planted with field crops, a 30:1 ratio ... constraints were said to be mainly technical and political. Foreign demand is not a constraint.' (Glassburner and El Amir, 1981: 15).

Another study which suggests ways of absorbing manpower and increasing income in Egypt's agricultural sector concludes that Egypt should specialise in nine products: cotton, millet, rice, berseem, potatoes, onions, sesame, bananas and courgettes (Arman, 1982). These rather extreme conclusions are a result of the methodology used in the study (linear programming) but are none the less interesting as trend indicators.

8. To the information in Table 2.5 it should be added that whereas the area given over to the cultivation of rice or maize remained steady throughout the second half of the 70s, after a rapid increase in preceding years, the land given over to the cultivation of fruit was increased by 285,000 to 360,000 feddans and that given over to vegetables by 819,000 to 1,044,000 feddans between 1975 and 1980 (CAPMAS, 1981: 32-4).

9. There is no doubt that a problem of food security does in fact exist, and any discussion centres on how it should be defined. Given that Egypt is not self-sufficient as regards foodstuffs, the threat to security must be defined. Sarris (1981) for instance suggests that food security may be defined as a function of the variability of international prices, or finally as a function of the variability of world production and therefore of international supply in quantitative terms. He shows how the different definitions suggest different agricultural policies. A recent American mission reported

that 'The goal of food security embraces or, in our opinion, should embrace the concept of giving priority to producing those commodities for which Egypt holds a comparative advantage - with the goal of exporting at least sufficient agricultural commodities to offset the expense of commodities which must be imported' (Ministry of Agriculture, USAID, 1982: 83). This position may be criticised from the point of view of its economic rationality and many Egyptians might feel that it characterises the American desire to make Egypt dependent on America for its food needs. This would allow the USA to exercise its political will on the country.

10. Mabro (1974: 58-62) has described the evolution of the Egyptian agrarian system and its capitalistic nature prior to the agrarian reform. In fact the agrarian reform did not really diminish the importance of salaried work in the sector.

11. Papanek and Ibrahim (1982). The study shows that there exists an enormous potential supply of female labour and that female participation rates could easily be increased.

12. Ibrahim (1982: 11-12) examines the case of Abu Hamad:

> '...official driver for a UN agency's office in Riyadh ... an illiterate in his late 40's, a third generation sedentarised bedouin ... (He believed) in the value of education for his children but not for himself ... He pointed out that he had enquired about how much money each person in the UN mission was making and had learned, to his satisfaction, that the head of the mission with a Ph.D. and several years of experience was making less money than he was earning himself from various sources.

> 13. 'The composition of duty-free imports shows a bias towards consumer goods. Raw materials for artisans and textiles amount to less than 25 per cent and even if some electrical equipment (tools) means of transportation (trucks and tractors) and metal products may be capital goods, more than half of the duty-free imports are clearly consumer

goods.' (Hansen and Radwan, 1982: 240).

Is the glass half empty or half full? The same data could be seen as telling us that more than 30 per cent of all duty free imports are factors of production, a relatively high rate of savings on income. It is also interesting to note that more than 30 per cent of all duty free imports are accounted for by factors of production.

14. The question of whether the Egyptian economy is characterised by an excess labour supply has often been discussed in the literature, since W.A. Lewis numbered Egypt amongst his examples of economies with labour surpluses. Lewis's interpretation was shown to be wrong as early as the mid 60s with regard to the agricultural sector and the most recent studies suggest that the unemployment problem in Egypt is not so much due to an enormous supply of labour, as to a non-correspondence between supply and demand (Hansen and Radwan, 1982: 7).

15. The real wage index in the agricultural sector (1960 = 100) increased slightly up to 1974 (= 110) since when it has risen rapidly, registering 236 in 1979 and 208 in 1980 (Hansen and Radwan, 1982: 110).

16. Birks and Sinclair (1980), on the other hand, argue that the labour market is divided and fairly rigid. This is backed up by Ibrahim (1982). Sabagh's (1982: 71) argument however still seems the most convincing. After having examined various empirical results, he concludes that, 'An analysis of the available data for Egypt as a whole and for some communities, suggests that Birks and Sinclair underestimate the possible effects of emigration on geographic and social mobility within Egypt ... Egypt does not have a particularly rigid occupational structure.'

17. The annual flow of emigrant construction workers towards other Arab countries rose from 6,000 in 1968 (2 per cent of the labour force in the construction trade) to 32,000 in 1973 and 62-78,000 in 1978. It had been estimated that by 1976 60 per cent of the construction industry labour force had left Egypt. In spite of this enormous exodus the number of workers in the construction industry has risen, thanks to increased

recruitment (Hansen and Radwan, 1982: 89).

18. Vermeulen (1982: 3), for example, notes that 'Large annual increases in the number of temporary emigrants - in numbers totalling perhaps as much as 40-50 per cent of the net annual increases in the labour-force - have helped to limit the need for new jobs within Egypt', but he feels that the Egyptian authorities will not be able to count on this factor to the same extent in the future: 'Net emigration rates almost certainly must decline over time even in the absence of any abrupt reversals of demand for labour among the Arab Gulf nations. Even if the pool of Egyptians who have been abroad for an extended period of time increases, return migration will increasingly offset the ongoing flow of new emigrants.'

19. This hypothesis often seems more credible than it actually is. In any case it is interestng to note that the eventual consequences would be somewhat less than disastrous. The same study notes farther on, that if employment in the public administration increases at the rates foreseen by the plan, a mass return of emigrants would lead to an unemployment level of 12.3 per cent.

20. Sherbiny and Serageldin (1982: 255) argue that (Egyptian) emigration to Saudi Arabia will continue to increase from the 95,000 emigrants in 1975 to between 370,000 and 530,000 by 1985. They also feel that there is no doubt that Egypt can afford itself the luxury of having two million Egyptian workers abroad in 1985.

21. According to estimates published by the Petroleum Intelligence Weekly (PIW, 27/4/81: 2), the cost of transporting Arabian light crude oil direct to Rotterdam was $0.9 if the crude was taken on board at Yanbu (Red Sea) and transported via the Cape by supertanker, and $0.86 if it was transported via the Canal by an 150,000 ton tanker. It would be even more convenient for a larger tanker to unload part of its haul at the beginning of the Sumed, go through the Canal half laden and reload at the other end of the pipeline. This would be more convenient than the journey around the Cape even for crude taken on board at Ras Tanura (on the Gulf). The convenience of the passage through the Canal is even greater if the port of destination is on the Mediterranean (e.g. for oil going

to Sicily the journey via the Cape costs $0.9, whereas the journey through the Canal costs $0.49 if the oil is taken on board at Yanbu). If on the other hand the oil is headed for America the Cape route is still slightly more convenient.

22. In 1975 there were 21,568 hotel rooms in Egypt of which 2,599 were in public hotels and 18,089 were in private hotels. By 1980 the respective figures were 30,234, 27,546 and 2,785 (CAPMAS, 1981: 216). Since then these figures have increased: there are at least 3,000 more rooms in Cairo alone.

23. According to the World Development Report (World Bank, 1981) the average annual population growth rate in Egypt over the period 1970–9 was 2 per cent. This is below that of Tunisia (2.1 per cent, Morocco 2.9 per cent), Algeria (3.3 per cent, Saudi Arabia (4.5 per cent) and Kuwait (6 per cent). These rates were obviously affected by the migrant flows.

24. For instance, Arman (1982: 8) notes that by 1985 35.3 per cent of the total population will be under ten years old, and this figure will rise to 39.9 per cent by the year 2000.

25. However 1979 was a bad year for the building industry, which grew by 3.2 per cent as against a 1975–9 average of 9.4 per cent (see ESU, 1981: 10).

26. They hypothesise that the population in the year 2000 will be 67 millions, a figure which is higher than any of the projections we have looked at, the highest being that of CAPMAS (62 millions: see Table 2.9). They also assume that income will have an annual average growth rate of 7 per cent; this figure is lower than those registered in recent years.

27. However, since joint ventures between private and public sector firms are treated as private concerns, independently of who holds the controlling majority, it might seem from a statistical point of view that the private sector is growing at the expense of the public sector.

28. The discussion which follows on the provisions of Law 43 is based for the most part on: CAPMAS (1982: Chapter 1); Clark (1981: 4–12); Driskoll, Hayek and Zaki (1978: Chapter 1, and appendix, which includes the text of Law 43 of 1974 and of Law 32 of 1977).

29. In fact many critics feel that the General Authority is inclined to pass any plan. Fouad Ajami (an American scholar) has written a strong article criticising this practice (1982: 489).

30. The public sector economic agencies are the following: The Egyptian General Petroleum Company (EGPC); the Suez Canal Authority; the railways, electricity, telephones, public transport, water, radio and television, post and ports (see Ministry of Industry, 1981: 4).

31. A summary of Heba Handoussa's writings on this subject is found in Kheir El Din and Lucas (1981: 5-8).

32. For, if the equation takes on a value greater than 1, the cost in terms of domestic resources is greater than the benefit in currency, while if it is negative, this means that the denominator is negative and therefore the activity will lead to a straight loss of currency.

33. A positive reading simply means that the value added at domestic prices is greater than that at international prices and that the activity is not so competitive at the international level as is suggested by the domestic prices. An ERP value between 0 and -1 means that the value added at domestic prices is positive and the value added at international prices is negative.

34. Work is currently being carried out on the Naga Hammadi plant to increase its capacity from 50,000 to 100,000 tons per year. Many Arab countries are investing in aluminium and there are doubts as to whether it should become a priority sector for Egypt. (See Ghantus, 1982: 155-8).

35. 'Export activity was more widespread among the companies interviewed than we expected. Nearly a third of the companies were either exporting the bulk of their output or exporting a substantial fraction (like a third). About another quarter were either exporting small amounts of their output or had plans to export that had some concreteness. This left about half which were selling only domestically, and either not intending to export or expressing only vague interest in future exporting.

> The substantial exporters were most frequent in the textile sector but were also found in engineering and metal products, chemicals, and foods. Indeed one inference we draw from the interviews is that the principal factor determining whether a company is export oriented is often the enterprise of individual owners, rather than any more general sector circumstances.' (Clark, 1981: 30).

36. 'The export coefficient of its (Egypt's) industries should be raised. It must also emphasise, and gradually move into the export of manufactured goods' (Muntasser, 1982: 11). 'Discussing various methods of hedging against adverse foreign exchange developments, the mission found it imperative that industries be established and developed with a view to earning foreign exchange' (Hansen and Radwan, 1982: 11). Curiously enough these last two authors make two surprising statements in another part of their book: the first is that to finance investments in an exporting industry 'by foreign loans (at market prices) would make little sense; debt service would swallow a substantial part of the future exchange earnings'; the second is that 'there is the question of creating the necessary incentives for the new export industries to be set up. It is in the nature of the problem that these will not be created by private entrepreneurs unless special incentives are given. We are dealing with investments which are socially but not privately profitable.'

37. For example:

> 'It is therefore feared that the foreign investment law will function in such a way that it will be possible for foreign enterprise and the multinationals to infiltrate the Egyptian market, drain away the surplus, and establish and perpetuate a pattern of extroverted 'development' ... There has been a definite shift in Egypt's economic policy. Some writers refer to this as economic liberalisation; others call it a retreat from economic nationalism... The country seems to be heading now towards a free enterprise system, and the change does not simply represent a 'retreat' from economic nationalism, but rather a process of re-

absorption of the Egyptian economy into the world capitalist system.' (Khalek, 1982: 266, 278).

38. As should be clear from what has already been said, Papanek bases his arguments on overly pessimistic assumptions concerning future levels of emigration and agricultural potential. As a consequence he exaggerates the role to be played by the exporting industries both as regards their capacity to employ and as regards their effect on the balance of payments. Moreover, as everybody can see, his 'model countries' today find themselves in particularly vulnerable positions as a result of the difficulties faced by the industrialised countries, whereas the outlook for the Egyptian economy, which depends far less on the dynamism of the OECD markets, is brighter.

Chapter Three

EGYPT'S SOCIAL EQUILIBRIUM AND GLOBAL OUTLOOK

EGYPT IN THE EIGHTIES: A SOCIOLOGICAL PROFILE

Introduction

Egypt's contemporary social structure displays much of what is common in many Third World countries of similar size, for instance, Iran, Mexico, Nigeria, Indonesia. Standard features of such countries include overpopulation, rapid demographic growth, unchecked rural-urban migration, oversized urban centres, mounting demands on services, strained infrastructure, deficit in the balance of payments, foreign debts, inflationary pressures, maldistribution of wealth, and sociopolitical unrest, to name but the most important.

Important differences do exist, however, among these Third World countries. Some are quantitative differences in order of magnitude; others are qualitative specificities emanating from the particular historical path of evolution, and from regional and global factors impinging on each country.

Egypt's social structure is a function of three sets of dialectics: a) the interplay between forces of continuity and forces of change; b) the tension between the indigenous and the exogenous; and c) the conflict between the lower and the upper halves of society. The three sets of dialectics are themselves interconnected and overlapping. But much of what can be said about Egypt's social order is subsumable under one of these three categories.

More concretely, Egypt's social transformation was

set in motion with the anchoring of Napoleon's ships at Alexandria in 1798. That French expedition is considered by many historians as the symbolic beginning of the Arab launching into the 'Modern Age'. Two worlds, the Arab and the European, are thought to have dramatically 'rediscovered' each other, after several centuries of virtual isolation. The 'rediscovery' was, however, a mixed blessing for Egypt and the Arab World. The latter was weak, fragmented, mismanaged, politically authoritarian, and socially 'traditional'. Egypt's economy was characterised by subsistence agriculture and stagnation. Its population, education, class structure, and value system were locked within the bounds of traditional equilibria. The West, on the other hand, had made its big leaps forward: its scientific and cultural revolutions had already been accomplished; its industrial capitalism was being established and its political revolutions were already under way.

The French foray in Egypt, short and militarily unsuccessful, nevertheless set the stage for a long and agonising societal transformation. Since that foray and the subsequent Western penetration into Egypt and the Arab World, four big waves of social change have had a deep impact on the social structure. The colonial experience, modern science and technology, the national struggle for emancipation, and oil are the hallmarks of the four tidal waves and their chain reactions in the transformation of Egyptian society.

Every generation since the 1800s has experienced the collapse of one or more aspects of the pre-modern social order; and the gestation, difficult labour, and occasional Caesarian birth of a new one. There have been many false pregnancies and several miscarriages. But through it all, the old structures never completely disappeared; they lay there, albeit in crumpled or twisted form, and have continued to coexist with new or with caricatures of modern structures. The continuous interplay between these elements, the old and the new, has kept Egypt in a permanent state of 'transition' for the last two centuries. Every generation believed it was the bearer of the burdens of 'transition', and often felt trapped or victimised by it.

Egypt's social order in the 1980s is a product of

previous orders intersecting with regional and global events over the last three decades. The symbolic points of its emergence may date back to the 1952 Revolution. But it has undergone several turns and twists, important among which are the defeat in 1967, the death of Nasser and succession of Sadat in 1970, the Arab sense of 'triumph' in their fourth war with Israel in 1973, the subsequent oil-price revolution, and the departure of Sadat from the scene in 1981.

To gauge the march, dynamics, and consequences of the long transition which started in 1952 is an immense task. It goes beyond the limited purpose of this profile. But such broad parameters must be kept in mind as we address the specifics of Egypt's present social order. Even the latter must be narrowed down to concrete dimensions. We therefore confine ourselves here to Egypt's demographic and urban transformation, class structure, socioeconomic bottlenecks, and the resulting varieties of social unrest. Other domestic, regional, or global aspects will be touched on only in so far as it helps elucidate our treatment of the above aspects.

Demographic transformation

One of the striking effects of Western penetration into Egypt has been the undermining of the country's demographic equilibrium. For thousands of years Egypt's population had covered between 2 and 5 million. The lower and upper limits had been set by unchecked fertility and mortality - both high - cancelling each other out and maintaining a balance between biological reproduction and economic production. Contact with the West brought about a gradual borrowing of modern means of 'death-control', i.e., public health measures and medical technology. Such means were readily adopted by Egyptians to whom, as to other peoples around the world, life and longevity are universal values. Means of 'birth-control' were introduced much later, and were not as readily nor as widely adopted. This ushered in what is known among social scientists as the stage of 'demographic transition' - characterised by high birth rates, declining death rates, and rapid population growth.

Population growth In 1800 Egypt's population was estimated by scholars of Napoleon's expedition at about 3 million. Seventy years later, it had grown to about 5 million, (Ibrahim 1977: 304-6). The first general census in modern Egyptian history was conducted in 1897, and was repeated every ten years till 1947. Between 1947 and 1982 three other censuses were conducted (1960, 1966, and 1976). Basic demographic data from the early and recent censuses are presented in Table 3.1. The figures tell the dramatic story of Egypt's population growth, which has been uninterrupted and accelerating.

If we take French estimates in 1800 (of 3 million), it means that Egypt tripled its population in the course of one century - for by 1879 the figure was 9.8 million. The latter figure was nearly quadrupled again in the first decades of the 20th century. Taking the two centuries together, Egypt's population grew steadily from 3 to 40 million in 180 years, i.e. nearly 14-fold.

This steady growth resulted solely from natural increase, since immigration has been negligible. The death rate has sharply declined - from about 40 per thousand in 1900 to about 12 per thousand in 1975 (CAPMAS 1978). Birth rates, on the other hand, have either remained the same or declined only very slowly - e.g. 52 per thousand in 1900, 44 in 1950, 43 in 1960, 35 in 1970, and 38 in 1975 (CAPMAS 1978; Fargani 1981: 434). This is why the rate of annual net increase of population accelerated from 1.3 per cent in 1897 to 2.5 per cent in 1966.

The rapid demographic increase has had several repercussions. As Table 3.1 shows, overall density per square kilometre has increased concomitantly. Only 4 per cent of Egypt's total area is inhabited; the rest is inhospitable barren desert land. Thus the growing population has to be crowded into the Delta and the narrow green strip of the Nile Valley, which together measure no more than 40,000 square kilometres (out of a total of one million square kilometres). Density in this settled area has gone up from 24 to 735 persons per square kilometre in the last eight decades.

Rural-urban balance For thousands of years, agriculture has been the mainstay of Egyptian society. Despite the

Table 3.1: Basic Demographic Data, Egypt

Year	Size in millions	Growth per year in inter-census period %	Density per km2 of total area	Density per km2 of population area	Urban population as % of total	Rural population as % of total
1897	9.8	1.34	9.8	242	20.1	79.9
1927	14.2	1.28	14.2	273	26.1	73.9
1937	15.8	1.14	15.8	306	27.4	72.6
1947	18.9	1.78	18.9	365	33.0	67.0
1960	25.9	2.38	25.9	499	38.0	62.0
1966	30.1	2.54	30.1	578	40.5	59.5
1976	38.2	2.31	38.2	735	43.3	56.7

Sources: CAPMAS and Ministry of Planning.

limited cultivable area, the great river has given Egypt a rich base for its hydraulic civilisation. Until 1800, nearly 90 per cent of its population lived off the land in rural areas. So long as the ecological balance between population and agricultural land was maintained, Egyptians had no or little inclination for internal or external migration. But once the traditional demographic equilibrium was undermined, this proposition no longer held. The steady population growth meant, among other things, mounting pressure on agricultural land. At the same time, Islamic laws of inheritance produced further fragmentation of land ownership so that plots became smaller and smaller as time passed. A growing number of Egypt's peasants have become unable to support themselves from such small plots. Many more have become outright landless.

This phenomenon is not confined to Egypt. It is a classical situation in many Third World countries. One of its obvious results is the flight from rural to urban areas. As Table 3.1 shows, the distribution of the population between rural and urban areas has been shifting, with a noticeable decline in the relative weight of the rural population in Egypt. Until 1900 almost 80 per cent of all Egyptians lived in rural areas. By the 1970s the figure dropped to 57 per cent. The relative share of the population living in Egyptian cities grew correspondingly from 20 to over 43 per cent over the same period. It is estimated that by the mid-1980s urban areas will claim half of all Egypt's population.

It should be noted, however, that urban growth in Egypt is not only, or even mostly, a function of rural migration. The average rate of urban growth in the last fifty years has been about 4.5 per cent annually. Two thirds of it is due to natural urban increase and only one third (1.5 per cent) is the result of net rural-urban migration (Ibrahim 1975).

The urban scene in Egypt today is dominated by two oversized cities, Cairo and Alexandria. Cairo, the capital, grew from half a million in 1900 to about seven million in 1976. This represents a 1300 per cent increase in about 80 years. To put it differently, while Egypt's total population grew fourfold, that of Cairo grew 13-fold over the last eight decades. Alexandria's growth, while not as dramatic was also quite rapid: from 300,000 in 1900 to 2,300,000 in the late 1970s, which is nearly an eightfold increase. Greater Cairo's share of all of Egypt's urban population is at present about 40 per cent; that of Alexandria is about 14 per cent. Thus, the two cities together claim more than half of Egypt's urban population and about a quarter of the country's total population (Morkos 1980: 37-9).

Middle size cities (50,000 - 100,000) have grown at a much more modest rate in recent decades. Their share of total population increased from 4.5 to 5.6 per cent between 1960 and 1976. Small cities (20,000 - 50,000) recorded a negative relative growth. Their share of urban population declined from 5.2 to 3.6 per cent during the same period. Towns (of less than 20,000) also dropped in relative share, from 5.2 to 3.6 per cent between 1960 and 1976 (Morkos 1980: 53).

All in all, then, Egypt's urbanisation has been increasing at a faster rate than the overall population, which itself has been growing rapidly. The urban rate of growth has been about twice as high as that of the total population. About one third of urban growth has been contributed by rural-urban migration. Urban growth has not, however, been spread evenly among Egypt's cities. The largest cities have appropriated the lion's share of this migration. In recent decades Cairo and Alexandria have been getting net migrants not only from rural areas but also from small cities and towns. In brief, there has been a trend toward urban concentration.

For its current level of socioeconomic development, Egypt seems to be overurbanised. Many observers have noted that its urbanisation is out-distancing its economic development in general and its industrialisation in particular. (Ibrahim 1975a). Compared to Western societies which launched industrialisation in the 19th century, Egypt is said to have twice as many urban dwellers as these societies had during their economic take-off. Indeed, it is argued that at present Egypt's overurbanisation is one of the factors stunting its economic take-off, in that much of its scarce capital must be diverted away from industrial development in order to relieve the strains on overtaxed urban infrastructure.

It has also been noted that the influx of newcomers from rural to urban areas adds very little to the productive capacity of Egyptian cities. Most of these newcomers are what sociologists call 'non-select migrants,' i.e., migrants with little or no education, little or no savings, and little or no skills. Yet their physical presence in large cities taxes the already overloaded service structures (housing, education, transportation, utilities, etc.). Because their supply has exceeded demand, most of the rural newcomers have not readily been incorporated into the modern sectors of the economy - a fact that retards their adoption of the typically 'urban way of life'. And, because they have descended on the cities in large numbers, the newcomers tend to cluster in the same quarters inside or on the edges of such cities. Their proximity to one another tends to reinforce rather than diminish their 'rural way of life'. This has given rise to a phenomenon now dubbed as the 'ruralisation' of Egyptian cities. The areas in which new rural migrants and the old urban poor concentrate have rapidly turned into slums - physically, socially and psychologically.

The first generation of rural migrants are more likely to tolerate this slum condition, since it still represents a slight improvement over their destitute existence in the rural areas from which they escaped. But for their children, the second generation, it is a different story. With some education, with no strong memory of rural conditions, and with higher levels of expectations generated by the 'demonstration effect' emanating from the well-established urbanities, they do not tolerate slum conditions so readily. As a result, the youth of these slums have grown quite restless in recent years. Along with their counterparts from lower-middle class areas of large cities, they represent today the most 'inflammable material' on the Egyptian political landscape. The food riot of January 1977 was a preview of potential things to come. By official count (Al-Ahram, 19-21 January 1977), most of the violence and the human casualties were in Bab El Sharia, Boulaq, Shubra and Imbaba, all of which are overcrowded and among the poorest districts of Greater Cairo.

Manpower issues Egypt's growing population displays a feature common to many other Third World countries, i.e., predominance of young age groups. In the last three censuses in Egypt, the population younger than 15 years old ranged between 40 and 45 percent of the country's total. This fact has several repercussions. Such young age groups are generally consumers, not producers. They place added burdens on the national economy. Patterns of resource allocation and investments are conditioned by the pressures to provide funds for education, health, and welfare institutions for Egypt's youngsters. One indicator of this situation is the 'crude dependency ratio' (calculated as: Population between 15 and 65 / Population outside 15-65 range x 100) which stood at 53 per cent in 1976, compared to an average of 25 per cent in Western societies. This means that the average adult in Egypt must support more than twice the number of 'dependents' as his Western counterpart.

1. Economic participation. The crude dependency ratio, high as it is in Egypt today, still conceals an even greater strain on gainfully employed Egyptians. This is easily detected from refined figures of the economically active among the population. Between 1947 and 1976, the economically active grew by 5 million, at a rate slightly lower than that for the population at large, which grew from 6.5 to 11.5 million, giving Egypt an economic participation rate of 34.1 and 31.5 per cent, respectively. The comparable rate in a country such as Switzerland is 48 per cent (1970).

Egypt's low rate of economic participation is due not only to the preponderance of children in the population but also to other sociocultural factors, such as those which have limited women's entry into the labour force. The participation rate for women is quite low, 9.2 per cent in 1976, compared to 53 per cent for men. Even this figure was reached only between 1966 and 1976; prior to that, the female participation rate was around 5 per cent.

We have reason to believe that the rate of participation went up somewhat for both men and women in the late 1970s and early 1980s as a result of growing demand in oil-rich Arab countries. This point is discussed later.

2. Characteristics of Egypt's labour force. The main trend in Egypt's labour force is the declining share of agricultural employment. As the countryside has lost in relative terms to urban areas, the agricultural sector has been losing to both the industrial and the service sectors. For the first time in Egypt's recorded history, the share of manpower in agriculture dropped to less than half, from 58 to 44 per cent between 1947 and 1976. The 14 percentage points drop went to industrial manufacturing (4.4 percentage points), services (3.5 points), construction (3 points), and commerce (2.4 points). The rise in the share of manufacturing employment reached its height in the Nasser years (13.1 per cent), then declined slowly in the Sadat years (1970-1981).

Another trend in Egypt's labour force has been the steady rise in the skill level. Non-manual occupations, ranging from professionals to sales workers, increased their relative share from 12.4 per cent in 1947 to 20.8 in 1974. Non-farm manual occupations increased their share from 24.6 to 31.1 per cent during the same period. Manual farming occupations, on the other hand, dropped from 60.5 to 45.6 percent between 1947 and 1974.

3. Employment patterns. The most recent labour force sample survey was conducted in 1980. Table 3.2 shows that the size of Egypt's labour force was 10.3 million. More than half (5.5 million) were salaried and wage earners, and about 40 per cent were self-employed or family workers. Over half of the labour force was still in rural areas (5.5 million), and the share of females was still slightly below 9 per cent of the total.

About 64 per cent of the gainfully employed males in rural areas were self or family employed, compared to only 31 per cent in urban areas. This is not surprising, in view of the nature of the agricultural activities dominant in the Egyptian countryside. As economic activities in urban areas are more elaborate and complex, we find the overwhelming majority of the labour force working as salaried employees for the government, the public sector, or the formal private sector (69 per cent). This phenomenon is even more accentuated in the female labour force. About 92 per cent of the female

Table 3.2: Labour Force (12-64 years old) by Sex and Area, 1980 (in hundreds)

		Males			Females		
Category	Total	Rural	Urban	(%)	Rural	Urban	(%)
Employed	55,673	22,667	27,341	66	839	4,826	70
Self-employed	29,193	18,220	9,944	24	511	518	08
Family worker	13,137	11,019	1,872	04	178	58	01
Sub-total	98,003	51,906	39,157	94	1,528	5,402	79
Unemployed	5,359	1,378	2,327	06	287	1,363	21
Never worked	4,859	1,312	1,942	05	275	1,330	20
Previously worked	500	66	389	01	12	33	01

Source: CAPMAS.

labour force in urban areas are salaried, and only about 8 per cent are self-employed or working for family-owned enterprises. In rural areas, over half of the female labour force (55 per cent) are also salaried or wage earners, about one third of these teachers, doctors, and social workers in government institutions. The rest (two thirds) are farm labourers and domestic workers.

4. Unemployment. Table 3.2 shows that in 1980 Egypt had 5.2 per cent of its labour force overtly unemployed; most of these had never worked before and were seeking employment for the first time. The unemployment rate among females was nearly four times that for males. The unemployent rate among males in urban areas is more than twice the rate in rural areas (20.1 vs. 16 per cent). This greater concentration of the unemployed of both sexes in urban areas may be a function of under-reporting in rural areas. It may also be the case that hidden or seasonal unemployment is obscured in official figures. But there seems to have been a genuine development in the labour market of rural Egypt since the late 1970s: rising complaints of labour shortages in the countryside have been widely reported in the mass media. Such reports are substantiated by the rising wages of agricultural labour, estimated to have gone up from 1 Egyptian pound per day in the mid-1970s to 3 in the early 1980s.

The official unemployment figures do not take into account hidden unemployment in both rural and urban areas. There seems to be a consensus that the overall unemployment rate has in fact gone down because of rising demand for Egyptian labour in oil-rich Arab countries. The fact remains, however, that substantial underemployment or hidden unemployment exists in the Egyptian labour market. In the countryside, this takes the form of seasonal unemployment. Some economists estimate the annual number of full-time equivalent days of work in rural areas to be about 200. This means that as many as 150 days of unemployment per man are concealed in official statistics. In urban areas, the prime case is that of underemployment in government and public sector institutions. As a result of a policy adopted in Nasser's years (since the early 1960s), the

Egyptian government is committed to employing all secondary school and college graduates. The policy may have been justified at the time, for it was the state that played the leading role in expanding and operating the economy. But in the 1970s, when its role in managing the economy began to decline, the government none the less kept up this policy. In the mid-1970s the number of state employees was 3.2 million, compared to 350,000 in the early 1950s. (Mohieddin 1982). This represents a tenfold increase, when both the labour force and general population barely doubled during the same period. The state employs about 200,000 graduates per year. Most of them are piled up in state bureaucracies without much real work to do. At least one third of all state employees are thought to be redundant, i.e., if they were laid off, total output would not be adversely affected. (Ayubi 1981: 88-91).

External labour migration One of the most striking socioeconomic events of the last decade in Egypt is the large scale labour migration to neighbouring Arab countries. Though such migration has always existed, there has been a quantum jump in its scale since 1974.

1. Size and evaluation of labour migration. In 1973, the number of Egyptians working in the Arab countries was about 100,000 (Farrag 1976). By the mid-1970s, the number had jumped to 400,000 (Birks-Sinclair 1980: 134-5). About one third of this number were in Libya, another third in Saudi Arabia, and the rest in various Gulf states (Kuwait, Qatar, Arab Emirates). By the late 1970s and early 1980s, Iraq, Oman and Jordan were also competing for Egyptian labour. Two Egyptian social scientists estimate that Iraq alone has over one million labour migrants from Egypt (Saad Eddin and Abdel Fadil 1983). Other oil-rich countries seem to have stabilised their importation of Egyptian labour. In 1982, the total number of Egyptians working abroad was estimated at between 2 and 2.5 million. Jordan, which is not an oil-rich country, claims about 200,000 Egyptian workers, who are making up for its own shortages resulting from a similar external labour migration.

No one can ascertain the exact number of Egyptians working abroad, but if we took the 1976 census figure of an active labour force of 11.5 million, and allowed for an annual 2 per cent increase, then by 1980 the size of Eygpt's labour force would be about 12.5 million. Since the actual figure of the CAPMAS Labour Force Sample Survey for 1980 is 10.3 million (Table 3.2), then the difference of 2.2 million must be approximately the number of Egyptians working abroad. This means that in less than one decade Egypt's external labour migration has skyrocketed from 100,000 to 2,300,000, a 2100 per cent increase.

2. Causes of Egyptian labour migration. The phenomenal growth of this labour migration was no doubt triggered partly by an equally phenomenal increase in demand from the oil-rich Arab countries. But there were also important factors within Egypt itself which prompted this big jump in external migration. These factors are demographic, economic, and socio-political.

First, Egypt is the most populous Arab country and has, by Arab standards, the largest well-trained deployable labor force in the region.

Yet, Egypt's demographic structure made it possible, but not inevitable, to become a labour-exporting country. In order to understand Egyptian labour migration one must refer to a second set of factors, which are economic in nature. Egypt's economic expansion and industrialisation, in full swing from 1955 to 1965, came to a halt in the early 1960s. The major cause of this was the defeat in the third Arab-Israeli war of 1967. The ten years prior to this defeat witnessed not only economic expansion but also active socialist policies: central planning, creation of a large public sector, worker participation in management, land reform, and rent controls. The share of industry in Egypt's GNP was steadily rising, and the transformation of the country's labour force to modern sectors looked irreversible. With such socioeconomic factors at work massive labour transfers to other countries was unthinkable. At that time, permitting Egyptians to work abroad was motivated mainly by nationalist and political, not economic, considerations. Numerous restrictions were placed on Egypt's manpower lest some of it should migrate and adversely affect Egypt's own development. But with the economic stagnation of the late 1960s and the death of Nasser in 1970, Sadat rose to power with a gradual retreat from socialism. By 1974 the country was reoriented under a new set of policies, among them the Open Door Economic Policy. Formalised in Law 43 of 1974, Law 32 of 1977, and numerous other decrees, the Open Door Policy gave wide freedom of movement to both private capital and the labour force. Exporting Egyptian labour, and attracting investments from outside the country's borders, have become integral parts of the Open Door Policy, evolved to deal with Egypt's economic problems (Dessouki, 1982).

The demographic-economic interplay discussed above was acted upon by a regime that seemed committed to the interests of the upper-middle and upper classes. Its vision was to modernise Egypt on a Western model, and to reintegrate its economy into the world's capitalist economic order. This vision was aided by regional and international factors. New alliances with conservative oil-rich Arab countries, as well as with the US and the West, were forged by the Sadat regime in the mid-1970s.

At the individual level, substantial wage differentials between Egypt and the oil-rich Arab countries were strong inducements. No longer checked by official policies, but in fact reinforced by them, such inducements triggered the massive labour migration of the 1970s and early 1980s.

3. <u>Social consequences of Egyptian labour migration</u>. As in most large scale societal processes, the consequences of Egyptian labour migration are quite complex. The 'positive' and 'negative' are so entangled that it is hard to assess their relative weight or trade-offs for the society at large in both the short and long run.

For the individuals the consequences seem, on the surface at least, to be mostly positive. Most of these migrants do indeed solve their immediate financial problems, e.g., saving enough to be able to find housing, to get married, or to acquire some durable goods.

Among the societal consequences of Egyptian labour migration is the large amount of remittances. In a country with chronic shortage of capital and hard currency, these remittances have been more than welcome. Their volume steadily grew from $100 million in 1970 to $268 million in 1974, to over $2,000 million in 1980. This represents a 200-fold increase in one decade. The amount of remittances equals or exceeds the combined returns of Egypt's cotton exports, the Suez Canal revenues, tourism, and the value added from the Aswan High Dam (18). The Egyptian balance of payments, as a result, showed marked improvements by the end of the 1970s. The trade deficit, which was 1,785 million Egyptian pounds in 1978 decreased to 1,466 million in 1979, an improvement of about 35 per cent (19).

However, the initial euphoria over exporting labour and receiving its remittances has given way to a more sober assessment in the last three years. Economists have been noting sectoral labour shortages in Egypt, especially in the construction industry, the skilled manual occupations, and farm labour during cropping seasons. Such shortages have led not only to the hampering of Egypt's own development programs, but also to a sharp rise in the price of services. Also, there have been several multiplier effects of remittances: inflationary pressures, the spread of conspicuous consumption, and the downgrading of Egypt's labour force (20).

On the social level, several consequences have been noted. Most important among them is the fact that migration to an oil-rich country has become the fastest way to achieve upward social mobility. This, in turn, is having a silent but deep impact, changing Egypt's class structure in both rural and urban areas. Secondly, migration is expanding the frame of reference of many Egyptians, especially the peasants and lower class urbanites, and is unfreezing hitherto rigid customs, traditions, and values. Temporary migration has become part of a new 'Egyptian Dream' for many young people. On balance, however, it has led to instability in the domestic labour market and in many Egyptian families. As more and more married males temporarily migrate leaving their wives and children behind, there has been what may be called an 'increased feminization' of the Egyptian family. This means that women become the mainstays and decisionmakers of the family. A whole generation of children is growing up in one-parent families, with the other parent no more than a periodic visitor. The long range effects of this phenomenon have yet to be assessed. Finally, since many of the labour migrants are young and ambitious, migration provides an outlet for what might otherwise be expressed in political activism at home. Had these usually restless young people remained in large numbers in Egypt, in the absence of channels to absorb their energy, they would most likely have been a source of trouble for the regime (21). Recent events in Egypt show that the ones who do remain behind become easy prey for recruitment into radical militant movements, a point to be discussed later.

Stratification Structure

In the absence of consistent data on income and property distribution over the last 50 years, it is difficult to draw an accurate picture of the changing class structure. Likewise, with no structural data on intergenerational mobility, it is hazardous to generalise with any pretension of accuracy about the volume and direction of such mobility across stratification lines of income, occupation, education and power. What we can do, however, is make approximations based on broad parameters of social change with regard to class structure, and on inferences from global occupational and educational data with regard to social mobility.

We propose to begin with the socio-political-economic setting on the eve of the 1952 Revolution, and carry through to Nasser's and Sadat's regimes. Even though it is often said that social history contains no surprises, it would be helpful to outline the march and retreat of Egypt's social policies. Such policies have had a direct bearing on income distribution and shifting positions of various strata. In other words, policies are, in a sense, the parameters of Egypt's stratification and income distribution.

Underlying parameters The 1952 Revolution inherited a society whose socioeconomic transition from 'traditionalism' to 'modernism' had begun a century and a half earlier. That transition, however, had lingered and been frustrated by external and internal factors which resulted in an accumulation of problems and bottlenecks in all aspects of life.

Egypt's substructure was characterised by four principal modes of production: capitalist-agricultural, capitalist-industrial, traditional-urban informal sector, and traditional-agrarian sector. The size and rate of growth of the four modes was quite unequal, with the capitalist-agricultural dominating in the countryside and the capitalist-industrial dominating in urban areas. This domination was indicated not so much by the human base involved as by the relative share of each mode in Egypt's national wealth (measured by GNP or national income) and in the wielding of political power.

The integration of Egypt's economy into the international capitalist system, and the slow and imbalanced growth of resources and institutions throughout the century preceding the 1952 Revolution, resulted in the accumulation of socioeconomic problems. The failure of the political system to cope with, much less solve, these problems was a principal factor behind the 1952 coup d'état by the Free Officers.

The Revolution of 1952 was to confront many challenges: a land-scarce economy, a surplus population, a lopsided production structure, substantial unemployment, capital shortage, dependence on the outside world, maldistribution of wealth, a half-paralysed bureaucracy, the task of national liberation, and the Arab-Israeli conflict. Some of these problems had reached crisis proportions on the eve of July 1952, and others were to explode later, i.e. during the march of the Revolution in the 1960s.

It is beyond the scope of this book to deal with how the 1952 Revolution attempted, failed, or succeeded in meeting these many challenges. But the sum of actions, measures, and policies undertaken by the new regime resulted in changes in the class structure of Egypt. The intensity and implications of the changes have varied over the past quarter century. It is possible to identify distinct phases during the twenty-five year period. (Mohieddin and Ibrahim 1981).

1. The hesitation phase. Between 1952 and 1956, the new regime was busiest trying to consolidate its

power, establishing its legitimacy, and gain full political independence from the British. Socioeconomic policies remained, by and large, a continuation of the old regime. A major exception, however, was the issuance and implementation of the Land Reform in September 1952, limiting land ownership to 200 acres per family. Although its social objective could not be minimised, the Land Reform Law was, to a large extent, aimed at weakening the landed aristocracy of the previous regime. Also among its aims was the hope that part of the great agricultural wealth could be directed to industrialisation through capital investments. Otherwise, the policies of the new regime centered on improving the performance of the existing socioeconomic institutions of the country. Two organs were established to upgrade their performance: the Permanent Council for National Production (PCNP) and the Permanent Council for National Services (PCNS).

The changes in the class structure during this phase (1952-56) occurred primarily at the top and near the bottom. The ruling elite was completely changed, as new members of the middle class replaced the old elite of landed aristocracy and big capitalists (Dekmejian 1974: 167-224). The landed aristocracy, but not the big capitalists at this point, lost a substantial part of its economic power base. The beneficiaries of this loss were landless and small peasants near the bottom of Egypt's class structure, as well as the rich peasants, or what Binder calls 'the Second Stratum'. (Binder, 1978).

2. The economic consciousness phase. Between 1956 and 1960, the leaders of Egypt's revolution became aware of the need to escalate their attention toward Egypt's economic problems. This awareness reflected itself in the following measures:

a) the stipulation in the new constitution (1956) that Egypt's economy was to be managed according to a comprehensive national plan; a commission was established in 1957 to prepare the First Five-Year Plan (1960-1965);
b) Egyptianisation of most foreign interests in Egypt, including the Suez Canal Company, banks and insurance companies; a public corporation, the

Economic Organisation, was established as a holding company for these interests, and was given a mandate to expand its activities, alone or in partnership with the private sector; several new projects were undertaken by the Economic Organisation in the cement, fertiliser and textile industries;

c) the establishment of a new Ministry of Industry, in 1957, to undertake the planning and implementation of an industrial programme in the interim period 1957-60, and subsequently for the First Five-Year Plan. What was assigned to the new ministry was accomplished mostly with investments provided by the state, especially in the area of heavy industry. The rulers had hoped that the private sector would carry out its share in medium and light industries. Both public and private sectors were guided by a policy of import substitution;

d) the government issues in 1958 laws of urban housing rent control, reducing rents by 25 percent and fixing new rentals according to rules favoring tenants; and

e) the government initiated a policy of expansion of agricultural cooperatives and agricultural credit to cover the entire country.

The global impact of these measures in the second phase was the opening up of channels of social mobility. The Egyptianisation of foreign interests in 1956-7 led to the exodus of thousands of foreigners who used to own and manage these interests. Egyptian professionals, mostly college graduates, moved up to fill the vacuum. The moderate expansion of industrial activities created a greater demand for highly trained managers, engineers, skilled and semiskilled manpower. The latter either existed but was hitherto underutilised, or had to be drawn and trained from middle and lower class pools. The rent-control measures had their redistributive effects on both sides of the class divide. Urban landlords lost, and middle and lower class tenants gained, the equivalent of 25 per cent of the rentals in annual incomes. Thus in terms of mobility and sheer improvement in standards of income, the less well-to-do strata gained markedly during the second phase, especially in urban areas, as their counterparts had gained in rural areas in the first phase.

3. The socialist transformation phase. The period between 1960 and 1966 witnessed the height of revolutionary actions changing Egypt's socioeconomic structure. If Egypt ever witnessed an explicit class conflict in this century, it was during the third phase, 1960-5. And if Egypt ever experienced a fairly successful and sustained socioeconomic growth, it was also during this phase.

Among the far-reaching measures effected in this phase were the following:

a) implementation of the First Five-Year Plan for socioeconomic development, aiming at a 40 per cent increase in national income (7 per cent annual growth), a more equitable distribution of income, and the creation of one million more job opportunities;
b) the expansion and consolidation of the public sector to lead the country's economic activities;
c) the nationalisation of all big business in industry, banking, insurance, construction, import-export, and tourism; this brought over 80 per cent of non-agricultural activities under state control;
d) the promulgation of a second Land Reform Law limiting land ownership to 100 feddans per family;
e) the issuance of a second rent-control law in urban housing, reducing rentals by another 25 per cent;
f) the stipulation in the constitution allocating 50 per cent of the seats in all popular elective bodies to workers and peasants;
g) decree of a mandatory election of at least two workers in boards of directors of all companies, and the appropriation of 25 per cent of annual profits for workers and employees in these companies; and
h) the initiation of a new policy of employing all university graduates and trade school graduates in state or public sector jobs.

The sum of these measures and policies together are known among students of Egyptian society as the Socialist Laws. Regardless of their strictly economic merits, their implications for the shape of Egypt's stratification structure and social mobility were quite significant. They had marked redistributive effects in favour of the middle and lower strata. The vast expansion of the public sector, resulting from both nationalisation and the creation of new industries, substantially increased the demand for new talents and skills. The demand was met by a corresponding expansion in public education at all levels. The policy of employing all graduates meant the entry of several hundred thousands into white-collar and civil service jobs. The representation of peasants and workers on elective bodies increased the political power of these two groups as never before. Thus, in terms of income, occupation, education, and power, the third phase of socialist transformation resulted probably in the biggest change in Egypt's stratification system in this century.

4. The stagnation phase. Between 1965 and 1970, Egypt suffered serious military and political setbacks. The defeat in the 1967 Arab-Israeli war, the drain of the Yemeni war, the termination of American economic aid, among other factors, had profound effects and slowed down Egypt's socioeconomic march. The envisaged Second Five-Year Plan never took off, as an increasing percentage of the country's resources were earmarked for military expenditure. The loss of the Suez Canal revenues and the Sinai oil fields, the massive destruction of Suez Canal cities, and the mass displacement of nearly one million people added to the strain on Egypt's economy. As a result, investments in socioeconomic development declined sharply, and Egypt's rate of growth for the period was no more than one per cent annually. The public sector stood still during this phase; and under some internal pressures, the private sector was allowed a greater margin for movement.

The impact on the stratification system was simply the halting of further improvements in the living conditions of the lower classes and of all those employed by the state. Social mobility declined and became limited to government employment of graduates who were not drafted into the armed forces. The only other major channel for income mobility was through migration to the West or to the oil-rich Arab countries.

5. The socialist retreat phase: the open door economic policy. Between 1970 and 1974, four major events took place: Nasser's death, Sadat's ascendance to power, the October War of 1973, and the institution of the Open Door Economic Policy. The latter, though in the making since 1968, took on explicit official endorsement after 1973. It called for revitalisation of the private sector, opening the country's doors to the flow of foreign and Arab capital, the partial dismantling of the public sector, revoking certain aspects of the Land Reform Law (specifically, those regulating land tenure), and indirect measures of Egyptian currency devaluation.

The sum of these policies amounted to a reversal of Egypt's socialist transformation. This phase can be characterised as one of mixed economy, progressively tilting toward capitalist 'laissez-faire, laissez-passer'.

The impact on class structure is not very clear as yet. There are indications, however, that some elements of the pre-revolutionary upper and upper middle class are resurfacing. Upward social mobility is mainly accomplished through: a) private sector activities, and b) temporary migration to neighbouring oil-rich countries where higher incomes are earned. Strata with fixed incomes seem to have suffered most in this phase.

Against this background, the elaboration of income distribution and changing class structure in Egypt may be understood.

Income distribution The overall picture of income distribution is far from clear, due to data shortage. If we infer such distribution from the 'Sample Household Budget Survey', we have to start from 1958, the first year the survey was conducted. We also have to settle for something less than income data per se, since it only accounts for family expenditure, without taking into account savings and/or investments. As an approximation, however, the survey offers the best available time-series data in this regard.

Table 3.3 presents household expenditure data over three time points, 1958-9, 1964-5, and 1974-5, broken down by rural and urban areas. The expenditure categories are in current prices. The 1964-5 and 1974-5 figures have to be deflated by about 35 and 190 per cent, respectively.

We can evaluate income distribution in several ways. The simplest is the degree of deviation from the average. In 1958-9 the income per capita was about 40 Egyptian pounds. For a household of 6 persons, the national average income per household would be roughly 240 Egyptian pounds. In rural areas, 87.6 per cent of all families were in expenditure categories of less than 250 Egyptian pounds; the equivalent figure for urban areas was 62.2 per cent. Phrased differently, less than 13 per cent of the rural population, and about 38 per cent of the urban population, were in expenditure categories roughly equal to more than average income per capita for the year 1958-9.

In 1964-5, the national average income per capita was roughly 51 Egyptian pounds, or slightly over 300 Egyptian pounds per household (400 in current prices). In rural areas, 75.7 per cent of all families were below the national average, compared to 87.6 in 1958. There were about 12 percentage points of improvement during the six-year period separating the two surveys. In other words, nearly one quarter of the rural population was better off than the national average, compared to only 13 per cent six years earlier.

Among urban families, 56.4 per cent were below the national average in 1964-5, compared to 62.2 per cent six years earlier. About 44 per cent of the urban population was above the national average, i.e. an improvement of about 6 percentage points.

As is to be expected, the absolute proportion of urban families above the national income average was greater than that of rural families both in 1958-9 (39 per cent vs. 13 per cent and in 1964-5 (44 vs. 25 per cent). But the relative improvement between the two dates was greater for rural areas (12 vs. 6 percentage points).

In 1974, income per capita in Egypt was about 100 Egyptian pounds, in current prices. The average figure per family would be about 550 Egyptian pounds. More than 84 per cent of rural families and 63 per cent of urban families were below the national average. This represents a deterioration in the income distribution map from that of 1964-5. The countryside worsened by 9 per

Table 3.3: Distribution of Households by Expenditure Categories, 1958-75

Expenditure category (in Egyptian pounds)	1958-59		1964-65		1974-75	
	Rural	Urban	Rural	Urban	Rural	Urban
Less than 50	10.6	0.3	3.0	1.3	2.0	0.4
50 - 100	29.7	3.8	12.6	5.8	6.2	1.4
100 - 150	24.6	19.1	22.5	11.9	7.8	4.0
150 - 200	14.6	16.3	19.0	14.5	11.2	5.3
200 - 300	12.5	20.0	22.8	22.8	24.4	15.5
300 - 400	4.2	12.0	10.4	15.1	19.1	15.8
400 - 500	2.0	6.5	4.1	9.0	11.3	14.7
500 - 600	0.9	3.3	2.4	5.6	4.4	12.0
600 - 800	0.6	4.2	1.9	6.2	6.5	12.8
800 -1000	0.14	1.4	0.3	3.5	3.0	6.9
1000 -2000	0.16	1.9	0.4	2.8	2.4	9.8
Over 2000	0.00	0.0	0.3	1.5	0.5	1.6

Source: Computed from Sample Household Budget Survey, 1958-59, 1964-65, and 1974-75

Table 3.4: Percentage Distribution of Household Consumption Expenditure, 1958-59, 1964-65, 1974-75

Percentage of expenditure according to	1958/59		1964/65		1974/75	
	Rural[a]	Urban[b]	Rural[a]	Urban[b]	Rural[a]	Urban[b]
Lowest 20%	6.4	5.6	7.0	5.9	5.8	6.3
Second 20%	11.3	9.9	11.9	11.7	11.3	10.7
Third 20%	15.7	13.6	16.1	15.3	15.7	15.8
Fourth 20%	22.8	23.2	22.4	20.2	21.9	17.1
Top 20%	43.9	47.7	42.7	46.9	46.1	50.9
Top 10%	28.2	27.9	27.5	28.2	31.0	29.3

Sources: a. Radwan, 1977: 4.3, Table 4.4
b. Computed from Sample Household Budget Survey (Cairo: CAPMAS, for 1958-59, 1964-64, and 1974-75).

centage points, and urban families by 7 points. Those families above the national average have declined from 25 and 44 per cent to 16 and 37 per cent in rural and urban areas, respectively, during the ten-year period 1964-74. The situation in 1974 reverted back to what it was in 1958-9, i.e. to the pre-socialist transformation phase.

Relative shares of different strata Another way of examining income distribution in Egypt is to divide the population into five groups, each comprising 20 per cent of the total from lowest to highest. Again, using Household Budget Surveys, Table 3.4 gives data on the relative shares of total expenditure at the same three time-points, 1958, 1964, 1974, broken down into rural and urban areas. The share of the lowest 20 per cent in rural areas was 6.4 per cent of total expenditure in the countryside in 1958. It rose to 7 per cent in 1964-5, but declined to 5.8 per cent in 1974-5. By contrast, the share of the top 20 per cent declined from 43.9 in 1958 to 42.7 in 1964-5, but rose again, to over 46 per cent. Thus, while the lowest fifth of the population lost 1.2 per cent in its relative share between 1964-65 (the height of the socialist transformation) and 1974-5 (the phase of socialist retreat), the top fifth gained 2.2 per cent.

In 1958 the lowest strata, comprising 40 per cent of the total rural population, accounted for 17.7 per cent of total rural expenditure. Six years later the figure was 18.9 per cent, but by the end of the following ten years it dropped to 17.1 per cent. The bottom 40 per cent of the rural population, in other words, were worse off in 1974 than they were sixteen years earlier. At both points they were accounting for far less than the upper ten per cent in rural areas. In 1958 the latter accounted for 28 per cent of total expenditure, then enhanced its share to 31 per cent in 1974-5.

As a matter of fact, except for the top 20 per cent, all other strata seem to have suffered a decline in their relative shares of total rural expenditure between 1965 and 1975.

In urban areas, the same pattern holds. The

lowest fifth had a very slight gain from 5.6 to 6.3 per cent of total urban expenditure between 1958 and 1974, i.e. less than one per cent. By contrast, the top fifth raised its share by 4 per cent, by far the largest proportionate change between 1964 and 1974, i.e. during the phase of stagnation and socialist retreat.

The impact of the socialist transformation was not felt in urban areas until the mid-1960s. Although all lower strata benefitted somewhat, the lower middle class gained relatively more. The second and third fifths raised their combined share of total urban expenditure from 23.5 in 1958 to 27 per cent in 1964-5. This gain was at the expense of the two strata above, whose combined share dropped from 71 to 67 per cent between the same dates. While the upper 20 per cent of urban families more than recouped their losses by 1974-5, the fourth fifth continued to lose. Its share of total urban expenditure dropped to 17.3 per cent. This is by far the greatest loss that any of the five strata experienced at any time. Between 1958 and 1974, its share declined from 23.2 to 17.3 per cent, a net loss of nearly 6 percentage points. We suggest that the fourth fifth of urban families is comprised of top civil servants in the government. As any group on fixed incomes, they tended to suffer as a result of inflationary pressures in the late '60s and early '70s. Naturally, this would reduce their relative expenditures.

Poverty and income distribution. In a Third World country such as Egypt, income distribution does not acquire its full social meaning unless it is related to people's needs. The poor are often thought of as those who cannot satisfy their basic needs. But the question of what is 'basic' is quite relative. Nevertheless, it is possible to estimate the monetary value of the least costly diet that fulfills the minimum nutritional requirements as set by specialised international agencies such as the Food and Agriculture Organisation (FAO) and the World Health Organisation (WHO).

The Egyptian economist Samir Radwan calculated the cost of minimum diet, clothing, and housing for rural Egyptian families. (Radwan 1977: 40-6). He used this minimum as a benchmark to establish a 'poverty line' for the years 1958-9, 1964-5, and 1974-5. His attempt is quite ingenious; and we only regret that he did not do the same for urban households. To complement his work, we estimated that an urban household would require about 30 per cent more than a rural counterpart in order to meet typically urban needs, especially those of housing and transportation in the city.

Table 3.5 shows the two respective poverty lines for rural and urban areas in three successive periods. In 1958-9, 35 per cent of all rural families were below the poverty line. By that date, the first Land Reform Law had been implemented, and no doubt several hundred thousands (Ibrahim 1982a: 375-434) as land recipients and tenants had benefitted from it. Our estimation is that the percentage of poor families before the 1952 law was well over 40 per cent of all rural households. By 1964-5, the second Land Reform Law was in effect. Thanks to this and other policies (credits and cooperatives), there was a further reduction in the percentage of poor families to 27 per cent of the rural total. During the next ten years, however, economic stagnation and the socialist retreat affected the situation in the countryside. The percentage of households below the poverty line jumped to 44 per cent, 17 percentage points over the 1964-5 figure, and 9 points over the 1958-9 figure.

In urban areas, poverty was the lot of 30 per cent of all households in 1958-9. There was some improvement in 1964-5, as the figure dropped to 28 per cent. But, again, during the next two phases of stagnation and socialist retreat, urban poverty climbed to nearly 35 per cent of all households. Part of this rise must be due to the influx of some of the rural poor to urban centres.

Citing a joint Egyptian-American study, El-Gritly (1977), draws an even dimmer picture of income distribution in urban areas in 1976. Table 3.6 gives data which indicate that as many as 56 per cent of urban families fall below the 400 Egyptian pounds category of annual income. This means that about 50 per cent of all urban families are below or very near the poverty line.

It is quite obvious that income distribution in Egypt has become a function of: a) the overall economic

Table 3.5: Estimation of Rural and Urban Poverty in Egypt, 1958-75

Variable	Area	1958-59	1964-65	1974-75
Poverty line as measured in Egyptian Pounds	Rural	93.0	125.0	270.0
	Urban a	121.0	163.0	351.0
Percentage of families below poverty line	Rural	35.0	36.8	44.0
	Urban a	30.0	27.8	34.5

a. Our own computation on the basis of 30 per cent increase in minimum living expenditure in urban areas.

Source: Radwan, 1977: 42.

Table 3.6: Income Distribution Among Urban Families in Egypt, 1975

Income categories (Egyptian pounds)	Percentage
Less than 150	37.0
150 - 400	19.0
400 - 1000	20.0
1000 - 1600	14.0
Over 1600	10.0

Source: El-Gritly, 1977: 120.

growth, and b) state policies. Overall growth naturally increases average income per capita, and tends to have a trickling effect on the lower strata of the population. State policies accentuate or distort income distribution. The Land Reform Laws of 1952 and 1961 had marked redistributive effects in favour of the lower strata of Egypt's population up to 1965. The same is true for the urban population, which benefited directly or indirectly from both economic expansion and the Socialist Laws of 1961.

Those significant effects, however, were not substantial enough to become self-propelling toward further equalisation without steady growth or state intervention on behalf of the poor. When both factors ceased to operate between 1965 and 1970, there was a slight increase of inequality. The trend toward inequalisation picked up after 1970 when the state began to intervene on behalf of the well-to-do.

Other indicators of stratification. In a detailed study by this author (28), we established that educational and occupational stratification in Egypt has closely followed that of income. Manual occupations have subsided in favour of non-manual occupations (see Table 3.7). Farming activities have steadily declined in favour of non-farming activities. In other words, an increasing portion of the labour force has been moving up occupationally, with all the implications this entails in terms of income and prestige. This upward occupational mobility was, however, greatly affected by the prevailing socioeconomic policies in the various periods following the 1952 Revolution. Between 1952 and 1966 most of the upward movement was channeled into professional, managerial, and manufacturing occupations. Then there was a slowdown or complete halt of occupational mobility in the years following the 1967 War, up to the early 1970s. After 1973, upward occupational mobility accelerated again. But with a new socioeconomic orientation under President Sadat, most of the upward mobility was channeled into sales occupations. The latter include those commercial and finance occupations which seem to flourish under a free enterprise system.

With regard to education, the stratification has

Table 3.7: Distribution of Labour Force by Occupation, 1947-1974 (in thousands)

Occupation	1947		1960		1966		1971		1974	
	N	%	N	%	N	%	N	%	N	%
1. Professional and technical	189	2.7	285	3.7	400	4.8	462	5.5	522	5.7
2. Administrative and managerial	63	0.9	85	1.1	150	1.8	162	1.5	91	1.0
3. Clerical workers	140	2.0	285	3.7	458	5.5	429	5.1	507	5.5
4. Sales workers	476	6.8	626	8.1	525	6.3	480	6.9	769	8.4
Total non-manual	868	12.4	1,281	16.6	1,533	18.3	1,497	17.9	1,189	20.8
5. Craftsmen, production, processing* and operators	1,490	15.5	1,491	19.3	1,733	20.8	1,547	18.4	1,999	22.2
6. Service workers	630	9.0	688	8.9	701	8.4	765	8.3	826	9.1
Total non-farm manual	1,720	24.6	2,179	28.2	2,434	29.1	2,312	27.6	2,825	31.1
7. Farmers and related workers	4,232	60.5	4,103	53.1	4,198	50.4	4,337	51.6	4,126	45.6
Total manual (5, 6 and 7)	5,952	85.1	6,282	81.3	6,632	79.5	6,649	79.2	6,951	76.7
8. Not specified	175	2.5	170	2.2	200	2.4	227	2.7	235	2.5
Total	6,995	100.0	7,733	100.0	8,365	100.0	8,373	100.0	9,075	100.0

* Including transportation workers.

Sources: 1947, 1960, 1966 Population Censuses; CAPMAS, Labour Force Sample Surveys, 1971 and 1974, Cairo.

been steadily shifting upward. Tables 3.8 through 3.10 reflect the trends in absolute and relative terms. School enrolment alone rose from 2.2 million in 1952 to 6.8 million in 1977. For 1982 it is estimated at 8.5 million. This represents a fourfold increase in thirty years, compared to only a twofold increase in total population. Thus, while only one out of every ten Egyptians was in school in 1952, the proportion was one in five thirty years later. The growth has been most impressive in higher education. Between 1952 and 1977 there was a fivefold increase, from 79,000 to 454,000. This compares to a threefold increase in primary education, and a fourfold increase in preparatory and secondary education (see Table 3.8).

The sociopolitical significance of these figures explains much of the fermentation that Egypt witnessed in the late 1970s and early 1980s.

Class configurations: the case of Cairo. Fragmentary indications of the Egyptian class structure can be gleaned from the data on income, education, and occupation presented above. However, these fragments have not yet been pulled together systematically to obtain a cohesive picture of the situation in the country as a whole. Ibrahim (1982a: 424-7), conducted a small scale survey in 1979 to depict the stratification configuration of the city of Cairo. Although limited to Cairo, we suggest that the data capture most of the picture for the other major cities, i.e., urban Egypt. Below is a summary of the profile of six strata which were identified in the Egyptian capital.

1. The lowest stratum: the destitute. This category comprises mostly families whose annual income is less than 300 Egyptian pounds, who live in one room, own no durable goods or only a radio, and whose breadwinner is unskilled, a production or service worker. He is likely to be illiterate, born to an illiterate father who was equally poor, a worker or poor peasant. The urban poverty line in 1975 was 350 Egyptian pounds. Given an inflation rate of at least 10 per cent anhually in the following four years, the urban poverty line in 1979 would be well over 500 Egyptian pounds. This would suggest that these 11 per cent of Cairo's families are

Table 3.8: Distribution of Population (over 10 years old) by Educational Level, 1947 to 1976 (in thousands)

Educational Level	1947		1960		1966		1976	
	N	%	N	%	N	%	N	%
Illiterate*	10,900	78.0	12,726	70.5	13,770	65.3	15,611	56.5
Read and write	2,911	20.8	4,356	24.2	5,886	27.9	6,923	25.1
Intermediate certification	113	0.8	801	4.4	1,193	5.7	4,475	16.2
College or higher certificate	57	0.4	170	0.9	235	1.1	606	2.2
Total	13,972	100.0	18,053	100.0	21,084	100.0	27,615	100.0

* Including not classified.

Sources: Population Censuses, 1947, 1960, 1966, 1976, CAPMAS, Cairo

rockbottom poor. If not illiterates like their fathers and grandfathers, the children of these destitute families only read and write, with very few past primary school. All in all, this stratum epitomises the 'culture of poverty' in which low income is only one manifestation of several in a multitude of vicious circles gripping several successive generations.

2. The low stratum: the poor. This category comprises over 10 per cent of Cairo's families whose annual income is between 300 and 500 Egyptian pounds. The typical family lives in one or two rooms, with a breadwinner who is illiterate or barely literate, and who is a semiskilled worker, vendor, or in a clerical occupation. The breadwinner is generally born to an illiterate worker or a peasant, and has moved up slightly over his father. His children have gained more education and, if working, they are in skilled or clerical occupations, with very few going to college or joining professional or executive ranks. In sheer income alone, these families are immediately below the poverty line. But socially and culturally, they are not as caught up in its vicious circle. Many of them do not 'feel' poor.

3. The low-middle stratum: the border line. This category comprises nearly 27 per cent of Cairo's families. Their annual income is between 500 and 1000 Egyptian pounds per family. The typical family lives in two rooms and owns a few durable amenities such as a radio, gas stove, and a black and white television. The breadwinner is likely to be literate or have an intermediate education, and be a skilled worker or in clerical or sales occupations. In most cases, he is better off than his father educationally and occupationally. Nearly half of the heads of household are from rural backgrounds. Their children have attained as much or slightly more educationally. These families 'feel' middle class and try to lead a middle class lifestyle. Since their income is immediately above the poverty line, they are bound to feel hard-pressed.

4. The middle stratum: the upwardly mobile. This category comprises 36 per cent of Cairo's families. The typical family has an annual income of around 1000 Egyptian pounds, lives in three or four rooms, and has

more than half of the durable items. The heads of households in this stratum are likely to be young professionals, middle executives, or in senior clerical or sales positions. Most of them have had college education. More than half of them are newcomers to the middle class and have ascended to it from a lower stratum in which the father was a peasant, a worker, a clerk or salesman. Individuals in this stratum have experienced more upward mobility than any other group. Their children seem to have more opportunities than the strata below, but not more than their fathers had a generation ago.

5. The upper middle stratum: the secure. This group comprises 15 per cent of Cairo's families. The typical household has three to five rooms, almost all the durable items, and around 2000 to 3000 Egyptian pounds in annual income. The head of the family is likely to be college educated and an established professional or executive. Most individuals in this stratum are born to fathers who had at least intermediate education, and were themselves in one of the middle strata a generation ago. Their children are continuing on the upward track for the third generation, both educationally and occupationally.

6. The highest stratum: the rich. This is the smallest group, consisting of about one per cent of Cairo's families. The typical household comprises five rooms or more, enjoys all the urban amenities, possesses all the durable goods - private car, colour television, air conditioners, etc. The family income averages more than 5000 Egyptian pounds per annum. The typical head of household is a college educated, well established professional, senior executive, or a businessman. Almost all individuals in this stratum were born to college educated fathers and have college educated sons. In other words, this group seems to be locked in the highest stratum for the third generation in a row.

This six strata configuration is based on objective criteria of income, education, occupation, and lifestyle. The latter involved a complex scale with items on size and location of residence and possession of durable goods (e.g. cars, television, refrigerator, air conditioners, etc.). There may be degrees of arbitrariness in the indices or in the cutting points along the stratification continuum, but this is unavoidable in this sort of attempt. More important for our general purpose and for the analyses in the next section of this chapter is to keep an eye on strata 3 and 4 above. It is from amongst their ranks that most of Egypt's social activities and much of the political dynamism comes.

THE POLITICAL BACKGROUND

In the previous section we examined Egypt's social structure and noted the various problems which block the country's capacity and potential. These problems were at the root of the dramatic events which culminated in the assassination of Sadat. They are likely to persist throughout the process of economic and social development, and if adequate attention is not paid to them they could slow down or indeed halt the development process. In any case, in order to examine the social situation in Egypt we must consider the political background against which it is set. This section describes the political struggle currently going on in Egypt. Although the institutional transition from Sadat to Mubarak was carried off without major shocks to the system, this has not minimised the social problems and political constraints facing Egypt's ruling classes.

The Current Situation

Present-day politics in Egypt is better understood when approached in its historical context. We can distinguish between three main phases in the evolution of Egypt: the liberal constitutional phase 1923-52, the one party phase 1952-74 and the controlled or limited political pluralism phase 1975-82.

The first phase started with the legal independence of the country and ended with the army takeover of power. It was characterised by the existence of political parties and the free enterprise system. The insistence of the king to rule autocratically and unconstitutionally, the refusal of the British to evacuate their forces from

Egypt, and the failure of successive governments to meet the new social and economic demands resulting from urbanisation, education and the growth of a new middle class in the post second world war era, undermined the legitimacy of the system. Social and political tensions in the late 1940s led to great unrest and widespread political alienation and the need for reforms was advocated strongly by a growing number of intellectuals. In the first six months of 1952, Egypt had five different cabinets, one lasting only 18 hours. On July 23, the army moved and a new chapter of Egypt's political life was initiated.

The Nasserist phase was characterised by the absence of political competitiveness, the existence of a single political organisation (The Liberation Rally 1952-56, The National Union 1956-62, and the Arab Socialist Union 1963-76), controlled political participation, centralisation of power, supremacy of the executive over the legislature and suppression of political dissent. There was an obvious imbalance between politics and administration, and output institutions (bureaucracy, police and army) far outgrew input institutions (political parties and interest groups). The government penetrated almost all intermediary associations, bringing them under its legal and financial control. A crucial factor to the stability and survival of the regime was Nasser's charismatic appeal.

In the 1970s (see above), Sadat introduced a number of major changes into the body politic of Egypt: from national planning and socialism to more reliance on market forces and private enterprises, from one party system to controlled political pluralism, and from a pro-Soviet foreign policy orientation to an essentially pro-American one. There was also the change in political alliances at the regional level and then the break with Arab countries since 1979. At a symbolic level Sadat changed the name of the country (from the United Arab Republic to the Arab Republic of Egypt), its flag and its national anthem.

At the beginning of this new phase which sees the country in the hands of a new President, Hosni Mubarak, whose social and political ideas remain somewhat of a 'black box', we must review the political movements currently active within Egypt and the objectives that they have set themselves. In order to do so, we will first of all examine the figure and the role of President, then we will consider the nature of the ruling class, and finally we will consider the political dynamism injected into Egypt by the opposition parties and the Islamic groups. Particular attention will be paid to this last point and to the significance of the Islamic opposition in relation to the social evolution that was discussed in the last section.

Searching for New Legitimacy: the Establishment of a New Personality Cult

The president as a 'person' and the 'presidency' as an 'institution' lie at the heart of Egypt's political system. The president is nominated by the Parliament and voted upon, uncontested, by the people in a referendum. He is elected for a six year period which is renewable. Generally, the president has always enjoyed sweeping powers and his activities have overshadowed all other organs of the state.

Notwithstanding the many differences in economic and social policies between Nasser and Sadat, Egypt's political system has displayed a noticeable element of continuity, that is, the obvious lack of political institutionalisation. Despite an extensive, rather cumbersome bureaucracy (or perhaps because of it), Nasser always had the final say in vital decision making. His power, beyond those things no politician can afford to do if he desires to stay in power, was tremendous. It is true that Nasser had much more of a free rein in deciding international policy issues than he did in domestic ones where he faced a number of strong political counterforces. For example, he was always cognizant of the power of the military and made special efforts to win them over to his side. Yet the fact remains that he had power above and beyond that of an ordinary president - he was virtually the heart of the government. The same was true of Sadat, whose power was just as extensive. Sadat, like Nasser before him, completely decided the course the government was to take.

As Egypt's vice-president in 1970, Sadat was in

line to succeed president Nasser if anything was to happen to him. With Nasser's death in September, Sadat assumed the presidency in a smooth legal transfer of power as provided by the 1964 constitution. Sadat's new position, however, was due to the grace of God and Nasser, and did not reflect his public standing in the country. His legitimacy was derived from his role in the Free Officers' movement and from his long association with Nasser. Between October 1970 and May 1971, Sadat was no more than a figurehead while real power rested with a number of Nasser's associates, headed by vice-president Ali Sabri, who clearly expected Sadat to do what they told him (Sheehan, 1971:6).

The power struggle of May 1971 represented a major change in Egypt's political evolution. By purging his opponents, Sadat completed the consolidation of his power and became the master of his own house. In the behaviour of his opponents, he perceived an attempt to restrict his right to make presidential decisions. In defeating them, he defeated also an alternative conception of a political system in which the president would be accountable to a larger group (Hinnebusch, 1981: 444). Sadat legitimised his move in the name of democracy which he summarised in three principles: rule of law, government by institutions and political freedoms.

The May events triggered the move towards increased liberalisation, as manifested in the gradual lifting of restraints on the freedom of expression, tolerance of dissent and ending of arbitrary arrests. Together with the move towards democratisation came a process of dismantling many of Nasser's policies, a trend that paved the way for a total de-nasserisation process by the mid-1970s. Sadat frequently contrasted his policies and regime implicitly and explicitly with that of his predecessor. He sought to exploit such a trend so as to consolidate and emphasise his regime's legitimacy, explaining to the Egyptian layman how he (Sadat) was attempting to redeem the country from the evils of the past regime. Real changes, however, were not initiated until after the October war of 1973 which consolidated Sadat's legitimacy and enabled him to break explicitly with Nasser.

The years following the October war saw extensive

changes amounting to a total redirection of the course of the 1952 revolution. Legitimacy for the regime has been sought through new pronouncements and policies such as Egyptian nationalism, democracy, ODEP, the 1973 war and later peace. The motto 'Egypt first' was upheld to replace the vigorous pan-Arab ideology. A relaxation of both the state controls on the economy and the austerity programme launched by Nasser was also promoted by Sadat whose dramatic 'opening' of the Egyptian economy was introduced to attract foreign capital and technology to rejuvenate Egypt's economy. This relaxation of controls appealed to many in the middle and upper middle classes who found in it new opportunities for quick and easy enrichment (Dessouki, 1982a: 75-83).

By 1976, Sadat had already set the guidelines for the introduction of controlled multipartyism. In 1974 he initiated a national debate to discuss the role and the future of the Arab Socialist Union, in 1975 the Arab Socialist Union national congress resolved to establish manabir (political groupings) within it, and in 1976 a committee to discuss the future of political life in Egypt recommended the establishment of three manabir to represent right, centre and left. This measure of democratisation was coupled with widening of the spectrum of permissible opinion in the press, as well as the revitalisation of the national assembly to enjoy a greater latitude in criticising government policies and functionaries. A greater degree of autonomy was also given to the press where direct censorship was abolished and editors were made responsible for what was published. President Sadat's cautious liberalisation of organised political participation as well as his reinforcement of the roles of both the press and the assembly were measures taken to enhance the structural legitimacy of the regime.

In November 1977 Sadat created a new powerful source of legitimacy for his rule: this came about with the launching of his peace initiative and his visit to Jerusalem. Popular support for the move towards peace was demonstrated by the massive crowds that gathered to welcome Sadat on his return. For a while, Sadat had become the hero of war and peace; the very favourable international reactions to his initiative made the Egyptian layman even more proud of him.

In addition to his moves in the domestic and international spheres, Sadat sought to project a favourable public image. Unlike Nasser, he did not base his leadership on personal charisma, but rather on the traditional authority of a family head: in his public appearances, Sadat posed as a benevolent patriarch, stressing his deep commitment to the welfare of his people and expecting in return respect and obedience. He consistently addressed delegates of the People's Assembly, high ranking officials and commanders of the armed forces as 'my sons', commending and reprimanding them in a paternal fashion. Newspapers addressed him as 'the head of an Egyptian family' which looks up to him in reverence and loyalty.

Sadat also emphasised his village origins declaring great attachment to his village background, its values, norms and moral modes. Al Ahram (17 October 1970) once described his humble house in his home village of Mit Abul Kom projecting the image of a man of the people, a simple Egyptian from a peasant background.

Islam, the religion of the majority, was also employed by Sadat to promote a favourable public image. In his autobiography, he described his relationship with God as one of close friendship and deep attachment. The mass media called him 'the believing president'. In addition, Sadat sought to advocate the revival of orthodox piety and to encourage religious institutions while constantly securing the allegiance of the Azhar sheikhs.

The New Political Elite

The main feature of Egypt's ruling elite is its fragmentation; it does not constitute a cohesive group ideologically or organisationally. It is difficult to underline what really, other than sharing prominent offices, holds them together. Intra-elite cleavages and conflicts over policies persist throughout. Having no power base, members of the elite derive support from the president and remain in their positions at his pleasure. Finally, there exist no systematic channels for elite recruitment. It seems that a primary consideration is personal connections and not organisational loyalties (Springborg,

1979; Akhari, 1982).

Analysis of the ministerial elite under Sadat shows that the military remained the most crucial force in Egypt's political life. Sadat, however, successfully managed to confine them to a professional role. The universities constituted the second major source of recruitment of the elite. Egypt's top economic managers tended to be coopted from the universities. The number of Ph.D.'s who served as ministers were 52 (33 per cent). Bureaucracy is a third important route for the elite.

If we go by profession, engineers represented 20.5 per cent of all ministers as compared to 14.5 per cent under Nasser. Lawyers decreased from 15 per cent under Nasser to 7 per cent under Sadat. New channels which narrowed in the 1950s and 1960s flourished again: those of private business and professionals. In the late 1970s about 25 per cent of the new ministers reached office via this route: primary examples include Fikry Makram Obeid and Mansour Hassan.

Two important tendencies deserve particular emphasis in this context. The first is the tendency towards civilianisation. For the first time since 1952, civilians could become prime ministers (Mahmoud Fawzi, Aziz Sidky and Mustafa Khalil) and even vice-president (Fawzi). Under Sadat the ratio of the military ministers to civilians was 32:163 (20 per cent) as compared to 44:131 (33.6 per cent) under Nasser.

The second tendency is the new alliance between the state elite and business. The lower middle class elements which Nasser appointed in the 1950s and 1960s transformed themselves in the 1970s into state bourgeoisie and they gradually acquired wealth and social status. The ODEP gave them opportunities that hardly existed before. They were not only given the chance to acquire and accumulate wealth, but to invest it with foreign and Egyptian capital. This was reinforced by the marriage and business alliances that were taking place between old and new elites.

The inner group of decision makers included millionaires such as Osman Ahmed Osman and Sayed Marei, both connected to Sadat by marriage. For the first time since 1952, the business interests had strong inroads into the ruling elite. The business elite further organised itself into a number of associations and clubs.

Political Dynamics (Political Parties and Dissent Groups) and the Systemic Crisis

The democratisation process of 1976 (Dessouki, 1978a) resulted in three political parties. The Liberal Socialists Party, headed by Mustafa Kamel Murad, advocated more liberalisation of the economic system. With weak representation in the Assembly and limited popular following, it rarely challenged the regime. Its weekly al-Ahrar (the Liberals) has been occasionally an outlet for diverse opposition views.

The left party, the National Unionist Progressive Party (NPUP), headed by former free officer Khaled Muhi el Din, warned against the erosion of socialist gains, the dismantling of the public sector, and the removal of subsidies on certain food items. Formed as a loyal left, it soon managed to elude the aim of the government and drew together a number of tendencies - marxists, nasserists and Islamic leftists. Its weekly al-Ahali which became the main opposition paper in 1977 was frequently confiscated by the government. Eventually the paper stopped publication in 1978, and only came back in 1982 after the assassination of Sadat and the completion of Israeli withdrawal from Sinai.

The centre had the backing of the government and its party, Egypt's Socialist Party (ESP), headed by Mamduh Salem, the then prime minister. In 1979 Sadat established a new political party, the National Democratic Party (NDP), which attracted most of the ESP membership and the latter quietly disappeared. The NDP issues the weekly Mayo (May) which defends and justifies the government policies. In 1982, Mubarak was elected as the party's president.

In addition to the three original parties established in 1976, two more parties existed. The first was the Neo-Wafd Party headed by Fouad Serageldin, the secretary general of the old Wafd, the majority party between 1923 and 1952. The party attracted a great deal of attention and popular enthusiasm which was perceived as a dangerous sign by the government. The New-Wafd was established in 1978 and survived for 100 days only. In May, Sadat called for a referendum whose results meant the political disqualification of Mr Serageldin. The party reacted angrily by dissolving itself. The other is the Labour Socialist Party (LSP), headed by Ibrahim Shukry. Sadat actively intervened to help with the establishment of this party, clearly with the intention of having a loyal opposition. It seems however that opposition has a momentum and logic of its own; soon the LSP developed as a genuine political opposition and its weekly al-Shaab (the people) criticised governmental policies almost in every respect.

Political Dynamism and Dissent Groups. The elections of 1976 gave the right 12 seats, the left 2 seats and the centre 280 seats, with the remaining 56 going to independents. In January 1977 it became impossible for the regime to conceal the downgrading of the social situation. Massive demonstrations erupted in Cairo, Alexandria and other major cities in reaction to price increases and the reduction of subsidies on some basic goods. It seems that these events were a turning point in Sadat's view of democratisation. He accused leftists of inciting the people and making false and slanderous accusations against the regime during the election campaign of three months earlier. He grew impatient when writers criticised inflation, rampant consumerism, the new parasitic wealthy classes and the increasing gap between rich and poor in society as being the frustrating results of the ODEP.

The peace initiatives and relations with Israel were another topic which Sadat was not ready to have discussed in public. Thus, the regime issued a series of laws limiting the freedom of opposition and called for referendums to give popular sanctioning to these policies. When the 1979 assembly elections were held, measures were taken to ensure that opposition elements would have no chance in it.

Another source of opposition was the professional syndicates, particularly those of engineers, journalists and lawyers. Through cooptation and incentives, the regime managed to get a loyal and supportive leadership in the first two. As to the lawyers, they proved more resistant, and therefore the elected council of the syndicate was dissolved by an act of the parliament in August 1981. The act was politically motivated, its constitutionality was doubtful and the president blessed the event as a 'rectification movement'. Earlier, in the election of the new board of directors of the judges' club the government's list was defeated and the minister of justice, recognising the failure of his efforts, submitted his resignation. In retaliation, president Sadat appointed one of those 'rejected' candidates as the new minister of justice.

Important as the opposition of political parties and professional associations may have been, the real challenge to the regime came from the Islamic groups. Sadat was eventually assassinated by a member of al-Jihad (Holy Struggle) group. These fundamentalist groups represent the most radical wing of a much broader religious trend normally referred to as the Islamic resurgence (Dessouki, 1981; Ibrahim, 1981a). We can distinguish between at least three main groups. The first, led by Omar al-Tilmisani, is the Muslim Brothers which used to publish the monthly al-Da'wa (The Call). It seems that the comeback of the Muslim Brothers' activities was sanctioned by Sadat and there were signs of cooperation between their leaders and the regime in the early 1970s. Al-Da'wa, however, became a major outlet of political dissent and this invited its closure by the government in September 1981.

The second group is al-Jama'at al-Islamiya (Islamic Associations) which existed primarily in university campuses. They began their activities in the late 1960s and became the most cohesive student group by the mid 1970s. They collaborated with the regime against communist and nasserist elements, then became the regime's arch enemy. They controlled virtually all the universities' student councils and criticised the unislamic policies of the government. In 1980 Sadat suspended all Islamic associations accusing them of promoting religious fanaticism, extremism and communal unrest.

The third group is represented by a number of small clandestine paramilitary groups, most of which grew out of the Muslim Brothers. It includes Jund Allah

(Soldiers of God), al-Jihad (Holy Struggle), Shabab Muhammed (Mohammed's Youth) and al-Takfir wa al-Higra (Repentance and Holy Flight). The last group distinguished itself in July 1977 with its kidnapping and execution of Sheikh Muhammad H. al-Dahabi, a former minister of al-Azhar and al-Awqaf. Six hundred suspects were arrested, 50 were tried in a military court, 6 were sentenced to death and 31 received prison terms.

Although numerically weak these paramilitary groups were capable of initiating terrorist activities and they symbolised an important current of ideological opposition to the regime. Their emphasis on corruption and the high life of the rulers struck a sympathetic chord in the people.

In 1980 there were signs that opposition forces were gathering momentum and moving into a united front. The deteriorating economic situation of the poor and limited income groups, the tales about corruption and abuse of power in high circles including the president's family and closest associates, the commmunal strife, increasing dependence on the US, Israel's intransigent policies and Sadat's one man rule - all gave ammunition to opposition groups to mount strong criticism against the regime. The ruling party could not develop itself into a credible political force to deal with the opposition. This was partly because of Sadat's monopoly of the political process and also due to the party's lack of ideological and organisational cohesion. The NDP consists of broad social forces, held together less by ideology and organisation than by personal connections, pragmatic concerns for career and patronage. In 1981 the opposition became too effective to be brushed aside or ignored. On September 5, 1981, three months after bloody communal riots in a low income district of Cairo, Sadat initiated the largest crackdown of his eleven year rule which involved the arrest of some 1563 persons including a number of imams of the mosques and coptic priests, the shutting down of seven newspapers and journals, the dissolution of 13 religious societies and the seizure of the Muslim Brothers' funds and assets. All private mosques were to be administered by the government. Finally, patriarch Shenuda III was stripped of temporal power and a papal committee of five bishops was appointed to take over his duties. The list of arrested people included all shades of political persuasion and it seemed as if Sadat had declared war on all his opposition, right or left, religious and secular, at once. His regime appeared isolated from all main currents of political life in Egypt. These decisions were a symptom of the systemic crisis his regime was facing; a crisis that found an outlet a month later when the president was assassinated.

The Islamic Movement and its Sociopolitical Roots. On several occasions in this chapter we have had cause to consider the Islamic movement and its sociopolitical roots. As regards its role as a force of opposition, the Islamic movement is the political incarnation of a political, social and economic malaise which cuts deeply into several social classes in Egypt. The movement is widespread and exists at various levels in all the Arab countries, although its success in Iran and the forms it has assumed in that country would be difficult to repeat elsewhere. In Egypt, the resurgence of the more or less institutionalised Islamic groups (see under last heading) is due to many factors. These groups are the product of a crisis, characterised by economic difficulties but above all by a state of moral and ideological confusion and growing social unrest. It is worth noting the moral and psychological components of this crisis, which are as important as they are misunderstood. The defeat in 1967 was for all Egyptians, and especially for the younger generations, a traumatic event. Besides the military defeat, the outcome of the war belied all that Nasser had symbolised for the Arabs and the Egyptians: that is, revolution, nationalism and secularism, not to mention the role that Nasser and Egypt had played in the pan-Arab context. Many Egyptians went through a phase of soul-searching and introspection. From the police interrogations of the militants emerge memories of psychological experiences of desperation which often found comfort in a return to religion and later on militancy (Sivan, 1982: 184). On the other hand, the government, which had to explain in one way or another what had gone wrong, also resorted to moral or religious explanations of the defeat.

And in fact Nasser himself turned to Islam and the will of God (Dessouki, 1981a: 114). Religious activities were encouraged, as a diversion. In December 1967, Egypt's semi-official newspaper Al-Ahram gave wide coverage to a march organised by the Sufi orders. In the immediate post-war period there was an apparition of the Madonna in Cairo and it was the militants of the Arab Socialist Union who controlled the crowd which gathered, (ibid.) Many attributed the defeat to the fact that religion and the faith had been neglected due to westernisation, atheism, socialism, capitalism and other evils of modernisation. And when in October 1973 the Egyptian army was victorious in a significantly different political and cultural climate this was seen as a sign of the reformation and divine protection.

The Egyptian soldiers, having crossed the Canal, praised the name of God, 'Allah Akhbar' (Kazziha, 1979: 27, 32), and it was not by chance that the war had been fought in the month of Ramadan (Dessouki, 1981a: 114). Sadat, too, encouraged this return to religion, and as we saw above he used it to consolidate his position. But Sadat also changed the policies which had characterised Egypt's political and cultural identity: he took Egypt from socialism to capitalism, from the radical-nationalist Arab alliances to the alliance with Saudi Arabia, from the 'strategic' alliance with the Soviet Union to a new friendship with the USA, and finally, from the sworn conflict with Israel to the journey to Jerusalem and his 'friend' Begin. All of this led to personal traumas, cynicism, ideological confusion, a feeling of uprooting and alienation: in other words to a situation in which Islam seemed, especially to the younger generations, to be the only firm reference point in an increasingly confused society.

Besides these psychological and cultural factors, the concomitant problems of social order are very important. As we have seen, the economic and social transformations brought about by Sadat and the constant inflation which accompanied them led to a major redistribution of income. The most impoverished classes were low and medium low income classes, which account for about two thirds of Egypt's urban population. The youth of these classes find it increasingly difficult to move up the social ladder but nevertheless they will continue to be the nerve centre of Egyptian society and above all of its economic organisation. It is to these youngsters that the law assures a job in the bureaucracy. These jobs invariably involve travelling far from the urban centres and pay a miserable stipend compared to what the youngsters of the wealthier class can earn by being able to find jobs in the sectors tied to the development of the ODEP. The same youngsters have to suffer the problems of overpopulation, overurbanisation and infrastructural decline which among other things often force them to continue to live with their parents even after they marry because they cannot find a house of their own. From these culturally alienated and socially degraded lower middle classes comes the main body of the Islamic militancy, which in Egypt is an essentially urban phenomemon, of the lower middle classes (Williams, 1978; Humphreys, 1979).

We have concentrated on Islamism as a political movement, because this phenomemon cannot but weigh heavily on whatever economic policy the new president, Mubarak, wishes to implement. We saw in the first chapter that the containment and reorganisation of public expenditure and in particular of expenditure on transfer payments will be a necessary qualification of any development policy that the Egyptian authorities hope to adopt. We also considered the necessity of a political and social limit to such a containment of public expenditure for reasons of social control. The existence of the Islamic opposition must surely have the effect of considerably raising that limit. This is one of the most difficult problems facing Egypt's new leader in his attempt to guide the country towards greater development and overcome the social conditions which are today at the root of the opposition of the Islamic movements.

SECURITY, FOREIGN POLICY AND PUBLIC EXPENDITURE

Foreign policy is certainly an important factor for Egypt. Some experts go so far as to attribute special weight to foreign policy in Egyptian politics. They contend, in fact, that it is also always designed to attract resources to help square the country's balance of payments. This would help explain Egypt's resounding turnabout from the USSR to the USA and also the peace agreement it concluded with Israel. In both cases, one of the major objectives would have been to attract more US resources. Although it is certainly true that the country's internal and financial situation affects Egypt's international choices, in reality, its foreign policy seems to be determined by a more complex combination of factors. Its ambition to lead the Arab world, prestige, regional security, a strong national conscience, its intention to project itself externally - for example, in Africa - play an equally important role in shaping Egyptian foreign policy.

The issue of what factors influence Egyptian foreign policy and to what degree will not, however, be addressed here. The scope of this section is to analyse instead the factors which currently and concretely condition the foreign and internal policy choices of the Egyptian leaders, drawing special attention to the security dimension. In this sense, it can be said that today the Egyptian leadership is faced with three sets of interrelated challenges: a) the need to revise Sadat's policy of cultivating a close relationship with the United States for the purpose of exerting pressure on Israel and at the same time developing Egypt's military (and economic) strength; b) the need to reassess Egypt's regional status and role and the related policies; c) the need to appraise local threats such as those posed by Libya and Ethiopia.

Egypt's Relations with the United States

Egypt's policy toward the United States, as described above, has not been exclusive to Sadat. After the 1967 defeat, when it became clear that the Soviets could not give the Arabs the expected edge over Israel, all the principal Arab countries decided to adopt, more or less gradually, a similar policy. But it was Sadat who most resolutely began to implement this strategy, in 1972, by severing Egypt's ties with the Soviet Union, after it had become clear that Moscow would not deliver the arms

Cairo had requested.

The crucial point is that, along with its economic and strategic interests in the region, what keeps the United States so deeply involved is its special relationship with Israel. This means - to use one of Sadat's most famous expressions - that 'the core and crux' of Middle East politics, namely the Arab-Israel conflict and the Palestinian issue, cannot be resolved without the cooperation of the United States. Consequently, the major goal was to become just as important an ally of the United States as Israel so that sooner or later the US would have to tackle the problem of restraining Israel and finding a solution to the Arab-Israeli conflict in order to meet the demands of its Arab friends and avoid tensions among its allies in the region. Oil was considered one of the most important means for exerting pressure on the United States. For this reason, a strong Saudi-Egyptian axis worked reasonably well for some time.

The new strategy had the advantage of not requiring a buildup of Egypt's military capacity to the point where it would be superior to Israel's (which is what Egypt had hoped to achieve through its alliance with the USSR). The military option was in fact to be complemented by the political leverage the Arabs thought they would acquire thanks to their alliance with the United States. None the less, the Arab military option had to be kept at a credible level, otherwise it was feared that Israel - because of the special place military force holds in its security concepts - could never be seriously restrained even by US political pressure. Agreement on the need to keep the military option effective while seeking to strengthen ties with the United States was at the basis of the Eygptian-Syrian entente. Even Saudi Arabia agreed to this policy. Generally speaking, this inter-Arab consensus on the conditions deemed necessary to make the strategy work was one of the major conditions for its success.

It is important to keep this point in mind when analysing developments in the period following the 1973 war. Although Sadat made great strides in consolidating friendly relations with the United States, he was not nearly as successful in exploiting the relationship to strengthen Egypt's military capacity; and he neglected the importance of keeping inter-Arab consensus alive and strong. The bilateral ceasefire agreements he reached with Israel in the framework of his step-by-step policy were interpreted quite correctly by Syria as a move that weakened the Arab military option and hence hindered the political process that was supposed to force Israel to agree to a comprehensive settlement. At the Riyadh summit in October 1976 it seemed that Saudi diplomacy had been successful in making Egypt rethink its policy and in smoothing over the inter-Arab divergencies (Dishan, 1978: 147-50). Syria suspended its anti-Egyptian campaign and in turn Egypt agreed to let Syria have the upper hand in Lebanon. Both reiterated the need to maintain a credible military option. But renewed tensions led to another collapse of the understanding when in August 1977 Sadat suggested to the US Secretary of State, Cyrus Vance, without first consulting Assad, that preparations be made for the Geneva conference by setting up a working group of all the parties involved that would meet in the United States. This was interpreted by Syria as a factor that weakened both the Arab strategy and the inter-Arab understanding, and as a result the entente broke down once again.

Besides this, after the 1973 war the Egyptian armed forces had been rebuilt to a certain extent, but with the notable exception of the air force and without any significant modernisation (Schuefter, 1978: 87). By 1977 Egypt had not only lost its military option against Israel; its military standing with respect to Syria and other countries of the region also appeared to be on the decline, particularly from the qualitative point of view. The United States had in effect refused to become the arms supplier the Egyptian strategy had foreseen it would become. In other words, Sadat had given absolute and constant priority to the strengthening of Egypt's political ties with the United States thinking that at a later stage the US would also become the country's major source of arms. This proved to be an unbalanced and unproductive approach. In the end it weakened Egypt instead of providing it with more leverage vis-à-vis the other actors of the Middle East scene, trapping Egypt in a political stalemate.

By the end of 1977 it was in fact evident that Egypt had reached a stalemate. The second Sinai agreement was due to expire in September 1978. Egypt was thus faced with the dilemma of whether to renew it and lose face in the Arab world or let it lapse and risk military tensions with Israel that it was totally unprepared to cope with. There was also the fact that the Carter administration was preparing a conference in Geneva with the USSR and the other interested Arab parties at a time when Egypt was becoming increasingly aware that it was too weak politically and militarily to make its weight felt in the Arab world, particularly against Syria. For these reasons Sadat decided to play a completely different game, and therefore initiated the process to conclude a bilateral peace agreement with Israel.

This peace with Israel can be considered a sharp reversal of the strategy inspired and pursued by Egypt up until then, for with it Sadat dropped all efforts to ensure a certain degree of parallelism between the 'political process' and the 'military option'. Leaving aside the implications in terms of internal politics, the decision to abandon definitively all efforts to recreate a military option implied complete reliance on the United States' willingness and ability to compel Israel to reach a satisfactory settlement. Whatever the case, the United States has so far been unwilling or unable to restrain Israel and convince it to reach an agreement capable of restoring Egypt to a position of leadership in the Arab world.

Sadat's death left Egypt totally dependent on the United States and with no leverage with which to influence the superpower's policy towards Israel and the Middle East. It seems, however, that Sadat viewed the Reagan administration's new policy toward the region as an opportunity to rebuild the military option he had gradually lost over the preceding ten years. In spite of the fact that it initially ignored the Arab-Israeli conflict, Reagan's strictly East-West perspective obliged the United States to establish military relations with its allies in the region, supply them with arms, military assistance and economic aid, and embark on negotiations to gain greater military access to their territories and facilities. The dilemma inherent in this policy is how to preserve a military balance favourable to Israel while at the same time strengthening the Arab allies. The debate over whether to supply Saudi Arabia with AWACS and other military equipment has highlighted the implications of Reagan's policy. Those who think Israel's opposition to the AWACS deal is exaggerated, considering that they already have a tremendous qualitiative edge over the Arab countries, fail to understand what Israel has clearly grasped: that the Arabs are seeking to build up their military capability not for the purpose of ensuring military victory over Israel but to make a plain Israeli military victory impossible in order to ensure US political involvement in the region both in peacetime and in the event of a war.

It is therefore clear that in the last months of his life Sadat saw in the new American policy an opportunity to relaunch his strategy. Egypt eagerly adhered to Reagan's 'strategic consensus' policy, seeing it as a chance to confirm its close relationship with the United States and at the same time as a way of acquiring for Egypt, thanks to the increased military supplies and assistance that were part and parcel of the new American policy, the leverage it had lost over the preceding years. Sadat's expectations were not, however, fulfilled. He returned empty-handed from his trip to the United States to meet the new president; that is, without that privileged relationship at the political and military level that could have transformed the significance of the relationship Egypt had established with the US over the preceding decade. It was at this point that Egypt quite opportunely initiated a policy of diversification of its arms suppliers. The country's procurement programme now includes arms and military equipment from France, the United Kingdom, and minor producers such as Italy. The Egyptian arms industry has also been given a big boost with the idea of exporting part of the output to Egypt's regional partners (Cremasco, 1981). The recent launching of the Alphajet, an interceptor, attests to the success of this venture.

The shift in the Reagan administration's policy

following the Israeli invasion of Lebanon once again put Egypt in an awkward position. Reagan's proposal goes beyond Camp David, and summons into the picture the moderate Arab states that had been excluded from the US-Egypt-Israel triangle, at a time when post-Sadatian Egypt is still anchored to its Camp David policy and has not yet re-established normal relations and sufficient authority with the other Arab countries. Moreover, the process to reacquire adequate military weight has just started and there is still much to be done before it gives Egypt the leverage it seeks in its relations with both the United States and the other Arab countries. In this sense, the risk Mubarak is running is similar to the one Sadat ran when the United States and the Soviet Union, with their joint declaration of 1 October 1977, convened the Geneva conference to negotiate a settlement: in a new multiparty negotiation Egypt may once again feel too weak to be able to assert its leadership in the Arab world, its national interests, and its leadership in the Arab world, its national interests, and its special relationship with the United States.

The new leadership's lack of clearly defined foreign policy goals and its sometimes ambiguous attitude are a reflection of the unwieldiness of the legacy left by Sadat. Egypt has moved closer to the moderate Arabs, it is more cautious and reserved in its relations with the United States, and it is colder towards Israel; but none of this gives us a clear indication that a new policy is being forged. It is also true, however, that the constraints on Egyptian foreign policy are particularly daunting and almost insuperable. For the short term Egypt has no alternative but to resort to cautious and, in certain circumstances, ambiguous diplomacy. It is clear, however, that if Egypt wants to resolve its problems, it will have to begin as soon as possible to strengthen its economy and at the same time rebuild its military capacity to a credible level. An increase in military expenditure is however bound to make it all the more difficult to strengthen the economy.

Egypt's Regional Role and Local Threats

There are two sides to Egypt's regional security dimension. For one thing, the state of Egypt's military force affects both the regional balance and the country's inter-Arab status. From what was pointed out in the preceding sections, it should be clear that the preservation of a credible military capacity is of the utmost importance to Egypt's role in the regional context. It should also be noted that the regional military balance has become rather unfavourable to Egypt (without, however, overlooking the fact that Egypt is still the only Arab country to possess all the economic, industrial and social inputs which make armed forces significant in a modern sense). The other side of the security dimension is that regional military capacity is not only an inter-Arab factor. Egypt's ability to cope with extraregional international threats, such as international terrorism (Egypt's special security forces' raid on Nicosia airport in 1977), Khomeini's Iran, Black Africa (the expeditionary corps against the invasion of Zaire from Angola in 1977), revolt (its presence in Oman following Iran's withdrawal), and Soviet-backed marxist regimes (support to Somalia, Sudan and Oman against the threats posed by South Yemen and Ethiopia), is a factor which strengthens its hand in the regional contest for power but which is also, and above all, an essential underpinning of its special relationship with the United States. In 1977-78 Egypt's internationalistic policy was translated into an attempt to create a NATO-like Arab coalition, under the leadership of Egypt and Saudi Arabia, to contain the Communist threat from Ethiopia which it was feared might spread rapidly throughout the Red Sea region. But on that occasion too, the expected American support failed to materialise and the Ogaden war turned out to be a political and military defeat for the Arabs. Egypt currently plays an international role by means of the aid it provides to a group of key countries, Oman, Somalia and Sudan, which are also very important in the context of the US's drive to gain military access to the region.

Needless to say, a military presence is crucial if Egypt is to maintain adequate political status in the region and it intends to recreate a military relationship with the United States. This would entail, however, an increase in the state budget.

When discussing the regional security situation, mention should also be made of the minor or 'localised' threats. Although the Ethiopian threat does present a local aspect, the only truly local threat to Egypt, by virtue of its special relationship with Sudan, is Libya. This threat has taken different guises in the course of time: constant and multiform pressures on Sudan and the Nile Valley; intermittent border tensions with Egypt which in 1977 led to short battles (which, by the way, made evident the uncertain state of the Egyptian armed forces).

From a strictly local point of view the Libyan threat cannot be considered very serious. Though extremely vocal, Libya's attitude has always proved to be very cautious, and in the summer of 1977 it was Egypt that wanted to teach Libya a lesson and thus show the other Arab countries its strength and the United States the importance of its role in the region. It is none the less true that Libya is the most determined of Egypt's enemies and that for a long time it has been trying to undermine Egypt, especially from the political point of view, by threatening Sudan and supporting Ethiopia and, more recently, also South Yemen. Another aspect worth mentioning is that Libya is a big repository of Soviet arms and equipment. This can be considered an objective threat, but not one involving regional or local aspects.

The local factors are not decisive, but they too suggest that Egypt will have to improve its military readiness both for specific security reasons and as a sound basis for its foreign policies. They thus confirm Egypt's need to make a difficult and delicate choice between financial and foreign policy requirements.

Islamism as a Regional Factor

The assassination of Sadat confirmed that Islamism constitutes a very risky and dangerous political and social factor for Egypt and the other countries of the region. One might wonder if the Islamic movement, which in different ways and to differing degrees affects all the countries of the region, should be considered not only an internal but also a foreign policy issue and hence a factor to be dealt with in the framework of the country's security policy. This question assumes special relevance if seen in the light of the socioeconomic transformations which Egypt will have to embark on if a positive process of development is to be initiated. Such transformations are bound to create tense socioeconomic situations which, however transitory they may be, could easily be exploited by the Islamic opposition. An ill-pondered change in the subsidisation policy, for instance, could ignite a process of this sort, as the January 1977 events have proved. The regional extension of the Islamic movement might lead one to think that a necessary precondition to changes in Egypt's economic and social policies would be a certain degree of control and influence over this movement, by means of the country's foreign policy as well.

But, in reality, it may be misleading to call Islamism a regional movement, for it is made up of a large number of extremely diverse and often unrelated groups. Even the international links of the old and widespread Muslim Brotherhood tend to be random and sporadic. What is spreading throughout the Muslim world is imitation and activism, not organisation and structures.

It is important to underline the tenuous nature of the international structures of Islamism in order to make it clear that foreign policies designed to check it can play no more than a secondary role, affecting its development only marginally. It could be argued that the rise of Islamism as a political movement is simply a reaction to the intrusion of external, alien factors which have had a negative impact on Islamic society, and that Islamic revivalism is basically a search for cultural identity and social dignity prompted, among other things, by the frustration experienced in trying to compete with the outside world. In other words, the movement is an expression or reflection of the Arab world's predicament today; a problem which is certainly not unique to Egypt, and which in any case does not interest us here.

Another reason why foreign policy measures can

have only a limited impact on the Islamic movement in the region is that the Egyptian Islamic movement has its own roots, even if it is now supported by the wider regional environment. Moreover, its development was encouraged first by Nasser, to offset the frustration of the 1967 defeat, and then by Sadat, to counter opposition and comply with Saudi demands. For this reason, even if a foreign policy designed to check Islamism were successful, it might only serve to weaken Egyptian Islamic activism without significantly curbing or eliminating it.

The four main centres from which Islamism is projected internationally are Pakistan, Saudi Arabia, Iran and Libya. There are also some individual religious leaders (preachers and so on) who depend exclusively on the activism of believers and followers. While Saudi Arabia and Pakistan are not directly and consciously subversive in their Islamic projection, some of the individual religious leaders are. But the most serious and delicate problems at the international level are currently posed by Iran and Libya.

Notwithstanding the theories elaborated by Qadhafi in his 'Green Book', Libya's Islamic projection is definitely less inspiring than Iran's. It cannot compare with the tremendous revolutionary wind blowing from Teheran across the entire region. Tripoli will never be able to win the hearts of the masses. Its policy consists in specific actions designed to promote conspiracies, rings and subversion. What is more, its projection is always instrumental to short term foreign policy goals, such as undermining Egypt, whose significance is decidedly inferior to what is at stake in the overall revival of Islamism. The nature of Libya's projection is revealed in a disconcerting series of subversive activities in foreign countries, mainly Egypt. And its relations with Sudan show that Libya is ready to act as a catalyst when social malaise and/or riots give it the chance to do so.

The internal security problems created by low Libyan-inspired violence and subversion should be dealt with mainly by the internal security forces and intelligence services. None the less, at the international level, it is the Libyan state that is a threat to Egypt.

This makes Egypt's ability to deter Libya very important if the government is to have adequate freedom of action in dealing with its social problems without the risk of giving Libya the opportunity to exploit potentially explosive situations.

Iran is quite a different case. The underprivileged masses and the organised groups of Muslims in Egypt undoubtedly consider Teheran a guiding light, especially since the Islamic movement seized power. In the last analysis, the biggest difference between Libya and Iran is that Iran - a populous and composite country - does not project its revolutionary Islamic zeal by means of subversion. Rather, it is doing so by means of a long and destructive war with Iraq. This war is perceived not so much as a national war but rather as a campaign to assert Islamism. An Iranian victory would have far-reaching consequences not only in Egypt. For this reason, Egypt cannot be indifferent to the Iran-Iraq war. And in fact it is already supporting Iraq by sending spare parts and other Soviet material out of its old stocks. A significant rapprochement between the two countries, at the political level too, is now under way.

It should be obvious from what has been pointed out so far that checking the spread of Islamism throughout the region is essentially a question of containing Iran. The problem presents certain military aspects, which Egypt is unprepared to cope with, but it is mainly a political problem. Egypt's current inability to formulate a more active and clearly defined foreign policy is reflected in its vacillating attitude toward the Arab countries, including Iraq. Egyptian political backing of Iraq, in the framework of a new alliance with Saudi Arabia and the moderate Arab states, would be just as meaningful as an expeditionary force. But such support, which would reinforce the internal policy aimed at containing the Islamic movement at home, would have to be given covertly in view of the general conditions and constraints which have led Egypt to adopt a wait-and-see foreign policy.

Foreign Policy, Security and Public Expenditure

As was pointed out, Sadat left his country with a foreign policy that is extremely difficult to manage. For a long time Sadat counted increasingly on the 'political process' he thought the alliance with the United States would carry to a successful conclusion. But the Camp David process was left incomplete. The United States lacked either the will or the ability to work to alter the political and military balance in the region. American backing proved uneven and vacillating from both the political and military point of view. Egypt's gradual loss of a credible military option only deprived it of all leverage, without this being offset by a greater US ability or willingness to moderate Israel.

The new regime seems determined to change this state of affairs (Dessouki, 1982b) and pull Egypt out of the powerless situation it finds itself in today. There is, however, a basic continuity with the past in the goals the new president has apparently set for Egypt. Mubarak is not intent on upsetting the country's present alliance system. He certainly does not want to lead Egypt toward a new form of nationalistic radicalism. And he is not thinking of repudiating the peace with Israel. He seems to want to conserve all this while at the same time seeking to regain that margin of autonomy that Sadat had lost, first with respect to the United States and then with respect to the other protagonists of the regional scene.

Mubarak may be criticised for not proceeding more explicitly and resolutely (Ibrahim, 1982b), but it is also obvious that his goal of rectifying Sadat's policy under the banner of continuity cannot be achieved in short order because of the many constraints that condition his policy. Closer ties with the moderate Arab countries are of course essential if Egypt hopes to regain a certain measure of autonomy in its relations with the United States. The establishment of closer ties with them is, however, conditional on how the Palestinian issue develops, which in turn depends on US policy, however ineffectual it may be. But Egypt no longer has any trump cards to play to influence US policy. Egypt's return to the Arab fold would be guaranteed if it went back on the Camp David accords, even without going so far as to break off relations with Israel. But in this way it would return defeated, in the sense that it would have to disavow the policy it had hitherto followed, thus losing all authority in the region. Instead, Egypt wants to go back to the Arab fold only if it can regain a dominant position. Mubarak's predicament is that he is still conditioned by the Camp David policy. If he went back on it, he would risk undermining Egypt's relations with the United States, with no assurance that Egypt would be able to regain a position of leadership in the region. Egypt thus has a chance of solving the Camp David dilemma only if the United States changes its policy. And even if it does, there would still have to be some sort of continuity with the Camp David process in Egypt's new policy. Otherwise, its inter-Arab position would be in jeopardy. For this reason, Egypt backs President Reagan's September 1982 proposal for negotiations in which Jordan would play a key role, on the condition that it be seen as a continuation of the process set in motion with the signing of the Camp David accords.

Caught in the grip of these contradictions, Egypt has decided to follow for the moment the course of discreet diplomacy aimed at re-establishing close relations with the moderate Arab countries. At the same time, the president is making significant gestures such as refusing to make a trip to Jerusalem and attending King Khalid's funeral. Diplomatic relations will be formally re-established in due course. Mubarak's middle term objective is instead to lay the foundations for a concrete strengthening of Egypt's political position. His attention seems to be focussed mainly on building up the economy and the nation's military capacity. With regard to the economy, Mubarak has confirmed Sadat's Open Door Economic Policy (ODEP), but has also emphasised the need to direct efforts to increasing productive investments and reducing consumption. Though less publicised, steps are also being taken to concretely strengthen Egypt's military capacity in order to regain that credibility and autonomy which seem to be the new president's central concern. The rebuilding of a military option could be considered primarily a response to the subjective demands of public opinion. The Israeli bombing of the Tammuz nuclear power plant in Iraq and the Israeli attack on Lebanon, with the destruction and massacres that followed, deeply shook the Egyptian people. There is no doubt that they once again feel seriously threatened by Israel. But the recreation of a military option also meets certain objective requirements of support to Egypt's foreign policy. The removal of the possibility of an armed conflict in the Middle East was considered by the United States an end in itself rather than the precondition for finding a comprehensive solution to the Middle East issue. At the same time, Israel's behaviour worked regularly to discredit Egypt's policy and confirm the Syrian point of view that Israel's purpose in reaching an agreement with Egypt was to put the strongest Arab armed forces out of action so that it would be free to attack the other Arab states militarily with little risk of serious reprisals. Finally, as we have seen, Egypt's weakness in the framework of the Arab-Israeli conflict is reflected in a series of weaknesses in those regional situations, that go from inter-Arab relations to containment of Iran, in which military strength counts just as much as political influence. A reversal of the situation in which Egypt currently finds itself seems therefore to hinge greatly on its ability to recreate a credible military capacity.

The problem is that an increase in military expenditures will inevitably create serious difficulties for a country that also needs to reduce public spending and make room for productive state and private investments in order to stimulate economic development. The need to increase military expenditure seriously reduces the government's leeway in trying to strike a balance between international openness and the heavy burden of the state budget. It is however a requirement that cannot easily be evaded since on it depends the regaining of that confidence which Egypt will need finally to embark on a process of real growth of individual incomes and of the country's wealth.

BIBLIOGRAPHY

AJAMI, F. 'The Open Door Economy: Its Roots and Welfare Consequences', in G.A. KHALEK and R. TIGNOR (eds.) 'The Political Economy of Income Distribution in Egypt' (Holmes and Meier, New York 1982), pp. 468-516.

AKHAVI, S. 'Egypt: Diffused Elite in a Bureaucratic Society', in I.W. ZARTMAN, et al. 'Political Elities in Arab North Africa', (Longman, New York 1982) pp. 223-66.

ALTMAN, I. 'Islamic Movements in Egypt', "The Jerusalem Quartely", no. 10 (1979), pp. 87-105.

ARMAN, I.M.I. 'A Model to Develop Egyptian Agriculture To Solve the Problem of Unemployment and Low Per Capita Income in Egyptian Agriculture', Institute of National Planning, memo no. 1318 (Cairo, January 1982).

----- 'Manpower and Employement of Egypt 1980-2000' Institute of National Planning, memo no. 1320 (Cairo, March 1982a).

AYUBI, N.M. 'The Evolution of the Political and Administrative System in Egypt', in S.E. IBRAHIM (ed.) 'A Quarter of a Century in Egypt, 1952-1977' (1981, in arabic).

BACON, R.W. and ELTIS, W.A. 'Britain's Economic Problem: Too Few Producers' (London 1976).

BINDER, L. 'In a Moment of Enthusiasm, Political Power and the Second Stratum in Egypt, University of Chicago Press, Chicago & London (1978).

BIRKS, J.S. e SINCLAIR, C.A. 'International Migration and Development in the Arab Region' (ILO, Geneva 1980).

BOUTROS-GHALI, Y. and TAYLOR, L. 'Basic Needs Macro-economics: Is It Manageable in the Case of Egypt?', "Journal of Policy Modelling", no. 2 (September 1980).

CAPMAS, 'The General Population and Housing Census 1976, The Preliminary Results' (Cairo, March 1977).

----- 'The Population Problem and the Issue of the Fertility Rate' (Cairo 1978, in arabic).

----- 'Labor Force by Sample Survey' (Cairo, May 1980).

----- 'Statistical Yearbook' (Cairo, July 1981).

----- 'Status of the Open Door Policy in the ARE up to 31/12/1981' (Cairo, February 1982).

CLARK, P.G. 'Private Sector Industrial Development Strategy', Boston University, Industrial Sector Strategy Assessment (December 1981), (mimeo).

CHOUCRI, N. and ECKHAUS, R. 'Interactions of Economic and Political Change: The Egyptian Case', "World Development", (August-September 1979), pp. 783-99.

COLITTI, M. 'Natural Gas and Economic Development', EGPC-IEOC, Atti del Convegno "Natural Gas and Egypt's Economic Development" (Cairo 1982).

CREMASCO, M. 'The Middle East Arms Industry: Attempts at Regional Cooperation', "Lo Spettatore Internazionale", vol. XVI, no. 4 (1981), pp. 297-312.

DAVIS, P. and LAPITTUS, J. 'Food and Energy Subsidies, 1979' (Cairo 1980, mimeo).

DEKMEJIAN, R.H. 'Egypt under Nasser', Albany, State University of New York Press (1974).

----- 'The Anatomy of Islamic Revival', "Middle East Journal", vol. 34, no. 1 (Winter 1980), pp. 1-12.

DESSOUKI, A.E.H. 'The Transformation of Party System in Egypt' in DESSOUKI, A.E.H. (ed.) 'Democracy in Egypt', Cairo Papers in Social Science, vol. 1, no. 2 (January 1978a).

----- 'Policy Making in Egypt: A Case Study of The Open Door Economic Policy' "Social Problems", vol. 28, no. 4 (April 1981), pp. 410-16.

----- 'The Resurgence of Islamic Organizations in Egypt: An Interpretation' in CUDSI, A. and DESSOUKI, A.E.H. (eds.), 'Islam and Power', (Croom Helm, London 1981a), pp. 107-18.

----- 'The Shift in Egypt's Migration Policy: 1952-1977', "Middle East Studies", vol. 18, no. 1 (January 1982), pp. 53-68.

----- 'The Politics of Income Distribution in Egypt' in KHALEK-TIGNOR (eds.) 'The Political Economy of Income Distribution in Egypt' (Holmesand Meier, New York 1982) pp. 55-87.

----- 'Waiting for Mubarak', "The New York Times" (May 16, 1982b).

DETHIER, J.J. and ESFAHANI, H. 'Macro Effects of Alternative Price Policies in Egypt', Agricultural Development Systems Project, University of California, Economic Working Paper n. 46 (September 1981).

DISHON, D. 'Inter-Arab Relations', in LEGUM, C. (ed.) 'Middle East Contemporary Survey', vol. 1, 1976-77 (Holmes and Meier, New York 1978), pp. 147-178.

DRISCOLL, R., HAYEK, P.F. and ZAKI, F.A. 'Foreign Investment in Egypt: An Analysis of Critical Factors with Emphasis on the Foreign Investment Code', Fund for Multinational Management Education (New York 1978).

EL AYOUTI, M.K. 'Exploration and Gas Discovery in Egypt', EGPC-IEOC, Atti del Convegno "Natural Gas and Egypt's Economic Development" (Cairo 1982).

EL GRITLY, A. 'Twenty-five Years: An Analytical Study of Egypt's Economic Problems, 1952-1977' (Cairo El-Hayya El-Misriyya El-Aama Lil-Kitab, 1977).

ENI 'Energia e Idrocarburi' (Roma 1982).

ESU (Economic Studies Unit), Ministry of Economy, Foreign Trade & Economic Co-operation 'Recent Development in the Egyptian Economy' (January 1982, mimeo).

FADIL, M.A. 'Development, Income, Distribution and Social Change in Rural Egypt 1952-1970', Cambridge University Press (Cambridge 1975).

----- 'Informal Sector Employment in Egypt' (Cairo 1981, mimeo).

FARGANI, N. 'Development and Labour Force' in IBRAHIM, S.E. 'A quarter of a Century in Egypt, 1952-1977' (1981, in arabic).

FARRAG, A. 'Migration between Arab Countries', (ILO, Geneva 1976).

FODA, A.S. et al. 'Banking Sector Survey' (USAID, Cairo 1982).

FRY, M.J. 'Saving, Investment, Growth and the Cost of Financial Repression', "World Development" (April 1980), pp. 317-28.

GEMMELL, N. 'The Role of the Non-Market Sector in Egypt's Economic Growth, 1960-76', "Oxford Economic Paper" (March 1981), pp. 207-223.

GHANTUS, E. 'Arab Industrial Integration' (Croom Helm, London 1982).

GLASSBURNER, B. and EL AMIR, R. 'The Economics of Agricultural Intensification: Strategies for the Attainment of National Goals', ADS Economic Working paper (May 1981).

HANSEN, B. and RADWAN, S. 'Employment Opportunities and Equity in Egypt (ILO, Geneva 1982).

HINNEBUSCH, R.A. 'Egypt under Sadat: Elities, Power Structure and Political Change in a Post-Populist State', "Social Problems", vol. 28, no. 4 (April 1981).

HUMPHREYS, R.S. 'Islam and Political Values in Saudi Arabia, Egypt and Syria', Middle East Journal", vol. 33, no. 1 (Winter 1979).

IBRAHIM, S.E. 'Urbanization in the Arab World', "UN ECWA Population Bulletin" (July 1975).

----- 'Over-urbanization and Under-urbanism, the Case of the Arab World', "International Journal of Middle East Studies", no. 1 (1975a), pp. 1-23.

----- 'Population in the Arab World', in IBRAHIM, S.E. and HOPKINS, N. (eds.), 'Arab Society in Transition', American University (Cairo 1977).

----- (ed.) 'A Quarter of a Century in Egypt, 19521977', Arab Development Institute, Beirut (1981, in arabic).

----- 'Anatomy of Egypt's Militant Groups', "International Journal of Middle East Studies", vol. 12 (1981a), pp. 423-53.

----- 'The New Arab Social Order, A Study of The Social Impact of Oil Wealth', Westview Press, Boulder (Co.), Croom Helm (London 1982).

----- 'Social Mobility and Income Distribution in Egypt', in KHALEK-TIGNOR 'The Open Door Economic Policy in Egypt: Its Contribution to Investment and its Equity' (1982a), pp. 375-434.

----- 'Qui va capter l'âme de Hosni Mubarak?', "Maghreb-Machrek", n. 97 (1982b), pp. 28-38.

IISS 'The Military Balance 1982-83' (London, 1982).

JONES, L.P. 'Improving the Operation Efficiency of Public Industrial Enterprise in Egypt', Boston University, Industrial Sector Strategy Assessment (September 1981, mimeo).

KAZZIHA, W. 'Palestine in the Arab Dilemma' (Croom Helm, 1979).

KERR, M.H. and YASSIN, E.S. (eds) 'Rich and Poor States in the Middle East', Westview Press, Boulder (Co.), (1982).

KHALEK, G.A. 'The Open Door Economic Policy in Egypt: Its Contribution to Investment and its Equity', in KERR and YASSIN 'Rich and Poor States in the Middle East' (1982), pp. 259-284.

----- and TIGNOR, R. (eds.) 'The Political Economy of Income Distribution in Egypt' (Holmes and Meier, New York 1982).

KHEIR EL DIN, H. 'Insufficiency of Saving or Shortage of Foreign Exchange? A Test of Alternative Contraints on the Growth of the Egyptian Economy', ESU, Ministry of Economy, Foreign Trade & Economic Co-operation (August 1980, mimeo).

----- and LUCAS, R. 'Comparative Advantage in Egyptian Manufacturing', Boston University, Industrial Sector Strategy Assessment (December 1981).

KORAYEM, K. 'Distributing Disposable Income and the Impact of Eliminating Food Subsidies in Egypt', Cairo Papers in Social Sciences, vol. 5 (April 1982).

LEWIS, B. 'The Return of Islam', "Commentary" (January 1976).

LUCIANI, G. 'The Mediterranean and the Energy Picture', Istituto Affari Internazionali, doc. 16 (Roma 1982, mimeo).

MABRO, R. 'The Egyptian Economy, 1952-1972', Oxford University Press (1974).

MCKINNON, R. and MATHIESON, D.J. 'How to Manage a Repressed Economy', Essays in International Finance (Princeton, 1981).

MINISTRY OF AGRICULTURE (A.R.E.) 'Economic Evaluation of Land Reclamation', Technical Report no. 19, Cairo (March 1981, mimeo).

----- USAID 'Egypt: Strategies for Accelerating Agricultural Development' (July 1982, mimeo).

MINISTRY OF INDUSTRY, General Organization for Industrialization, 'The Industrial Program of the Ministry 1980-85' (March 1981)

MINISTRY OF PLANNING 'The 1978-1982 Five Year Plan', vol. 2 (Cairo 1977).

MINISTRY OF TRANSPORT, Transport Planning Authority (A.R.E.), 'Egypt National Transport Study', prepared by Netherlands Engineering Consultants, Main Report (1981).

MOHIELDIN, A. 'The Development of the State of Agricultural Wage Labor in the National Income of Egypt', in KHALEK-TIGNOR 'The Political Economy of Income Distribution in Egypt' (1982), pp. 236-67.

----- and IBRAHIM, S.E. 'State Socialism and Economic Development in Egypt' in IBRAHIM, S.E. 'A Quarter of a Century in Egypt, 1952-1977' (1981, in arabic), pp. 329-36.

MORKOS, W.S. 'Trends and Patterns of Urbanizations in Egypt', "Population Studies", Cairo, vol. 7, no. 52 (January-March 1980), pp. 37-79.

MUNTASSER, E. 'The Arab Economy and Its Developing Strategy: A New Arab Economic Order', in KERR-YASSIN 'Rich and Poor States in the Middle East' (1982), pp. 99-128.

PADCO Inc. et al. 'The National Urban Policy Study', prepared for the Advisory Committee for Reconstruction, Ministry of Development of the A.R.E. (January 1982, mimeo).

PAPANEK, G. et al. 'A Report of the Industrial Strategy Assessment Project for the U.S. Agency for International Development' (1982, mimeo).

----- 'Employment: A Crucial Problem for the 1980a', in BOSTON UNIVERSITY, Industrial Sector Strategy Assessment 'Labor Markets and Industry in Egypt: Analysis and Recommendations for Employment Oriented Growth (June 1982a, mimeo).

----- and IBRAHIM, B. 'Economic Participation of Egyptian Women', Boston University, Industrial Sector Strategy Assessment (May 1982, mimeo).

RADWAN, S. 'The Impact of the Agrarian Reform on Rural Egypt' (ILO, Geneva 1977).

REYNOLDS, SMITH & HILLS Inc. 'General and Organizational Structure Analysis and Pre-Feasibility Review for Suez City Free Zone', prepared for the General Authority for Investment and Free Zone, Cairo (June 1979, mimeo).

RUSTICI, G. 'The Policy of the Egyptian Government for Promoting Gas Exploration and Exploitation', EGPC-IEOC, Atti del convegno "Natural Gas and Egypt's Economic Development" (Cairo 1982).

SABAGH, G. 'Migration and Social Mobility in Egypt', in KERR-YASSIN 'Rich and Poor States in the Middle East' (1982), pp. 71-98.

SALEH, M. 'A Study of the Possible Agricultural Factors Affecting the Population Growth Rate in Egypt, 1960-80' (Cairo 1982, mimeo).

SARRIS, A. 'Agricultural Crop Patterns and Egyptian Food Security, Some Preliminary Results', ADS Economic Working Paper no. 49 (November 1981).

----- et al. 'Supply Response for the Major Crops in Egyptian Agriculture', ADS Economic Working Paper no. 48 (November 1981).

SCHUEFTAN, D. 'Major Trends in the Arab-Israeli Conflict', in LEGUM, C. (ed.), 'Middle East Contemporary Survey', vol. 1, 1976-77 (Holmes & Meier, New York 1978), pp. 85-109.

SHEEHAN, E.R.F. 'The Real Sadat and the Demythologized Nasser', "New York Times Review" (January 18, 1971).

SHERBINY, N.A. and SERAGELDIN, I. 'Expatriate Labor and Economic Growth: Saudi Demand for Egyptian Labor', in KERR-YASSIN 'Rich and Poor States in the Middle East' (1982), pp. 183-88.

SIVAN, E. 'Mubarak's Egypt', "The Washington Quaterly" (Winter 1982), pp. 183-88.

SPRINGBORG, R. 'Pattern of Association in the Egyptian Political Elite', in LENCZOWSKI, G. (ed.) 'Political Elities in the Middle East', American Enterprise Institute for Public Policy Research (Washington D.C. 1979), pp. 83-108.

THOMAS, S.T. 'The Political Economy of Food Subsidies: Egypt 1960-80', The Fletcher School of Law and Diplomacy (1981, mimeo).

USAID 'Industrial Free Zones: Financial Analysis and Evaluation Design' Cairo (October 1980, mimeo).

US Embassy '<u>Economic Trends Report: Egypt</u>', Cairo (September 6, 1982, mimeo).

VERMEULEN, B. '<u>Labor Markets and Industry in Egypt</u>', Boston University, Industrial Strategy Assessment Project, Cairo (June 1982, mimeo).

WILLIAMS, J.A. '<u>A Return the Veil in Egypt</u>', "Middle East Review", vol. IX, n. z. (Spring 1978).

WORLD BANK '<u>Arab Republic of Egypt, Economic Management in a Period of Transition</u>, vol. 6 (1978).

----- '<u>Arab Republic of Egypt, Domestic Resources Mobilization and Growth Prospects for the 1980s</u>' (1980).

----- '<u>World Development Report</u>' (Washington D.C. 1981).

----- '<u>Staff Appraisal Report, El Dikheila Port Project, Arab Republic of Egypt</u>' (May 1982).

----- '<u>Interim Report on a Human Resources Oriented Development Strategy for Egypt</u>' (July 1982a).

INDEX

Index

Index